New River Gorge, Meadow River and Summersville Lake

Rock Climbers' Guidebook Comprehensive

Third Edition

By
Steve Cater

Published By
King Coal Propaganda

New River Gorge, Meadow River and Summersville Lake Rock Climbers' Guidebook
Third Edition, 2006
by Steve Cater

ISBN   0-9678270-4-3

Printed in China by Twin Age Limited, Hong Kong.

Warning- Please read this notice before using this book!

As with many things in life, rock climbing has inherent risks and dangers that could result in death and disfigurement to participants. The author, publisher and distributors of this book are not responsible for damages or injuries to any persons or property arising from the use of this book. This book is not a substitute for experience! Seek professional instruction if you are a beginner or unsure of your abilities. Every attempt has been made to make this book as accurate as possible but inaccuracies do exist so be cautious and use your best judgment in all situations. Climb at your own risk and climb safely!

For additional copies of this book.
http://www.caterbooks.com
or contact
scater72@hotmail.com

New Routes, Omissions and Corrections

If you discover mistakes or omissions in this book please contact the author. Any new route activity should also be reported to the email address below.

scater72@hotmail.com or stevecater@caterbooks.com

Cover Photo: Robert Thomas on the classic Quinsana Plus. Photo: Mike Turner.

Back Cover Photos: top left- USGS archive photo near Beauty Mountain. Top right-Rachel Babkirk on the classic route *Discombobulated* at Endless Wall (Photo: Steve Cater). Bottom left- Christina Austin on Pockets of Resistance (Photo: Dan Brayack). Bottom right- Will Niccolls on G-String (Photo: Eric Horst).

John Burcham Photography - jb@johnburcham.com

Mike Turner Photography- www.newriverphoto.com

Aerial Photography- USGS and West Virginia State Geographic Information Systems (GIS) Technical Center

A born climber's appetite for climbing is hard to satisfy; when it comes upon him he is like a starving man with a feast before him; he may have other business on hand, but it must wait.

- A Tramp Abroad, Mark Twain

He who climbs upon the highest mountains laughs at all tragedies, real or imaginary.

- Friedrich Nietzsche, Thus Spake Zarathustr

For one brief moment, he felt as if silence had become articulate, whispered its secret and shared a presence with him so eloquent that his mind and heart were thrilled by the revelation.

-The Vandalians, Thomas Cater

Table of Contents

Forward

This is the third edition of the New River Gorge climbing guide. Approximately 500 routes have been added to this guide since the second edition and for the first time the Meadow River has finally been added and many routes from South Nuttall. In recent years the Park Service purchased most of the Meadow River so access is now guaranteed. The Meadow has some great climbing on gorgeous stone so these additions should expand possibilities for rock climbing. Routes at South Nuttall have also been added. South Nuttall is the southern rim of the gorge. It is an extensive cliff but has remained mostly undeveloped due to remoteness and the shady aspect. These additions increase the number of routes and options for climbing in the New River Gorge and surrounding area.

If you take a quick look at the index, you will notice that the majority of routes at the New were established by a handful of climbers. Without the dedication and drive of these few climbers, the New would probably be unknown in the climbing world today.

In 1992 Frank (Hassan) Saab and I cranked out a guidebook to the New. I had been cataloging the routes for about one year and Frank had previous experience using page layout programs. We worked on a borrowed computer and printer and sat in a kerosene heated shack breathing in foul fumes for weeks. In the mornings it was so cold the computer would not boot up. Jake "The Snake" Slaney slept on the floor with the printer just inches from his head. At night, it would take the printer hours to print and Jake would be kept awake with the buzzing and clicking of the printer as it churned out the New's finest. We were totally winging it but having a great time. Although the book wasn't the greatest, it helped consolidate the New as a rock climbing area and opened it up to many climbers throughout the U.S.

The evolution of this book has been long and arduous. The layout is based on previous guidebooks especially my last two guidebooks "New River Gorge Select Rock Climbs" and "New River Gorge Rock Climbers' Guidebook". With each guidebook I have attempted to make improvements creating an easy to use and functional book. This book arranges the climbing areas and routes in a logical progression from left to right throughout the entire gorge. This should dramatically reduce the amount of confusion for climbers. Especially climbers new to the area.

We should all be thankful for the hard work and effort required at establishing new routes and keeping things moving forward. The efforts of climbers, National Park Service, Access Fund and New River Alliance of Climbers have combined to make the New River one of the best recreational rock climbing areas in the country. Hopefully things will continue in a positive direction with input from all concerned interests.

This book would not be possible without input from my friends and climbers. I am very thankful for the invaluable information and work contributed by Kenny Parker, Eric Horst and Rick Thompson. They have been intimately involved with development of the New as a rock climbing area almost from the beginning and have had significant input in the creation and cataloging of routes for current and future users of the New as a rock climbing resource. Also a special thanks to John Burcham (jb@johnburcham.com), Mike Turner (www.newriverphoto.com), Dan Brayack and Dan Hague for the use of their photos throughout this book.

Enjoy the stone, climb safely and may peace be with you,

Steve Cater, 2005

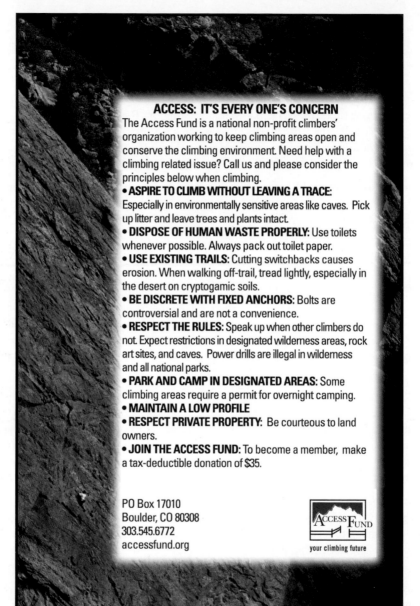

1

I n t r o d u c t i o n

The New River Gorge stretches roughly 60 miles through the rugged hills of West Virginia. One of the most spectacular sections is located near Fayetteville, WV. It is here that the colorful Nuttall Sandstone forms miles of pristine, unbroken cliffline.

Rock climbing at the New is relatively, well... new. While other popular East Coast climbing areas, such as the Gunks and Seneca Rocks, were being developed forty or more years ago, the New experienced major development in the past twenty years. The brief climbing history has allowed the area to develop at its own pace, resulting in a crag which contains a wide spectrum of routes, from modern sport climbs to traditional gear routes.

In the late 70's and early 80's, rumors in the climbing community began to circulate of extensive sandstone cliffs and good quality rock high on the rim of the New River Gorge. At the time, Seneca Rocks was the focus of climbing in the mideast. Its unique atmosphere overshadowed other areas, thereby attracting most of the attention and action.

During the late 70's two local climbing lads, Rick Skidmore(R .I.P.) and Nick Brash, began exploring cliffs and establishing routes near the Bridge Buttress and Beauty Mountain. Their early efforts uncovered excellent routes, such as *Zag* (5.8) in 1975 and *Supercrack* (5.9) in 1981. Compared to the rest of the country, the area lagged far behind in difficult grades. In 1978, Greg Anderson established the *Tree Route* at Bridge Buttress. This was the first 5.10 at the Gorge and remained one of the most difficult lines for several years. It wasn't until 1983 that a young Doug Reed, Vernon Scarboro and Tom Howard established the first 5.11 at the New. *Englishman's Crack* (5.11a) refers to an unknown English climber who was believed to have climbed at the Gorge in the early 70's.

Photo from late 1800's above Supercrack.
Photo: USGS Photo Archive

Development started slowly but picked up in the mid- 80's. A handful of dedicated climbers such as Mike Artz, Eddie Begoon, Andrew Barry, Cal Swoager, Kenny Parker, Rick Thompson and others journeyed regularly from Pittsburgh and Virginia to sample the New's untouched offerings. As the number of 5.10s and 5.11s grew steadily, the New gradually earned the reputation of a "Hard Man's Crag." Unlike many areas where the easier lines fell first, route activity at the New focused on the most obvious lines—difficult or easy. Naturally protected cracks, corners and faces received most of the attention, with an occasional bolt or pin placed when things became sketchy. The use of fixed gear was kept minimal to help instill the "feeling of fear that the first party experienced." On several recent occasions, parties have accidentally retro-equipped old established routes, apparently thinking no one could have climbed the lines without fixed gear. The absence of bolts has led many of todays gym-rats to look up at these routes in disbelief. It goes without saying that some of these lines were quite bold.

During the mid 1980's, exploration and development of surrounding cliffs uncovered many classic lines. Endless Wall, Beauty Mt., Bridge Area, Bubba City and Junkyard Wall developed in splurges. One of the first visits to Endless Wall was in 1981 by Tom Howard and partners. They established several routes during this excursion, such as the classic *The Undeserved* (5.10b). But it wasn't until 1985 that major development began at Endless Wall. Beauty Mountain received some of the earliest ascents in the Gorge such as the classic *Supercrack* (5.9) and *The Butler Done It*, which was aided in 1979 but freed in 1983 by Peter Absolon and renamed *Welcome To Beauty* (5.11b). But without a doubt Junkyard, named after the sprawling pile of junk near its base, and the Bridge Area received most of the attention in the early days. Many of the classic 5.10s and 5.11s such as *Agent Orange* (5.11c) and *Labor Day* (5.10c) were established during the mid 1980's. Even with profuse route activity and a growing reputation, the New was rarely visited by climbers. On a good weekend it was rare to see other parties at the cliff. In the late 80's, this began to change. The printing of the first guidebook in 1987 and several articles in climbing magazines resulted in a dramatic increase in climbers from nearby metropolitan areas. Fortunately, higher end grades and the New's remote location intimidated most beginning climbers. As it has turned out, these two factors have had a positive effect on the area by reducing the environmental impact of climbers and by keeping the cliffs relatively uncrowded.

One of the advantages of climbing at the New is the incredible diversity of routes. Slabs, cracks, corners, steep overhangs, vertical walls and anything in between can be found on the massive sandstone walls and aretes that rise above the trees. The diversity and harder grades are what attracted the more advanced climber. The first 5.12 was established in 1985 with Cal Swoager's top-rope ascent of *Let The Wind Blow* at Bridge Buttress. This was the first of literally hundreds of 5.12s to be established throughout the Gorge. Undoubtedly, the New has one of the best collections of 5.12s in the country. Routes such as *Pudd's Pretty Dress* (5.12d) at Central Endless, *Sanctified* (5.12d) at Kaymoor and *Sacrilege* (5.12b) at Endless are proof of the excellent rock and classic lines that have evolved at the Gorge.

Several years after the first 5.12 appeared, two 5.13s made their debut: Eric Horst established *Diamond Life* (5.13a) in Oct. 1987 at Bubba City and Doug Reed completed *Dissonance* (5.13a) at Upper Endless several weeks later. These two routes helped set the stage for extreme sport climbing at the Gorge. It was during the late 80's that a new trend developed. The number of trad lines on the walls dwindled and climbers began turning their attention toward the blank sections of rock which had repelled traditional style ascents. Realizing this vast amount of quality rock was not being utilized, several of the semi-local honemasters, (Doug Reed, Rick Thompson, Porter Jarrard and Eric Horst) began establishing a greater number of sport routes. One of the first was *Freaky Stylee* (5.12a) at Fern Point. Today it is one of the most popular 12a's—even with its sporty runout above the crux. Since its establishment in 1987, over 500 additional sport routes have been added to the tally.

Over the last few years, the total number of routes has grown at an enormous rate. In 1987, there were roughly 350 routes in the area. Currently the count is over 2,000 and growing. Computing a list of the 100 hardest routes, rock climber/librarian Harrison Dekker found that not one is graded below 5.12c. The area is excellent for training and a short stay, ticking off hard routes, will have you leaving the Gorge stronger than ever.

Since the trend of sport climbing began in the late 80's, the colorful walls and aretes have yielded some of the best routes in the Gorge. Lines such as *Chunky Monkey* (5.12b), *Jesus and Tequila* (5.12b), *Aesthetica* (5.11c), and *Quinsana Plus* (5.13a) have become instant classics. These routes and the quality rock attract a greater number of climbers every year. Why aren't there many 5.14s? The answer is simple; Not many local climbers are strong enough to put up 5.14 and secondly, the nature of the rock is not accommodating to routes of that grade. J.B. Tribout and Alein Ghersen have remarked that the rock at the New is very similar to that of Fontain Bleau in France. This bouldery nature of hard routes, lack of long sustained lines and totally blank rock in many places makes it difficult to locate the 5.14 pitch.

When I wrote the first edition of this book in 1995 I stated that "There is no doubt that a line will go at 5.14, it is just a matter of the proper soul finding the proper line". In the fall of 1997 Brian McCray established the route *Proper Soul* (5.14a) at the Cirque. Since then a variation of the route has been established called *Lord Voldemort* and there are now two 5.14s at Endless Wall. At Summersville Lake, a long standing project also went at 5.13d.

Considering the amount of rock, up and coming climbers eager to push the upper grades should not have a problem creating new test pieces at the New, Summersville and Meadow areas.

In the east, sandstone reigns, if you've danced you're way up any of the classic routes of the New River Gorge, you'll understand why the impeccable rock, perfect edges and varied climbing will, as "The Man" once said, "awaken in you the true nature of existence".

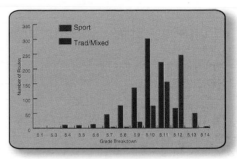

Grade Distribution

Guidebook History

This is the seventh published rock climbing guidebook to the New River Gorge. The first, *"New River Rock,"* was published in 1987 by Richard Thompson II. This book contained 465 climbs and within a matter of years it became outdated due to the huge increase of rock climbs. In the early 90's, a series of photocopied guidebooks by varying authors became very popular. These stapled booklets focused on individual crags but were sporadically produced and hard to keep track of, especially if you were out of toilet paper at the crag. By 1991 the demand for a new guidebook was dire. In the fall of 1991 Steve Cater and Hassan Saab produced the second comprehensive guidebook, *"Take Me To The River; Rock Climbers' Guidebook To New River Gorge"*. This guidebook contained over 1200 rock climbs including newer developed areas such as Bubba City, Kaymoor and Summersville Lake. Although this guidebook was sorely needed, its brief format made it difficult to use for many climbers. The New River Gorge area has also been featured in three other regional guidebooks for the eastern U.S. The first was *"Climber's Guide to the Eastern U.S."* by John Harlin (out of print), *"Sport Crags of the East"* by Steve Cater (out of print) and *"Rock Climbing Virginia, West Virginia, and Maryland "* by Eric Horst. Below is a list of printed books that focused on climbing at the New. This list does not include stapled booklets or mini-guides published in magazines.

"New River Gorge and Summersville Lake Rock Climbers' Guidebook" Second Edition (1999)- by Steve Cater. Out of print.

"New River Gorge Select Rock Climbs" (fall 1997)- by Steve Cater.

"New River Rock" Second Edition (summer 1997)- by Richard Thompson II.

"New River Gorge Rock Climbers' Guidebook" First Edition (1995)- by Steve Cater. Out of print.

"Take Me to the River" (1992)- by Steve Cater, Hassan Saab. Out of print.

"New River Rock" first edition (1987)- by Richard Thompson II. Out of print.

Location

The New River Gorge, Meadow River and Summersville Lake climbing areas are located in southern West Virginia. All of the cliffs in The New River Gorge are located within a few minutes drive of each other except for the Meadow River and Summersville Lake which are approximately 10 and 25 minutes north of Fayetteville on Rt. 19. The New River was designated as a National River in 1978 and much of the New River Gorge is located within the boundaries of National Park Service Land. Summersville is located on Army Core of Engineers land and the Meadow River is mostly within National Park Service Boundaries. The National Park Service has certain rules and regulations concerning the use of their land. For more information on these regulations or NPS facilities contact the National Park Service Headquarters in Glen Jean, WV at (304) 465-0508.

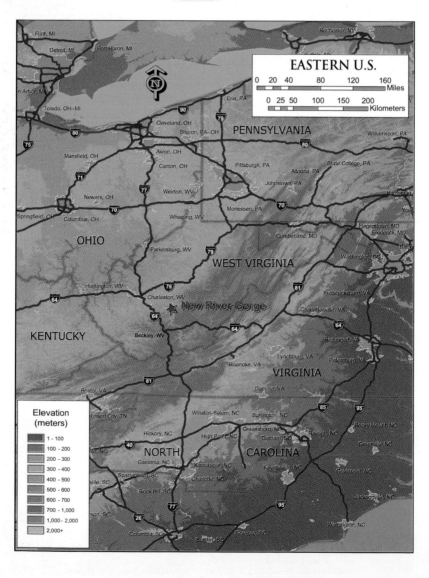

Climbing Area Locations

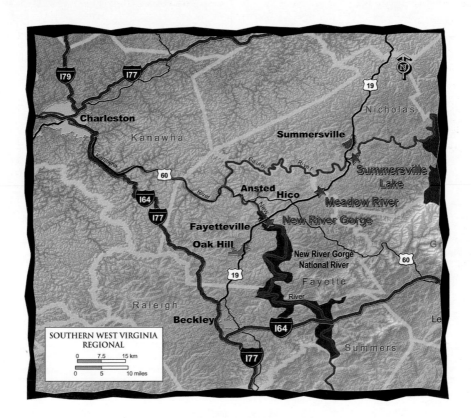

Drive Times

The New is centrally located to many major cities and is within one days drive of most major cities in the eastern United States and eastern Canada. Times are calculated using maximum speed limits.

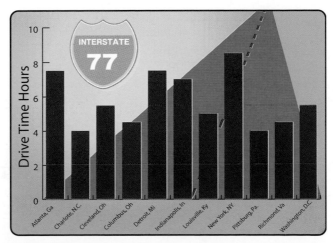

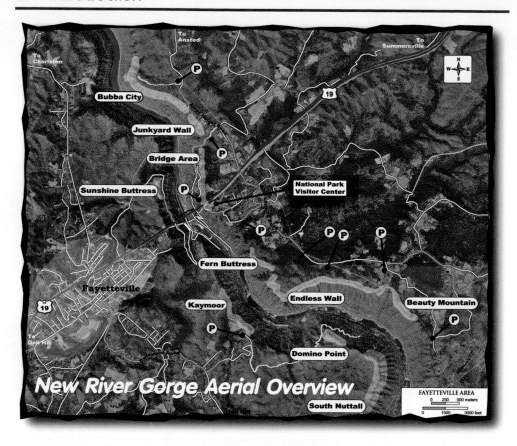

New River Gorge Aerial Overview

Summersville Climbing Area

Summersville Lake

Whipperwill

Bouldering Area

Rats Hole

Truck Stop

To Summersville

To Fayetteville

Summersville Aerial Overview

SUMMERSVILLE AREA
0   110   220 meters
0   500   1000 feet

Meadow River Aerial Overview

Main Meadow

Sunkist Wall

Upper Meadow

To Summersville

Road

Stringtown

Road

Sunday

Hico

To Ansted

To Fayetteville

Propps Ridge Road

Mine

MEADOW RIVER

MEADOW RIVER AREA
0   750   1500 meters
0   2500   5000 feet

0   0.4   0.8   1.6   2.4   3.2   4   4.8   5.6   6.4   7.2   8
Miles

Environment

The New River Gorge has experienced the ravages of coal mining and logging during the last 100 years. At one time the canyon walls were bare of trees and the smoke from coke smelters formed a dense thick cloud over the entire region. Coal miners, who worked their entire life for a few dollars a day and who were practically owned by mining companies, spent their lives crawling around in the dark depths of these mines sometimes to their deaths. Of course, all of this was in the name of progress. God bless America! Today a healthy crop of trees have revegetated the steep canyon walls and the air is relatively clean. Most of the mines have closed down and their ruins are scattered throughout the Gorge.

In more recent years the local economy has shifted its emphasis to tourism. It's estimated that over one million people pass through the area each year to enjoy the whitewater rafting, climbing, kayaking, hiking and mountain biking. This shift is bringing about a much healthier environment and life-style for many of the local residents. For example, Fayetteville and many of the small towns located next to the New River have been dumping raw sewage into the river for years. New regulations are requiring towns to have proper sewage treatment facilities. Hopefully sewage treatment facilities will be built for all areas and the watershed will be preserved.

At The Crag   http://www.accessfund.org/

Remember that the climbing areas at the New are for everyone so it is the responsibility of all climbers to attempt to lessen their impact at the cliff and to help maintain the climbing areas.

•Always pack out trash, old tape and cigarette butts. Also pick up what your friends or others have left behind.

•Stick to established trails to reduce erosion and do a little trail maintenance if you get the chance.

•Do not destroy any types of vegetation; this includes lichens and small trees on the cliff.

•Use gear anchors at the top of cliffs. Only tie-off to trees when necessary. Wrapping slings around trees eventually damages the tree bark and will weaken the tree.

•Bury human waste and burn or bury your toilet paper at least 50 feet away from the cliff and at least 50 yds. from streams.

•Do not deface the rock by painting or chipping.

•Use of motorized drills is prohibited on Park Service Land.

•Use camouflaged hangers and cold shuts. Avoid leaving bright colored slings and webbing in plain view.

•Keep your pet on a leash at all times. Not everyone thinks Rover is such a cute little puppy!

•Always park your car at least 5' off paved roads!

•Please do not undress, relieve yourself or fondle yourself or friends within view of the road, houses or natives.

•Ask permission from landowners before crossing private property.

Climate

http://www.nws.noaa.gov/

The New River Gorge experiences a wide range of weather conditions. As the old saying goes, "When the weather at the New is good, it's really good. But when it's bad, it's really bad." Most climbers who have visited the area have experienced the two extremes and unfortunately there are a few who have only experienced the "really bad." Like most climbing areas in the U.S., the prime season for rock climbing is during the spring and fall. The weather patterns during this time of year create the optimal conditions for rock climbing; stable high pressure systems from the north create cool dry conditions from mid-March through mid-June and mid-September through mid-November. Rainy spells occur during this time of year so don't expect totally dry weather. The least favorable conditions for rock climbing occur during the summer months and winter months. The summers at the New are hot and humid with temperatures rising into the mid 80's to lower 90's and 70% to 90% humidity- not exactly the conditions you want for redpointing that 5.12 project! Despite this, many people climb throughout the summer. The winters at the New River Gorge tend to be wet and cold with temperatures ranging from the 20s to upper 50s. It is common to have mild spells during midwinter where conditions

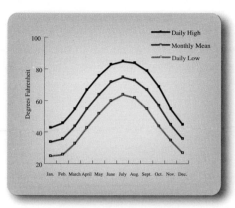

Average Monthly Temperature

are excellent with temperatures in the 50s and sunny dry weather. Fortunately, the New has a variety of cliffs that face in different directions providing an assortment of climbs to meet the conditions: Kaymoor faces north, providing shaded cliff and overhangs; Beauty Mountain faces southwest; Fern Buttress faces south; Endless Wall with its numerous corners, roofs and walls faces southwest and provides shaded and sunny climbs; Bubba City faces due south and Summersville faces southwest and is located on a lake. Your best bet is to check a national weather map and watch for the high pressure systems or call the local forecast in Beckley at (304) 253-4000.

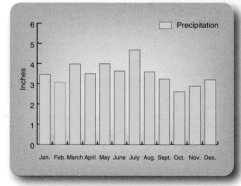

Average Monthly Precipitation

Star Ratings

Two stars ✪✪ is an excellent route and one star ✪ good quality. These ratings represent my personal opinion and general consensus of people I know. By all means, if a route looks good to you, do it! Be a free thinker and use these ratings as a reference. Don't limit yourself to only the one and two star routes, you could miss out on something that was overlooked. On the other hand if you have a limited amount of time and rarely climb at the New, the star ratings will be of great benefit.

Geology

The rock of the New is composed of a very hard band of conglomerate sandstone called the Nuttall Formation. This formation stretches for miles along the canyon rim of the New River Gorge and also outcrops in surrounding gorges such as Summersville Lake and Meadow River. The formation varies from 30' to 110' in height. Due to its high quartzitic composition, it's extremely resistant to the weathering process. It is believed that the rock was deposited over 320 million years ago in a riverbed type environment. The shear walls, corners, cracks and overhangs are the result of millions of years of erosion. Our life-span is but a split second of eternity for these rock walls. Our race and all we have built will be dust and meanwhile these cliffs will have hardly changed. Never the less, we should respect the formation and avoid damaging rock outcrops, vegetation and fauna.

Ethics

Please avoid defacing the rock by chipping or gluing. Do not place bolts on existing routes. Ground up or rap bolted ascents are common and there has never really been a conflict between climbers concerning the two methods. Please respect ground-up ascents or rappel bolted routes. Ground up ascents are usually more difficult to establish and take more time. If a climber is actively working on a project please be considerate and respect their attempts to complete the route even if it is something you could do in one or two attempts. Find your own line and equip it if you are that desperate. There are plenty of lines out there to complete.

New Routes

Many of the areas listed in this guidebook have very little room for new rock climbs. If you establish a new climb that needs fixed gear, be certain that you are not reequipping an older trad line. This guidebook has a majority of the routes at the New, however, some may have been accidentally overlooked. Check with local climbers and review other guidebooks for more information. In general, do not place bolts where gear may be easily placed and avoid placing pins. If bolts are required, use at least 3/8" x 3" stainless steel expansion bolts with camouflaged stainless hangers. For top anchors, use 1/2" camouflaged cold shuts and avoid using chains for anchors. Remember that it is illegal to use motorized equipment (drills) on Park Service Land.

Equipment

Cragging at the New is very diverse with a large selection of corners, cracks, slabs, aretes, vertical walls, steep faces and roofs. Holds range from small crimper edges to rounded sloping buckets and pockets. Most of the walls are 30' to 110' in height and range from slabby to extremely overhanging. A standard 50m rope is adequate for most climbs but there are a number of routes which require a 55 or 60 m rope to safely lower to the ground. Double ropes are recommended for some trad and mixed routes. For protection, a double rack of Friends, two sets of wires, two sets of small brass or steel wires, an assortment of TCUs and Tricams is recommended. For sport climbing, 12 to 15 quickdraws are adequate. For trad routes, 15 to 20 longer slings and runners will suffice. Always inspect fixed anchors and always use two.

Helpful Tips

Included is information that will help educate you and protect the resources that we are using. The information below is supplied as advice only. As with all rock climbing techniques, the climber is responsible for his or her safety and the safety of their partners. Use the tactics below where appropriate but always use common sense and the safest method possible. You, the climber, are ultimately responsible for any decisions made while climbing or rappelling.

Top-Roping

Top-roping is one of the safest ways to rock climb. One of the advantages to the New is that it is possible to set up top-ropes on practically any rock climb. This is great for climbers but bad news for any trees or plants growing at the top of a climb. Damaging erosion is occurring at the tops of the cliffs at some of the popular climbing areas. Please remember that once vegetation is removed from the top of the cliff, dirt and runoff will coat the rock resulting in dirt coated walls.

Use fixed anchors that have been placed at the top of routes. Always inspect the anchor and always use two. Use carabiners for top-roping to extend the life of the anchor.

Always wrap slings around the base of a tree. Trees smaller than your thigh should not be tied off. Never top-rope or rappel directly off a tree. When building anchors at the top of the cliff, if possible use gear placements.

Avoid trampling and crushing vegetation. Do not cut down trees or vegetation. Don't build fires at the cliff base. Use established trails. Pick up trash.

Lichens- A young climber once asked me how those dry leafs could stick to the rock. Those dry crunching things sticking to the rock are known as lichens. Avoid scraping lichens off the rock. Lichens are a fungus that grows symbiotically with algae. The result is a composite organism that characteristically forms a crustlike or branching growth on rocks or tree trunks. Lichens grow extremely slow and once removed will probably never regrow.

Peregrine Falcons- There is a voluntary closure of parts of Endless Wall during the spring for any Peregrine Falcons that happen to be in the area. This is a voluntary closure and usually there are no Peregrines breeding. Check with the Park Service for more details.

Map Symbols and Topos

The extensive cliffline of the New has always created problems for mapping. The numerous aretes and corners easily confuse the simple minds of modern day rock climbers. It is highly recommended that on first visiting a cliff, use the standard approach and access points described in this book so as to minimize confusion. When you first arrive at the base of a cliff, identify a climb and keep track of your location as you walk. Don't rappel into an area that you are not familiar with unless you intend on wandering around for an hour or so trying to figure out your location. This book contains a mapping system for the cliffs that should significantly reduce the amount of confusion. Cliffs are arranged in order from left to right starting with Bubba City. Route numbering also runs left to right. Cliffline is drawn from a bird's-eye perspective as accurately as possible and obvious features such as trees and boulders are identified. Each set of cliffline maps contains a small inset map located at the top of the page showing the entire cliffline with the current section of wall lightly shaded. Face topos of prominent areas are also drawn making it easier to identify your location and the location of climbs. Below is a sample of the maps and the symbols used throughout this book.

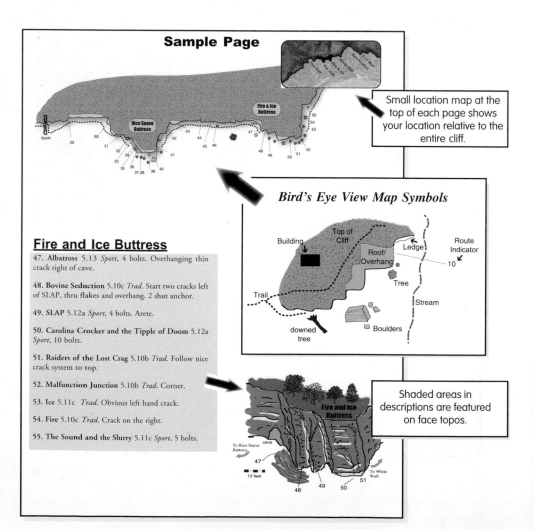

Sample Page

Small location map at the top of each page shows your location relative to the entire cliff.

Bird's Eye View Map Symbols

Building · Top of Cliff · Ledge · Route Indicator · Roof/Overhang · Tree · Trail · Stream · downed tree · Boulders · 10

Fire and Ice Buttress

47. Albatross 5.13 *Sport*, 4 bolts. Overhanging thin crack right of cave.

48. Bovine Seduction 5.10c *Trad*. Start two cracks left of SLAP, thru flakes and overhang. 2 shut anchor.

49. SLAP 5.12a *Sport*, 4 bolts. Arete.

50. Carolina Crocker and the Tipple of Doom 5.12a *Sport*, 10 bolts.

51. Raiders of the Lost Crag 5.10b *Trad*. Follow nice crack system to top.

52. Malfunction Junction 5.10b *Trad*. Corner.

53. Ice 5.11c *Trad*. Obvious left hand crack.

54. Fire 5.10c *Trad*. Crack on the right.

55. The Sound and the Slurry 5.11c *Sport*, 5 bolts.

Shaded areas in descriptions are featured on face topos.

Fire and Ice Buttress

To Rico Suave Buttress · Cave · To White Wall

10 feet

Brian McCray on Proper Soul (5.14a) at the Cirque. Photo: John Burcham.

Amenities

http://www.newrivercvb.com

The area in and around Fayetteville has a selection of campgrounds, motels, restaurants, fast food joints, drinking establishments and movie theaters.

Camping

There are several commercial campgrounds within a few miles of Fayetteville that are popular with climbers. Most of them are affiliated with river outfitters.

Chestnut Creek Campground- Located off Lansing Road near the Visitor Center.

Rocky Top Retreat- This is a primitive campground located at Kaymoor. This area is popular due to its quite surroundings, proximity to Kaymoor and its friendly proprietor, Roger. This campground has a porta-toilet, running water, tent sites (or sleep in your car). Nightly fees are about $5 per person plus $1 showers.

Mountain Lake Campground- Located near the Summersville climbing area.

Mountain River Tours- Located 5 miles north of the bridge on Rt. 19.

North American River Runners- Located in Hico 5 miles north of the Bridge on Rt. 19.

RiftRafters Campground- Located two miles south of the bridge.

Summersville Lake Dam- Free camp sites at the Fishermen Access and Camping Area located below the Summersville Dam. Drive north on Rt. 19 for about 15 miles and turn left onto Rt. 129 (Carnifax Ferry State Park exit). The campground is located at the base of the dam.

Mountain State Campground- Located on Ames Height Road just one mile north of the Bridge on Rt. 19. Fully equipped with hot showers, cabins and toilets.

Low Budget Camping- For the low budget climber the number of pull-off areas where you can sleep in your car or pitch a tent are slowly being whittled away. The Bridge Buttress Area was a popular sleep in your car area but the noise from tractor trailers and cars driving over the bridge plus the weekend crowd of partiers drinking beer all night make it difficult to sleep. The pull-off near Fern Buttress is also a good "sleep in your car" area but the author of this guidebook almost got heldup there one night so pack your own piece. The Junkyard pull-off is now a one-way paved road. Camping is permitted on National Park Service land but you must be at least 100 feet from the road, streams or cliff top. Please do not build fires on the cliff top or cliff base.

Lodging

Babcock State Park- 1-304-438-3003

County Seat B&B- 304-574-0823

Cozy Cottage- 304-574-0134

Dogwood Ridge B&B- 304-658-4396

Garvey House B&B- 304-574-3235

Hawk's Nest- 304-658-5212

Hillcrest Motel- 304-574-1329

Historic Brock House B&B- 304-872-4887

Holiday Inn- 304-465-0571

Laurel Creek Cabins- 304-574-0188

Laurel Ridge Cabins- 304-872-1602

Midland Trail Motel- 304-658-5065

Mill Creek Cabins- 304-658-5005

Morris Harvey B&B- 304-574-1902

Opposum Creek Retreat- 304-574-4836

Piney Springs Cabins- 304-658-4206

Quality Inn- 304-574-3443

Summersville Motor Inn- 304-872-5151

Super 8- 1-800-800-8000

The Lake House- 304-872-6602

Vanishing Creek Cabins- 304-574-3226

Whitehorse Inn B&B- 304-574-1400

Wisteria House B&B- 304-574-3678

Whitewater Inn- 304-574-3678

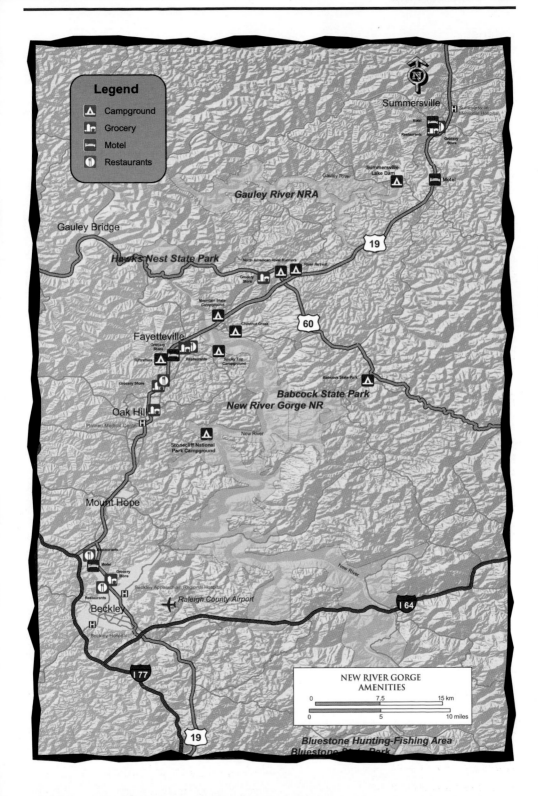

Legend
- Campground
- Grocery
- Motel
- Restaurants

Summersville
Summersville Memorial Hospital
Motel
Restaurants
Grocery Store
Summersville Lake Dam
Motel
Gauley River
Gauley River NRA
19

Gauley Bridge
Hawks Nest State Park
North American River Runners
River Retreat
Grocery Store
Mountain State Campground
Chestnut Creek
60
Fayetteville
Grocery Store
Raftsters
Restaurants
Rocky Top Campground
Babcock State Park
Babcock State Park
New River Gorge NR
Grocery Store
Oak Hill
Plateau Medical Center
New River
Stonecliff National Park Campground

Mount Hope

Restaurants
Motel
Grocery Store
Beckley Appalachian Regional Hospital
Restaurants
New River
Raleigh County Airport
I 64
Beckley
Beckley Hospital
I 77
19

NEW RIVER GORGE
AMENITIES
0   7.5   15 km
0   5   10 miles

Bluestone Hunting-Fishing Area
Bluestone State Park

Eateries

West Virginians are not known for their culinary diversity. Below is a list of recommendable and/or nearby eating establishments.

Biscuit World- On the corner of Rt. 19 and Court Street. Gut bomb!

Breeze Hill- Located near Lansing road 1/2 mile off Rt. 19.

Cathedral Cafe - Court Street in Fayetteville. Breakfast, lunch, dinner, good coffee and Wi-Fi.

Cowboy's - Main Street, Fayetteville.

Dirty Ernie's Rib Pit- Keller Avenue near Route 19.

Gino's Pizza- Located in downtown Fayetteville near the corner of Maple Ave. and Court St.

Godfather's Pizza- Located in the Little General in Fayetteville.

Gumbo's- South Court Street, Fayetteville.

High Country Cafe - North American River Runners. Hico, near the Meadow.

Pancake House- Located 2 miles south of the Bridge on Rt. 19. At one time, this was the breakfast hangout for the climbing scene until a cafe opened in Fayetteville. Truckstop-like atmosphere. Open 24 hours.

Peking Chinese Restaurant- Located on East Main St. in Oak Hill. Good Chinese food, alcoholic beverages and funky music.

Pies & Pints- 103 1/2 Keller Avenue. Beer and Pizza under Mountain bike shop.

Rio Grande- Mexican-American cuisine and your favorite alcoholic beverages with an endless supply of chips and salsa. Driving south on Rt. 19. turn right at the light just after you pass Kroger and K-Mart. It's located in the strip mall.

Sedona Grill- Located about two miles outside of Fayetteville. Lunch, dinner, beer and wine.

Smokey's On The Gorge- Located at Class VI on Ames Heights Road. Smorgasbord style service with good food.

Fast Food- There is a standard selection of corporate fast food joints in Oak Hill. Wendy's, Shoney's, Hardee's, Dairy Queen, Subway, Pizza Hut and just about all of the other places that serve processed, generic food products.

Groceries

For your shopping pleasure, in Fayetteville, there is a small health food store called the Healthy Harvest and a small grocery, Daniel's Fresh Market. In Oak Hill, a few miles south of Fayetteville on Rt. 19, there is a Kroger and Foodland. For clean water, the spring located 3/4 mile below Bridge Buttress and "The Pure Water Shed" located at Little General.

Cigarettes and Booze

Co-Mac Liquor- Also known as the den of sin caters to a wide array of legal vices. Located one mile south of town on Rt. 19 near the Dairy Queen.

Outfitters

Water Stone Outdoors- Located at the corner of Wiseman Ave. and Court St. in downtown Fayetteville. Outdoor retail store with large selection of climbing equipment, camping gear and clothing.

Contact: 304-574-2425 or www.waterstoneoutdoors.com

New River Bike and Touring- Located in Fayetteville. Fully equipped mountain bike shop and mechanic with all the peripherals. Contact: 304-574-BIKE or www.newriverbike.com

Rock Climbing Guide Services

New River Mountain Guides- Rock Climbing School and Guide Service. Contact: 304-574-3872 1-800-73-CLIMB or www.newriverclimbing.com

Hard Rock- Climbing guide service. Contact: 304-574-0735 or www.hardrockclimbing.com

Rock Climbing Shoe Resoler and Repair

Friction Fix- Contact: 304-469-2886 or www.frictionfix.com

Other Things To Do

Apart from rock climbing, the New is excellent for outdoor "*sports action*". If you plan on an extended stay, bring your mountain bike. The rugged hills and valleys are full of logging roads, trails and old railroad beds that are ideal for mountain biking and running. Miles of scenic trails vary from easy to extremely difficult. A few of the popular mountain biking trails and areas are the Kaymoor Trail, Keeny's Creek Trail and Babcock State Park. Stop in at Water Stone Outdoors, National Visitors Center or New River Bike and Touring for more information. The New River is also famous for tremendous whitewater action. Kayakers and rafters travel from all over the country to paddle the New River and the Gauley River. A day trip down the New or the Gauley will give you a new perspective on the cliffs. There are about twenty river outfitters in the area who specialize in river trips. And don't forget those gloves for sport rappelling. Yee-Haa!

For the less energetic, there are three movie theaters in Beckley. All are located on the same stretch of road off the Crossroads Mall, 12 miles south of Fayetteville on Rt. 19. The Raleigh Mall theater has $1 shows and the other two theaters have regular priced shows ($5.50). Charlie's Pub, located below Sherry's Beer Store in Fayetteville often has an interesting night scene with pool tables, juke box, pinball machines and plenty to drink in a smoke filled bar. The Comfort Inn also has a pub-like drinking establishment. Scenic airplane rides over the Gorge are also a good way to shake yourself up while checking out the miles of cliffline. Other interesting spots include the old town of Thurmond, Kaymoor Mine and Lewisburg.

Once a year on the second weekend of October, the New River Gorge Bridge is open to pedestrian traffic, rappellers and B.A.S.E. jumpers. If you don't mind the crowds, it is definitely worth watching the B.A.S.E. jumpers leap off the bridge.

The New River Alliance of Climbers (newriverclimbing.org) holds a rock climbers' rendezvous in May. This is a large get together of climbers and sponsors that happens every year. Bouldering comps, slide shows, gear demos and a party make it a great festival. Check the NRAC website for more details.

Emergency Information

If you participate in rock climbing, take responsibility for your actions. Don't expect to be rescued by some elite rescue squad in the event of an accident. Learn some first aid and rescue techniques so in the event of an accident you will not be clueless. Some sections of cliff are very remote and difficult to access by emergency rescue teams. Think about what you do, where you do it and potential consequences. Remember you are the master of your own destiny! Below is a list of emergency contact numbers.

For Ambulance, Police, Sheriff, State Police and Park Rangers.

Emergency - Dial 911

NPS *National Park Service,*
GLEN JEAN- 304-465-0508

H *Raleigh General Hospital,*
BECKLEY- 304-256-4186

H *Plateau Medical Center,*
OAK HILL- 304-469-8600

H *Memorial Hospital,*
SUMMERSVILLE- 304-872-2891

Hazards

There are a few hazards climbers should be aware of while at the crags.

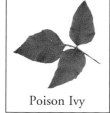

Poison Ivy

Poison Ivy- Shiny three leaf vine that often grows along the base of the cliff. After coming in contact with the plant or oil you have about 24 hours to remove the oils before they cause irritation. Wash with warm water and soap to remove oils. Be aware that clothing and pets may also transfer the oils.

Poisonous Snakes- Copperheads are the most common poisonous snake. In the past several years several climbers have been bitten. Contrary to popular belief copperhead venom is not deadly. In most cases the infection is worse than the venom. *Always look before sitting or placing your hands.* If you wear sports sandals, pay attention to were you are stepping. Copperheads are easily identifiable by their diamond shaped copper colored head. Seek medical attention if bitten.

Rattlesnake- Although less common these snakes are also found in this area. Rattlesnake venom is very toxic and if bitten it can be quite serious. Again be aware of where you sit, where you put your hands and foot placements. Seek medical attention immediately. If you do come across a rattlesnake or copperhead, kindly alter your course around it and let it go on its way.

Insects- Small black flies that bite appear sporadically throughout the year depending on the amount of rain. Mosquitos are also present but usually are not to bad. Standard bug juice will take care of these critters. Wasps are common during certain parts of the year and often sun themselves on sunny cliff faces. It is a good idea to bring a bee sting kit if you are allergic to bee stings.

Grizzly Bears- Just kidding!

Water- Do not drink water from streams without purification. Even then I would be cautious, although local springs are usually safe.

Thieves- Always lock your vehicle and do not leave valuables in plain sight. Lock valuables in trunk!

Drunks- Occasionally climbers camped near the Bridge Area are harassed by drunks. Avoid conflicts by not staying at this area or obvious party spots (areas with lots of beer cans and broken glass).

Monica Wang on Roy's Lament (5.9) at Endless Wall. Photo: Cater

In 1998 climbers, National Park Service and the Access Fund made dramatic improvements to the heavily used Bridge Buttress area. Photo: Cater

Recommended Routes

Below is a list of 25 favorite climbs of various climbers who have climbed extensively in the area.

Russ Clune (6'2", 170 lbs.) - Has climbed extensively throughout the world and currently lives near the Gunks in New York. Started climbing at the New in the late 1980's and has completed a great number of sport and trad lines at the New.

1-Party In My Mind. 2-Freaky Stylee 3-The Racisit. 4-Chunky Monkey. 5-Erotica. 6-Apollo. 7-The Mercy Seat. 8-Aethetica. 9-Pocket Route. 10-Agent Orange. 11-Jesus & Tequila. 12-The Sportster 13-Concertina. 14-Gift of Grace. 15-Leave It To Jesus. 16-Green Envy. 17-Disturbance. 18-The Undeserved. 19-Dial 911 20-Just Send It. 21- Nude Brut. 22-Titan's Dice. 23-Dining at the Alter. 24-Black & Tan. 25-Flash Point.

Porter Jarrard (5'9", 180 lbs.) - Porter established a great number of first ascents at the New River including many of the modern day classics such as Apollo at Summersville. He currently lives in Lexington, Ky near the Red River Gorge.

1-Apollo. 2-911. 3-Mercy Seat. 4-Titain's Dice. 5-Grace Note. 6-Sportster. 7-Chasin the Wind Direct. 8-Chorus Line. 9-Agent Orange. 10-Dining at the Altar. 11- Libertine. 12- Sanctified. 13- Slash & Burn. 14- Sacrilege. 15- Jet Cap. 16-Loud Noise. 17-Spectre. 18- Devil Doll. 19-Blood Raid. 20- Marionette. 21- Fall Line. 22- Fiesta Grande. 23-Supercrack. 24-Can I do it til I Need Glasses. 25-Quinsana.

Kenny Parker (6'1", 170 lbs.) - Parker has climbed extensively at the New since the early 1980's and has established many first ascents. He currently lives in Fayetteville, WV.

1-Springboard. 2-Burning Calves. 3-Stuck In Another Dimension. 4-Darwin's Dangle. 5-Transcendence. 6-Just Send It. 7-Linear Encounters. 8-Freaky Stylee. 9-Agent Orange. 10-Party In My Mind. 11- Raging Tiger. 12- Magnatude. 13-Chunky Monkey. 14- Narcissus. 15- Surge Complex. 16- Skinhead Grin. 17-Spectre. 18- Zealous. 19-Dissonance. 20-First Strike. 21- Celibate Mallard. 22- Hot Tuna. 23-Let's Make A Deal. 24-Can I Do it til I Need Glasses. 25-Chasin' the Wind.

Tracy Martin (5'8", 130 lbs.) - Lived at the New for several years and climbed many of the 5.10 to 5.11 range sport and trad routes. She currently lives in Colorado.

1-Flight of the Gumbie. 2-First Steps. 3-Muckraker. 4-Workman's Comp. 5-Jesus Is My License Plate. 6-Legacy. 7-Wild Seed. 8-Sheer Energy. 9-Sancho. 10-Aesthetica. 11-Satisfaction Guaranteed. 12-Fantasy. 13-Zag. 14-Four sheets to the Wind. 15-Roys Lament. 16-Supercrack. 17-Black & Tan. 18-The Entertainer. 19-Gemini Crack, right. 20-Mushrooms. 21-Tree Route. 22-Remission. 23-Rod Serling Crack. 24-Can I Do it Till I Need Glasses. 25-Rapscallion's Blues.

Doug Reed (6'3", 184 lbs.) - Doug Reed, also known as Mr. New River and Code Man, was the main driving force behind route development at the New for over ten years. He established hundreds of routes at the New and hundreds more throughout the south. He currently resides in North Carolina.

1-Four Sheets to the Wind. 2-Agent Orange. 3-The Prowess. 4-Freaky Stylee. 5-S'more Energy. 6-Pudd's Pretty Dress. 7-Can I Do it Till I Need Glasses. 8-Leave It to Jesus. 9-Jesus and Tequila. 10-Quinsana. 11-Party In Your Mind. 12- Dial 911. 13-The Racist. 14-Legacy. 15-Black & Tan. 16- Aesthetica. 17-Black Happy. 18-The Undeserved. 19-Celibate Mallard. 20- Disturbance. 21- Burning Calves. 22- Chasin' the Wind. 23-Lactic AcidBath. 24-Magnatude. 25-Apollo.

Steve Cater (5'11", 160 lbs.) - Steve wrote several guidebooks for the New and lived in Fayetteville for ten years. He first started climbing at the New in the mid 1980's and has climbed extensively in the area. This list is comprised of some of the more obscure classic routes.

1-Stuck In Another Dimension. 2-Cutting Edge. 3-Fat Cat. 4-Premarital Bliss. 5-New Age Equippers. 6-Linear Encounters. 7-Fall Line. 8-Meliflous. 9-Pudd's Pretty Dress. 10-Hellbound. 11-Zygomatic. 12- Dial 911. 13-Crescent Moon. 14-New Fangled Dangle. 15-Raw Deal. 16- Harbinger Scarab. 17-Devil Doll. 18-World's Hardest. 19-Crimes of Flashing. 20- Beast in Me. 21- Supercrack. 22- Under the Milky Way. 23-Sancho. 24-Thieves in the Temple. 25-Scenic Adult.

Jason Babkirk *"gitt'n jiggy with it"* on Welcome to Beauty (5.11a) at Beauty Mountain. Photo: Cater.

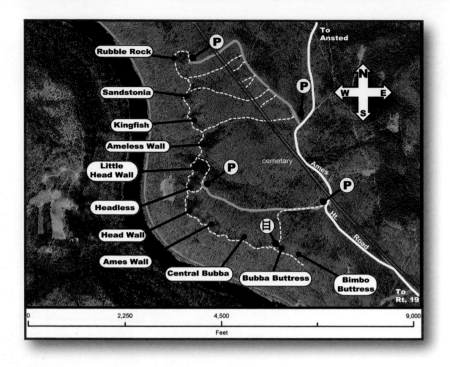

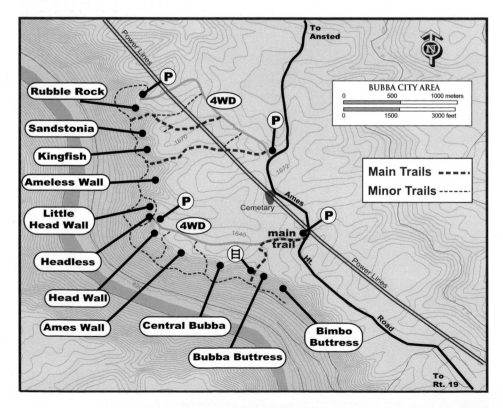

2
B u b b a   C i t y

333 • 177 sport • 156 trad/mixed

Bubba City is the most northern cliff at the New and is located downstream of Junkyard Wall. The main cliffs are Bubba Buttress, Central Bubba, Ames Wall and Head Wall. The majority of routes at Bubba were developed during the late 80's by a handful of climbers from Virginia and Pennsylvania. Bubba City is the location of the first 5.13 established at the New River Gorge. The climb *Diamond Life* (5.13a) was established at Central Bubba in 1987 by Eric Horst. The walls at Bubba range from 30' to 100' in height and the majority of routes are face climbs on vertical to slightly overhanging rock. The southern orientation of Bubba City makes it a good choice on cold days but it should be avoided during the hot days of summer.

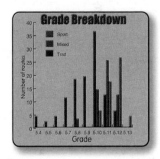

From 2001 to 2004 there was a surge of activity at Bubba. Numerous new sport routes plus the retro-equipping of old routes was carried out by Eric Horst, Eric McCaillister and a handful of other climbers. This effort has been an excellent contribution to the area. In 2003 a stapled guidebook was also published featuring the Bubba City area and contains many of the additions and changes. This guidebook also has attempted to include most of the additions. New routes and retro bolting are going on so some info in this book may not reflect the current bolt counts. Also keep in mind that new routes may possibly be added.

Access

The main access to Bubba City is from the Ames Height Road. To reach the parking area, drive 1.5 miles northwest on Ames Ht. Road and look for a pull-off and dirt road on the left. Park within view of the road, lest some "Bubbas" break into your car. Walk down the dirt road 600 hundred feet and keep an eye out for an obvious trail that branches off to the left. Follow this trail for 100 yards. It descends a small gully and emerges between Bubba Buttress and Central Bubba.

The group of cliffs downstream from Head Wall (Little Head Wall, Ameless Wall, Kingfish, Sandstonia and Rubble Rock) are most easily accessed from a parking area located 1/2 mile beyond the standard Bubba City parking area. Continue driving northwest on Ames Height Road, turn left at the second Gas Well and park here or continue 1/2 mile to its terminus. This is also a good camping area but don't leave anything unattended. It is also possible to reach this set of cliffs from Little Head wall but you have to do a little bushwhacking at times to access the cliffs. Another option is to park at the second parking area and walk down the dirt road. Several spur trails branch off from the road and make for a quicker, more direct route to several of the cliffs.

This section of cliff is downstream of the Head Wall. The most convenient access is from the spur trails off the gas well road located at the second pull-off. It's also possible to approach these cliffs from the Head Wall but the hike is long. Several shortcut trails branch off the logging road make the hike shorter.

Rubble Rock

1. Unnamed BC #2 5.10c *Trad*. This climb is located on the next section of cliff. It is the obvious long corner. Serious bushwhack.

2. Frilled Dog Winkle 5.11a *Trad*. Cracks and flakes.

3. The Hideousity 5.10a *Trad*. Corner to roof then cracks.

4. Gift from the Mayor 5.10b *Trad*. Face.

5. Metabolic Optimizer 5.11d/12a *Trad*. Right-leaning overhanging crack to ledge. Rappel from ledge.

6. Thing Foot 5.10b *Trad*. Seam to arete then left onto face.

7. Waka Jahwaka 5.11a *Mixed*, 1 bolt, 1 pin. Crack and flake system to ledge on left, Rappel from ledge.

8. Mercenary Territory 5.12a *Mixed*, 2 bolts. Move left and finish on *Waka Jahwaka*. Rappel from ledge.

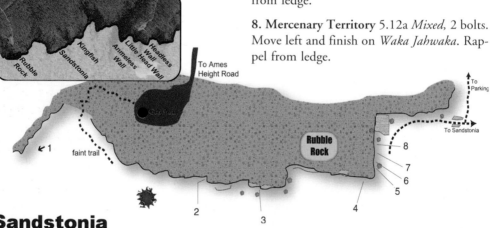

Sandstonia

This area has seen a great deal of new route activity. Please be cautious when lowering. Some routes require a **60m (200')** rope to lower safely. Cliff height varies from 45' to 110' feet. Always tie a knot at the end of the rope before climbing or have the belayer tie into the rope!

9. Hardcore Female Rash ✪5.10a *Sport*, 4 bolts. Left most route. Follow bolts through three overhangs.

10. Celtic Sun ✪5.9+ *Sport*, 5 bolts. Starts from ledge, up through two small overhangs into corner.

11. Assman 5.8 *Sport*, 5 bolts. After third bolt move left and finish on *Celtic Sun* anchors.

12. Five-Five My Ass ✪ 5.6 *Sport*, 4 bolts. Start

on Assman, up and right to anchor.

13. Bobby D's Bunny ✪✪ 5.6 *Sport*, 9 bolts. Starts right of Five-Five, move up and right passing small tree to anchors.

14. Geisha Girl ✪✪5.8 *Sport*, 11 bolts. Start at wide crack Moves left after first bolt and continue up broken face to anchors. 60m rope recommended.

15. Mrs. Field's Follies ✪✪ 5.8 *Sport*, 10 bolts. Start as Geisha but go straight up finishing over roof. 60m rope recommended.

16. Kinesthetica ✪✪ 5.10c *Sport*, 8 bolts. Up through overhangs finishing through high roof. 60m rope recommended.

17. Hep-C 5.10d *Sport*, 8 bolts. Up face finishing at anchors.

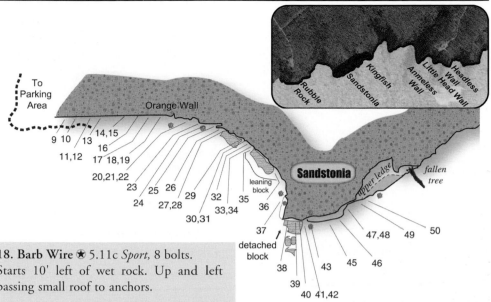

18. Barb Wire ✪ 5.11c *Sport*, 8 bolts. Starts 10' left of wet rock. Up and left passing small roof to anchors.

19. Badass Tattoo ✪✪ 5.10b *Sport*, 10 bolts. Same start as *Barb Wire* but move right after second bolt. Continue up corner and small roofs to anchor.

20. Bikini Line ✪ 5.11c *Sport*, 8 bolts. Starts right of wet corner. Up three bolts then move left passing through a roof to anchors.

21. G-String ✪✪ 5.11a *Sport*, 8 bolts. Same start as *Bikini*, after fourth bolt move right and follow bolt line straight up to anchors.

22. Booby Prize ✪ 5.10d *Sport*, 6 bolts. Same start as *Bikini*. After third bolt move up and right to finish on Clean Shaved anchors.

23. Clean Shaved 5.12a/b *Sport*, 6 bolts. Jugs up to smooth bulge and anchors.

24. Mike Tyson's Face ✪ 5.12a *Sport*, 7 bolts. Starts below overhanging face.

25. Butterfly Flake ✪ 5.7 *Sport*, 3 bolts. Right facing flake up to ledge.

26. Plumber's Crack 5.6 *Sport*, 5 bolts. Up wide left facing corner.

27. Pure Power 5.13a *Sport*, 5 bolts. Short route up overhanging arete.

28. White Henna 5.12b *Sport*, 4 bolts.

29. Shady Lady ✪ 5.7 *Sport*, 6 bolts. Starts on left side of right facing corner.

30. Lieback and Enjoy It ✪✪ 5.10d *Sport*, 7 bolts. Up to ledge, then climb dihedral to anchors.

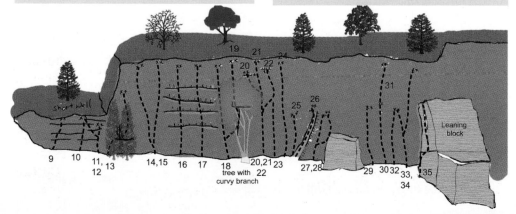

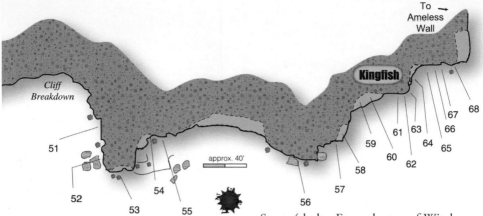

Cliff
Breakdown

To →
Ameless
Wall

Kingfish

approx. 40'

31. Weisenheimer Brainstorm ✪✪ 5.11a *Sport,* 11 bolts. From the top of *Lieback and Enjoy It,* continue out large roof.

32. The Good Book ✪ 5.10a *Sport,* 7 bolts. Starts at left facing flake, up to dihedral and anchors.

33. Crescendo ✪ 5.9+ Sport, 6 bolts. Starts on left side of detached flake.

34. Zeitgeist ✪ 5.10a *Sport,* 10 bolts. Climb Crescendo, after the last bolt move right and continue up overhanging face to anchors.

35. Lord of the Jungle 5.12a *Trad.* Short overhanging crack on leaning block.

36. Slip Sliding Away 5.4 *Trad.* Face.

37. Cool Crack 5.10a *Trad.* Crack. Rap from ledge.

38. Climb Free or Die 5.11a/b *Sport,* 4 bolts. Starts left of chimney, up arete and finish on ledge.

39. Jaws of Life 5.11a *Sport,* 10 bolts. Starts at chimney, up and left finishing on the left of the overhang.

40. To Bubba or Not to Be 5.11a *Trad.* Left facing dihedral up to ledge then pull roof at crack. 60m rope recommended.

41. Witches of Bangor 5.10c *Sport,* 5 bolts. Arete on upstream side of pinnacle.

42. She Got the Pussy, I Got the Drill 5.10d *Sport,* 4 bolts. From the top of Witches, continue out roof and face to anchors.

43. The Decameron ✪ 5.10b *Sport,* 9 bolts. Starts by right facing chimney. Up juggy face then move left to nice face and arete to finish at anchors. 60m rope recommended.

44. Mixed Emotions 5.8 *Trad.* Start as *Beef Boy,* traverse left 25' to corner after first crack.

45. Beef Boy Field Day 5.9 *Trad.* Start at crack behind tree, up to ledge then follow crack straight up to roof.

46. ISO 9000 5.11b *Sport,* 3 bolts. Starts under orange face, up face to anchors below roof.

47. Double Twouble 5.10c *Trad.* Corner to ledge then left crack to top.

48. Risky Business 5.11a *Trad.* Same as *Double Twouble,* finish on right crack at ledge.

49. Bass Ackwards 5.11c *Sport,* 5 bolts. Up face to shared anchors.

50. Pay It Forward ✪ 5.9 *Sport,* 6 bolts. Starts at chimney 18' right of Double Twouble. Climb up and right to anchors.

Kingfish

51. C. T. Crack 5.8 *Trad.* Crack to ledge, rappel.

52. Face Value 5.11a R *Trad.* Face and flakes to seam then face to top.

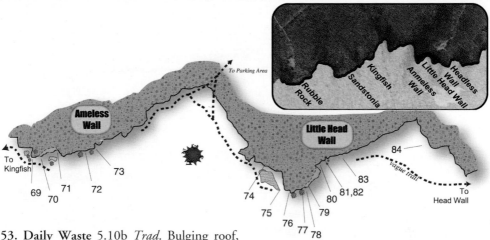

53. Daily Waste 5.10b *Trad*. Bulging roof, over roof then up and left.

54. Mid-Height Crisis 5.10a *Mixed*, 1 pin. Face moving up and right to ledge. Rappel.

55. Just Another Crack 5.9 *Trad*. Crack to ledge then rappel.

56. The Metamorphosis 5.9 *Trad*. Corner to cracks.

57. Ratz Holm 5.7 *Trad*. Corners to top.

58. Free Blast ✪ 5.12a *Sport*, 6 bolts. Starts on left side of roof, up arete and finish at anchors.

59. Bubba's Big Adventure 5.10a *Trad*. Left facing dihedral and corner to top. **Direct Start** 5.11b *Trad*. Starts 5' left of regular route.

60. Cafe Chic ✪ 5.10d *Sport*, 4 bolts. Easy start at dihedral, layback to roofs and anchor.

61. King of Swing ✪✪ 5.11b *Trad*. Crack to roof. Enjoyable crack climb under roof on good rock. Direct Finish- Out crack to top (5.11b).

62. Not Till Verdon 5.12b *Sport*, 6 bolts. Short flake to face, move right to arete.

63. Solitude Standing 5.10b *Sport*, 4 bolts. Face.

64. Fortitude 5.12c R *Trad*. Face. Boulder problem.

65. Good-bye Mr. Lizard 5.5 *Trad*. Crack and corner to roof, move left and finish through roof.

66. The Trial 5.8 *Trad*. Crack.

67. Silly Little Corner 5.6 *Trad*. Corner.

68. Iron Cross 5.12a *Trad*. Corner to roof and corner.

Ameless Wall

69. Plastic Sturgeons 5.10b *Mixed* 1 pin. Face and arete.

70. Face Life 5.10a *Mixed*, 1 pin. Corner. **Direct Start** 5.8 R *Mixed*, 1 pin. Face to pin.

71. Women Who Won't Wear Wool 5.10b *Trad*. Face to corner.

72. Blood Test 5.9 *Trad*. Crack.

73. Men Who Love Sheep 5.10b *Mixed*, 1 pin. Arete.

Little Head Wall

74. Stalking The Wild Toad 5.7 *Trad*. Corner.

75. Helmeted Warrior Of Love 5.7 *Trad*. Face to arete, then small roof and crack.

76. Comic Relief 5.7 *Trad*. Corner to crack and roof then right facing corner to top.

77. Utter Classics 5.11b *Sport*, 6 bolts. Bolt line up white face.

78. Technique Heavy Heifer 5.11a *Sport*, 6 bolts. Through low roofs to face.

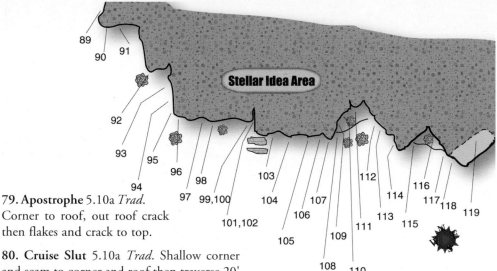

79. Apostrophe 5.10a *Trad*. Corner to roof, out roof crack then flakes and crack to top.

80. Cruise Slut 5.10a *Trad*. Shallow corner and seam to corner and roof then traverse 20' right following right facing corner to top.

81. Emergency Room Exit 5.10b R *Mixed*, 1 pin. Move left at pin, corner then finish on *Cruise Slut*.

82. Crazy Ambulance Drive 5.10b R *Mixed*, 1 pin. Starts on left side of arete, face to arete, move right at pin.

83. The Hunger Artist 5.10b *Trad*. Dirty face to cracks, finish on left crack.

84. An Affair with the Heart 5.7 *Trad*. Right facing flake left of an obvious arete.

Headless Wall

This is a small wall with four sport routes. It is located between Head Wall and Little Head Wall. From the Head Wall continue walking downstream one hundred yards.

85. Pyro Vixen ✪✪ 5.10a *Sport*, 6 bolts. Starts right of vertical seam, face to roof, move left up arete then right to anchors.

86. Ichabod Crane ✪ 5.10c R *Sport*, 5 bolts. Up flake thru small overhangs to face and anchors.

87. Mo' Verde 5.10a *Sport*, 5 bolts. Start at low overhang, up to corner, to tree, move up right and finish on Gimp Verde anchors.

88. Gimp Verde 5.8 *Sport*, 4 bolts. Line up right side of wall

Head Wall

89. Bubbatism by Fire 5.12a R *Trad*. Roof to left leaning corner.

90. Dementing Situations 5.10b *Mixed*, 1 pin. Start as *Inventing Situations* and move left to arete.

91. Inventing Situations 5.11d *Mixed*, 1 bolt. Slab.

92. Pump and Circumstance ✪ 5.12b *Sport*, 5 bolts. Obvious arete.

93. Stories without Words 5.12b *Sport*, 5 bolts. Finishes on *Rites*.

94. Rites of Summer ✪ 5.12a *Sport*, 6 bolts. Starts at short crack and wanders around face to anchors.

95. Stellar Idea ✪ 5.11b *Sport*, 4 bolts. Up face to small overhang then anchors.

96. Coughing Up Fleming 5.12a *Sport*, 4 bolts. Boulder problem start out low overhang.

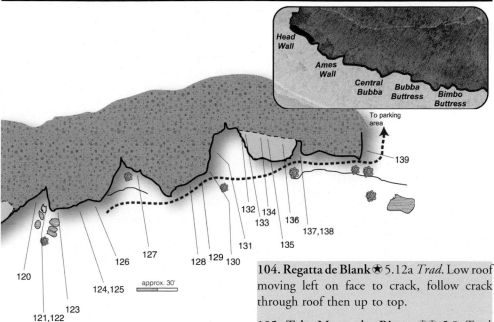

104. Regatta de Blank ✪ 5.12a *Trad*. Low roof moving left on face to crack, follow crack through roof then up to top.

105. Take Me to the River ✪✪ 5.9 *Trad*. Corner crack to ledge, con't on face to top.

106. Burning Down the House 5.12a *Trad*. Thin crack to ledge, finish at ledge and rap or continue up *Hubba Bubba*.

107. Dreams of White Horsts ✪ 5.13a *Sport*, 6 bolts. White arete, finish on *Hubba Bubba*. Bouldery moves.

108. Skewered 5.12c/d *Sport*, 5 bolts. Start from block, up seam to ledge and finish on *Hubba Bubba*.

97. Head with No Hands 5.11b *Trad*. Corner moving left to crack then up and right through roof.

98. Put Up or Shut Up ✪ 5.11c/d *Sport*, 6 bolts. Up face thru overhang to anchors.

99. Tour de Bubba 5.11b *Trad*. Start left of chimney, up and left passing two roofs and a crack.

100. Eclectic Mix 5.10c *Sport*, 5 bolts. Starts left of chimney, up face then arete stemming until reaching anchors on face.

101. Verde Suave 5.7 *Sport*, 5 bolts. Chimney, usually wet.

102. Tworgasminimum ✪ 5.10c *Mixed*, 1 bolt. Chimney moving right onto wall then up to short crack to top.

103. Little Creatures ✪✪ 5.10d *Trad*. Face to thin crack, moving right to double cracks in roof, con't to top.

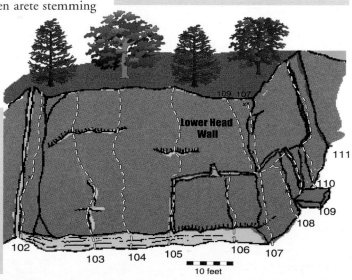

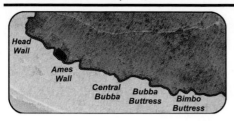

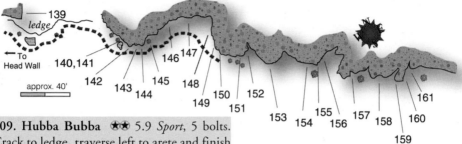

120. Masterpiece Theater ✪✪ 5.12d/13a *Sport*, 7 bolts. Up steep face just left of corner.

121. So Freakin' Fun ✪ 5.10d *Sport*, 7 bolts. Start as *Increderate,* then move left towards wide crack. Finish on *Masterpiece* anchors.

122. Increderate ✪ 5.12c *Sport*, 5 bolts. Starts

109. Hubba Bubba ✪✪ 5.9 *Sport*, 5 bolts. Crack to ledge, traverse left to arete and finish on left side of arete.

110. China Crisis ✪ 5.10d *Sport*, 4 bolts. Overhanging off-width.

111. Nasty Body O'Dour 5.7 *Trad*. Off-width.

101. Verde Bunyan 5.10c/d *Sport*, 3 bolts. Face to anchors under roof.

113. Sangre Verde 5.8 *Sport*, 4 bolts. Start under low overhang in right facing corner. Up thru crack in roof then to anchors.

114. All Things Considered 5.11a *Sport*, 6 bolts. Start right of chimney, up and right over bulge, then to arete.

115. Perpetual Motion ✪ 5.11b *Mixed*, 2 pins. Face to right side of arete.

116. The Law of Diminishing Returns 5.9 *Trad*. Corner and Crack.

117. On A Wing and A Prayer 5.11c/d *Sport*, 6 bolts. Corner and flake then move right to face.

118. Popeyean Forearms ✪ 5.12b *Sport*, 5 bolts. Starts on left side of roof, out roof up to short crack and anchors.

119. The Great White Shark ✪ 5.12c *Sport*, 4 bolts. White face to steep roof, traverse right and pull roof.

on left side of arete. Shares finish with *Critical Path*.

123. Critical Path ✪ 5.12a *Sport*, 7 bolts. Low roof to face.

124. Reaches from Hell ✪✪ 5.11c *Sport*, 7 bolts,. Right leaning crack to arete. Same start as *Skinhead Grin* but move left at 3rd bolt.

125. Skinhead Grin ✪✪ 5.11b *Sport*, 6 bolts. Start on *Reaches* and move right at bolt 3.

126. Skinhead Sin 5.11c *Sport*, 5 bolts.

127. Bubba Shitty 5.9 *Trad*. Crack.

128. Crankenstein 5.11a *Trad*. Crack to roof thru roof and corner to top.

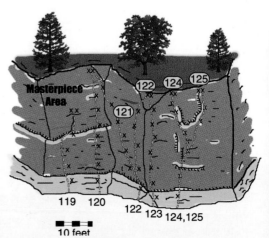

129. Feng Shui ✪ 5.12a *Sport*, 6 bolts.

130. Eurobubba 5.10c *Trad*. Flakes to roof up left to short crack then traverse left and con't up face to top.

131. Bubba Down Under 5.12b/c *Mixed*, 2 bolts. Face up and left.

132. La Pratique 5.8 *Sport*, 4 bolts.

133. Grimper de Pouvoir 5.12b *Sport*, 6 bolts. Starts on the left side of the large roof. Up and right thru roof.

134. L'Amour des Troits ✪✪ 5.12b/c *Sport*, 6 bolts. Starts under large roof, up crack to roof then continue out large roof.

135. Trois dans un Jour ✪ 5.12a *Sport*, 4 bolts. Up face to overhang then anchors.

136. Dieu est Partout 5.11c/d *Sport*, 4 bolts. Starts 10' left of arete.

137. L'Amour est Tout ✪ 5.11c *Sport*, 4 bolts. Start on below route. Move left at 1st bolt.

138. Vivre l' Amour ✪✪ 5.12a *Sport*, 5 bolts. Starts on left side of arete, thru bulge then arete to anchors.

139. Newvana 5.10d R *Trad*. Right side of arete and trend up and right passing through center of roof.

140. Forgotten But Not Lost 5.12c *Sport,* 8 bolts. Start on *Southern Exposure*, at 3rd bolt move left then straight up thru roof to anchor.

141. Southern Exposure ✪ 5.9 *Sport,* 3 bolts. Face and short flake.

142. No Bubbas Allowed 5.9 *Trad*. Crack to ledge then face.

143. Pony Ride 5.3 *Trad*. Wide crack.

144. Farewell to Bubba 5.10a *Trad*. Short left leaning crack.

145. Smoking Crack 5.8 *Sport,* 4 bolts. Crack and corner under large roof.

146. Czech Vacation ✪ 5.8 *Sport*, 5 bolts. Thin seam to horizontal move right then jugs to anchors.

147. Fiesta Verde 5.7 *Sport*, 3 bolts. Face up to short crack.

148. Bubbaduster 5.11a/b *Sport*, 4 bolts. Arete up to overhang and then anchors.

149. Highland Fling ✪ 5.11c *Sport,* 6 bolts. Starts in seam, up face to bulge and high roof.

150. Let Them Eat Pancakes 5.10b *Sport*, 4 bolts. Short crack to flake and roof. Finishes under large roof.

151. Keine Kraft ✪✪ 5.12b *Sport*, 5 bolts, Angular overhanging rock. Used to be 5.11d but a hold broke.

152. We're Having Some Fun Now 5.10b *Trad*. Face to right leaning flake.

153. La Vie en Rose 5.12a *Sport*, 3 bolts. Pocketed face. Stops 20 feet short of top at anchors.

154. Kama Futra ✪ 5.12c/d *Sport*, 5 bolts, 1 pin. Shares anchors with next two routes. Start at short left facing corner under roof.

155. A-Pocket-Leaps-Now 5.13a *Sport*, 6 bolts. Start at short corner under roof.

156. Pounded Puppies 5.11d *Sport*, 5 bolts. Starts at short left facing corner and angles up and left.

157. 'Til Tuesday 5.8 *Trad*. Broken crack system.

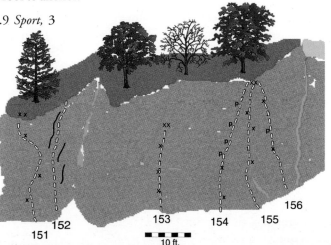

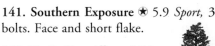

10 ft.

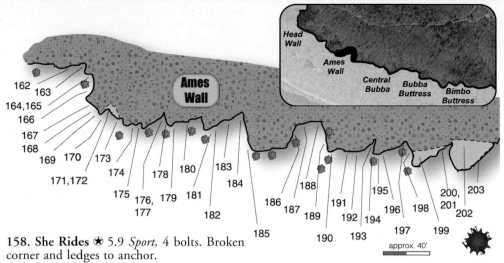

162
163
164,165
166
167
168
169 170 173
171,172
174 178 180 183
175 176, 179 181 184
177 182
185

Ames Wall

Head Wall
Ames Wall
Central Bubba
Bubba Buttress
Bimbo Buttress

186 187 188 189 190 191 192 193 194 195 196 197 198 199 200, 201 202 203

approx. 40'

158. She Rides ✪ 5.9 *Sport,* 4 bolts. Broken corner and ledges to anchor.

159. Powerful Opposition ✪ 5.12a/b *Sport,* 5 bolts. Starts on left side of arete.

160. Bubba the Vampire Slayer 5.12a *Sport,* 3 bolts. Face right of arete.

161. Bush Battle 5.5 *Trad.* Vegetated crack.

162. Where's Bohemia? 5.12c/d *Sport,* 3 bolts, 1 pin. Being reclaimed by vines and dirt.

163. Burning 5.12a *Mixed,* 2 bolts, 1 pin.

Ames Wall

164. Vertigo 5.12a *Mixed,* 4 bolts. Start on *F.U.B.* (gear needed) up to bolt on right, out right to arete to anchors.

165. F. U. B. 5.10b *Trad.* Face on left side of roof followed by crack.

166. F. A. B. 5.10c *Trad.* Roof into right facing dihedral and top.

167. Kick Ass and Ask Questions Later 5.11d *Sport,* 4 bolts. Left line of bolts finish on *Discogenic* anchors.

168. Discogenic 5.12c/d *Sport,* 5 bolts. Crack through roof.

169. Bubbaboey 5.11c/d *Sport,* 3 bolts. Left side of white face.

170. Chuckles 5.8 *Sport,* 3 bolts 1 pin. White face to ledge, traverse left to pin then anchors. Variation- Climb straight up past 3rd bolt (5.10d)

171. Scrubbing Bubbas 5.9 *Trad.* Corner to roof move left to ledge and continue up face.

172. Suggestions 5.11b *Mixed,* 1 bolt. Up *Scrubbing Bubbas* to ledge, move right past bolt.

173. Camalot 5.10d *Trad.* Up to roof and left facing corner, traversing left around arete.

174. Michelin Man ✪✪ 5.11d/12a *Sport,* 8 bolts. Overhanging start through bulges. Variation- At 6th bolt move right to seam (5.12b)

175. Radial Rimmed ✪ 5.10c *Sport,* 6 bolts.

176. Prickly Bubba 5.6 *Trad.* Same Start as *Isotope Cemetery,* staying in corner and wide crack.

177. Isotope Cemetery 5.10d *Trad.* Corner moving right onto face after passing low roof. Stay left of arete.

178. Cynarete 5.11a/b *Sport,* 5 bolts. Starts under arete and finishes to the left.

179. The Attacktician 5.10d *Sport,* 4 bolts. Flakes to right side of arete.

180. Parental Guidance Suggested 5.11a *Mixed,* 1 bolt. Face.

181. Stiff but Not Hard 5.10d *Sport,* 4 bolts. Starts on right side of arete.

182. Bubbalicious 5.8 *Trad.*

183. Air Wailing 5.8 *Trad.* Corner.

184. Gone with the Bubba 5.7 *Trad*. Crack just right of corner.

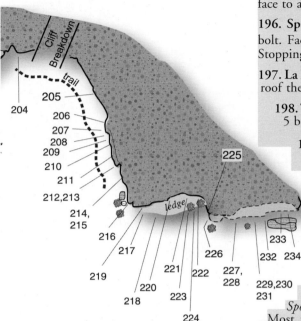

185. Bubba Black Sheep ✪ 5.12b *Mixed*, 1 bolt and 2 pins. Black face.

186. Tasty Flake ✪5.8 *Trad*. Left facing flake.

187. Ba Boschka 5.11a *Sport*, 4 bolts. Share anchors of *Tasty Flake*.

188. Bubba Does Debbie 5.10a *Trad*. Crack.

189. Arthur Murray Crack 5.10c *Mixed*, 1 pin. Crack.

190. Rock Waves 5.12b *Mixed*, 1 pin. Start on left side of arete, up then around right.

191. Fingers in Da Dyke ✪✪ 5.11b *Sport*, 4 bolts. Line up center of face.

192. Boschtardized ✪ 5.11c *Sport*, 5 bolts. Right line of bolts.

193. Lavender Chockstone 5.8 *Trad*. Dihedral.

194. Lycrascopic 5.11a *Sport*, 3 bolts.

195. Exobubba ✪ 5.11b *Sport,* 5 bolts. Thin face to anchors under roof.

196. Space Truck'n Bubbas 5.11c *Mixed*, 1 bolt. Face to right facing corner and thru roof. Stopping at roof is 5.10c.

197. La Bumba 5.9 *Trad*. Left facing corner to roof then undercling right.

198. The American Sportsman 5.12c *Sport*, 5 bolts. Slab up to small tree ledge.

199. Likme' ✪✪ 5.12a *Sport*, 5 bolts. Left side of orange wall.

200. Slip of the Tongue ✪ 5.11a *Sport*, 4 bolts. Step right at 3rd bolt on *Tongulation*. Variation of *Tongulation*.

201. Tongulation ✪✪5.11d *Sport*, 6 bolts. Right bolt line on orange wall.

202. Darwin's Dangle ✪✪ 5.11d *Sport*, 3 bolts. Out huge roof to belay. Most people stop here. Pitch #2- obvious crack.

203. Galapagos ✪ 5.12a *Sport*, 6 bolts. Right side of roof to vertical face.

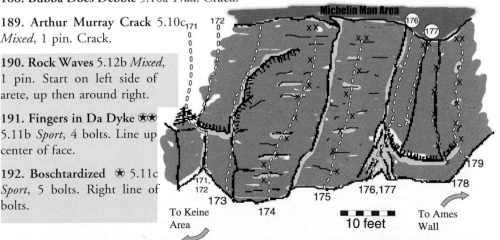

Central Bubba

204. Chicks in the Woods ✹ 5.11a *Sport*, 5 bolts. Left side of blunt arete.

205. Bubba's Lament 5.9 *Trad*. Left facing corner and crack through roofs.

206. Skinny Boys 5.10a *Trad*. Overhanging crack to ledge then clean streak to top.

207. Casper Says Boo! 5.9 *Sport*, 6 bolts.

208. Final Jepordy 5.11d *Sport*, 7 bolts. Starts left of prow.

209. Fat Chicks 5.10a *Trad*. Starts right on prow then moves around to the left.

210. White Bubbas on Dope 5.8 *Trad*. Dirty face.

211. Betty's Boop 5.8 *Trad*. Start at ledge, broken crack system and finish on *Rock'n Roll*.

212. Rock'n Roll Hours Variation 5.8 *Trad*. At bulge, traverse FAR left to clean face then up to top.

213. Arch Bubba Variation Finish 5.9 R *Trad*. Up to bulge, traverse left then left arching seam.

214. Trashed Again 5.10d *Trad*. Same start as *Eat at the Wye* but climb up black seam.

215. Eat at the Wye 5.10b *Trad*. Face to right angling flake.

216. Bubba Has Balls 5.10a *Trad*. Low roof to crack and arete, stay on left of arete.

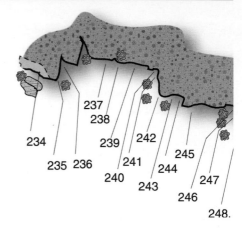

217. Mack the Knife ✹ 5.11d *Sport*, 4 bolts.

218. Dyno Please 5.11c *Sport*, 4 bolts. Bouldery moves up to high ledge (1 bolt). Then continue up left side of face passing 3 bolts.

These routes start from a high ledge.

219. Uber Alles 5.11a/b *Sport*, 4 bolts. Face on left side of ledge.

220. More Studly than Puddly 5.11d *Sport*, 4 bolts. Starts from high ledge. Up middle of face.

221. Absolute Reality ✹ 5.12c/d *Sport*, 5 bolts. Starts from high ledge. Right line of bolts up face.

222. Bumbling Bubbas 5.10a *Trad*. From ledge, left facing orange corner to crack.

223. D. S. B. 5.9+ *Trad*. Broken crack to Rainbow ledge.

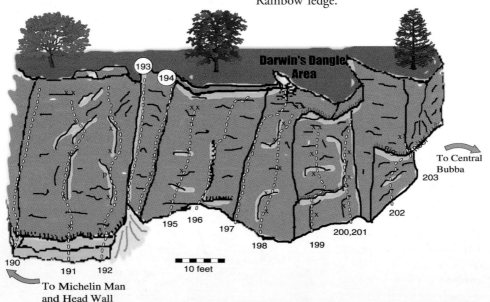

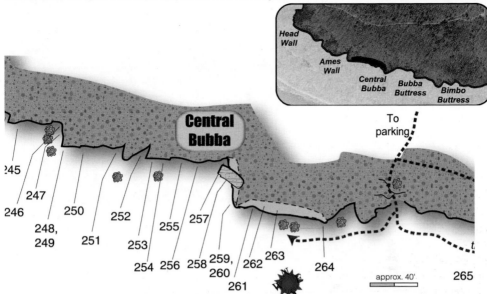

224. **Insistent Irony** 5.10b *Sport*, 3 bolts.

225. **Wasted Woute** 5.7 *Trad*. Wide crack to short flake.

226. **Bubbas on a Landscape** 5.11d *Sport*, 3 bolts. Bulging arete.

227. **Bubba Meets She-Ra** 5.10a *Trad*. Small left facing corner to roof, move left to arete then crack and face to top.

228. **Psychotic Turnbuckles** 5.10c *Trad*. Direct start to *Bubba Meets She-Ra*. Straight up through roofs.

229. **Bubba Meets Savannah** 5.11c *Sport*, 6 bolts. Start as *Look Who's Pulling*. Left hand bolt line.

230. **Look Who's Pulling** ✷ 5.11a *Sport*, 4 bolts. Right hand bolt line.

231. **Look Who's Crimping** 5.10d *Sport*, 3 bolts. Continuation from top of *Look Who's Pulling*.

232. **Hah! Direct Start** 5.11b *Trad*. Start directly below seam and straight up.

233. **Hah!** 5.11b *Trad*. Up and right through roofs to seam, seam to top.

234. **Arapiles Please** ✷✷ 5.12c *Sport*, 4 bolts, 1 pin. Steep face 10' left of arete.

235. **Whamawete** ✷✷ 5.11d *Mixed*, 1 pin. Arete. Good trad climbing route!

236. **Tosha Goes to the Gorge** 5.4 *Trad*. Right facing corner.

237. **Puddsucker** 5.11a *Mixed*, 1 bolt. Joins *Raptilian* at bolt 3.

238. **The Raptilian** 5.10d *Sport*, 4 bolts.

239. **Little Wing** 5.10b *Sport*, 3 bolts, 1 pin.

240. **Axis Bold as Bubba** 5.9 *Trad*. Left facing corner.

241. **Desperate but not Serious** ✷ 5.12a *Sport*, 4 bolts. Black face and dihedrals to anchor.

242. **Bubba Lou** 5.12c *Mixed*, 2 pins.

243. **Stop the Presses Rico Suave** ✷ 5.12c *Sport*, 5 bolts. Slightly overhanging face.

244. **Shear Strength** ✷✷ 5.11a *Mixed*, 3 pins. Orange dihedral.

245. **Where Fools Rush In** 5.12d *Sport*, 5 bolts. Starts right of dihedral.

246. **Pig Pen** 5.10a *Trad*. Dihedral.

247. **Into the Fire** ✷ 5.12b *Sport*, 5 bolts. Starts at short crack.

248. **Lean Productions** 5.12c *Sport*, 4 bolts. Starts on *Bubbacide*, continues straight up face.

249. **Bubbacide** ✷ 5.12a/b *Sport*, 4 bolts. Starts on face then right to arete.

250. **Diamond Life** ✷✷ 5.13a *Sport*, 5 bolts. Pocketed face. The first 5.13 at the Gorge.

251. **Sheer Energy** ✷✷ 5.11a/b *Sport*, 6 bolts. Corner up to anchors on right.

252. **Bedtime for Bubba** 5.9 *Trad*. Left facing corner.

253. **Hydroman** ✷ 5.11c *Sport*, 6 bolts. Up face through roof.

254. **Happy Campers** 5.11a *Mixed*, 1 pin. Up

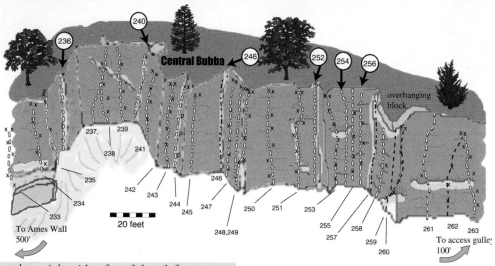

crack to right side of roof then left.

255. Brown-out ✪ 5.11d *Sport*, 4 bolts. Brown face to anchor.

256. The Golden Escalator ✪ 5.11a *Sport*, 3 bolts. Gold streak to top.

257. Bubba Bath 5.9 *Trad*. Dirty flake.

258. The Raging Tiger ✪ 5.10d *Mixed*, 1 bolt. Nice face climbing up to shuts under roof.

259. Jesus Wept 5.12c/d *Sport*, 5 bolts. Left bolt line.

260. The Cutting Edge ✪✪ 5.12b *Sport*, 8 bolts. Up and right to arete. Broken hold has made this one letter grade harder (It was 12a).

261. It's Brutal Bubba 5.12c *Mixed*, 1 bolt. Left facing corner to roof, left thru pockets.

262. Mind's Eye 5.13a *Sport*, 4 bolts. Joins *Rattle and Hum* at bolt 4.

263. Rattle and Hum 5.11a *Sport*, 4 bolts. Same finish as *Mind's Eye*.

264. Mr. Pudd's Wild Ride 5.11d *Mixed*, 1 bolt, 1 pin. Left facing corner to roof.

Bubba Buttress

265. Duck in A Noose 5.8+ *Sport*, 4 bolts. Starts in short left facing chimney. Continue up obvious flake to ledge and anchor.

266. Life-O-Suction 5.11a *Sport*, 4 bolts. Left of arete.

267. Harmonic Jello ✪ 5.12c *Sport*, 5 bolts. Broken hold at crux has made this a little bit harder.

268. Fired for Sandbagging ✪✪ 5.12a *Sport*, 6 bolts. Variation finish to Harmonic that moves left around the crux.

269. Face It Bubba ✪✪ 5.11a *Mixed*, 2 bolts. Crack to bolt move right to flake then up and left to finish.

270. Eight Ball in Side Pocket ✪ 5.12a *Sport*, 6 bolts. Bouldery move to bolt, continue up face to anchors.

271. Basic Bubba Crack ✪ 5.9 *Trad*. Crack and corner to roof, con't up crack to top.

272. Veni, Vidi, Vici 5.12a *Mixed*, 2 bolts, 1 pin. Bubbarete crack then face past bolts and pin.

273. Flexible Strategies ✪ 5.12b *Sport*, 7 bolts. Start on *Veni* crack then right to bolt. Up bolt line finish on *Veni*.

274. Bubbarete 5.10b *Trad*. Obvious hand-crack to start then traverse right to arete.

275. Immaculate Combustion ✪ 5.10d *Mixed*, 6 bolts, 1 pin. Slab trending up and left to ledge then straight up wall passing a bolt and pin.

276. Fierce Face 5.11b *Mixed*, 6 bolts. Start on *Immaculate* but move right at second bolt, up to ledge then center of face to anchors.

277. Bubba Safari 5.8 *Trad*. Crack to ledge, then right side of face to top.

278. Leaping Lizards 5.11c *Sport*, 4 bolts. Starts at short outside corner. Move up trending right to anchors.

279. Dubious Young Lizards ✪ 5.11c *Mixed*, 1 bolt, 1 pin. Lieback to left leaning crack.

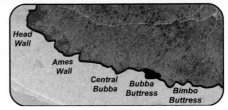

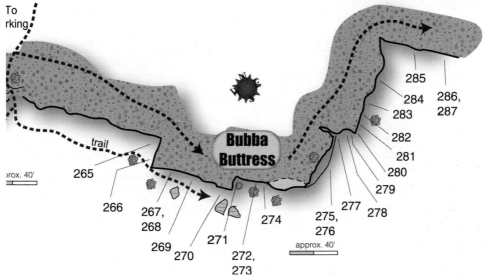

To rking

trail

approx. 40'

Bubba Buttress

265

266

267, 268

269

270

271

272, 273

274

275, 276

277

278

279

280

281

282

283

284

285

286, 287

approx. 40'

280. Dumbolt County 5.10b *Mixed*, 1 pin. Follows arete to top.

281. Truth or Contra-Expenses ✪ 5.11d *Sport*, 5 bolts. Twin cracks to bulge.

282. Reason Over Might 5.12a *Sport*, 5 bolts.

283. The Man from Planet Zog 5.11a *Sport*, 4 bolts. Right line of bolts.

284. Jaded Vision 5.6 *Trad*. Right facing corner.

285. El Routo De Los Contrivadores 5.8 *Trad*. Flake up to blunt arete and small roof.

286. Wunderkind 5.6 *Sport*, 4 bolts. Up small corner and roof to anchors.

287. Hi-C 5.10a *Sport*, 4 bolts. Same start as Wunderkind. After second bolt, move left.

288. Just Plain Dirty 5.4 *Trad*. Crack to ledge and top.

289. Exit if You Can 5.8 *Trad*. Left facing crack and flake system to tree.

290. Fossilized Faggots 5.8 *Mixed*, 1 pin. Crack through small overhang.

291. Mad Mac 5.11b/c *Sport*, 4 bolts. Short line up face through undercling.

292. Achtung Baby 5.11c *Sport*, 4 bolts. Short line right of Mad Mac. Shares same anchor.

293. Logotherapy ✪ 5.13a/b *Sport*, 6 bolts. Starts at short right facing corner. Up corner, overhang and pocketed face to bulge and anchors.

294. Cumberland Blues ✪✪ 5.11b *Mixed*, 1 pin. Arete and bulges to right leaning flake and small roof.

295. Perpendiculus 5.10c *Mixed*, 1 pin. Corner to roof, undercling out right to dihedral.

296. Beginner's Climb 5.6 *Trad*. Broken crack system and ledges up to anchors under small roof.

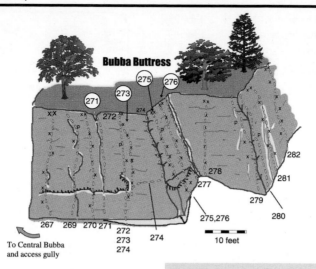

Bubba Buttress

To Central Bubba
and access gully

10 feet

297. **Pound of Prevention** 5.8 *Mixed.* Face to ledge and pin then right to nice dihedral. Var.- Finish left of regular route up seam, 5.11d.

298. **Thank God I'm Bubbafied** 5.8 *Trad.* Chimney.

299. **Leave It to Bubba** 5.9 *Trad.* From ledge, up to short crack and roof, traverse left around corner to other crack and to anchors.

300. **Fred Sandstone Flake** 5.9 *Trad.* Variation finish on *Leave It To Bubba.* Straight up to right leaning flake after roof, follow flake up and right to top and anchors.

301. **Werewolf** ✹ 5.10a *Trad.* Up center of face and pull roof at small crack to anchors.

302. **Exhaust Pipe** ✹ 5.8 R *Trad.* Up center of face, move right to orange corner.

303. **Doo-Wah-Woof** ✹ 5.4 *Trad.* Start as above but move right on ledge, up corner crack system to small ledge under roof then top.

304. **Creamy** 5.8 *Trad.* From ledge on above route follow right edge of wall up wide flake, finish near Daisy Cutter anchors.

305. **Daisy Cutter** ✹✹ 5.7 *Sport,* 5 bolts. Start inside obvious chimney at right side of wall. Up face then short crack. Climb flakes then move out left to face.

306. **The Cluster Bomb** ✹ 5.11b *Mixed,* 1 pin. Start right of chimney, move up and right to small roof and flake, continue up and right on face to top.

Beer Wall

307. **Near Beer** 5.6 *Sport,* 4 bolts. Starts from ledge. Up past broken rock to small overhang, then left to wide crack and then anchors.

308. **Gilded Otter** ✹ 5.7 *Sport,* 5 bolts. Dihedral to bulge and ledge then roof to anchors.

309. **Micro Brew** ✹ 5.5 *Sport,* 5 bolts. Obvious flake and corner to finish on anchors of *Gilded.*

310. **Spatenweiss** ✹ 5.11d *Sport,* 6 bolts. Up to overhang, thru overhang and finish on anchors of *St. Pauli.*

311. **St. Pauli Girl** ✹✹ 5.10c *Sport,* 5 bolts. Bolt line up steep orange face.

312. **Bubbaweiser** ✹ 5.10d *Sport,* 7 bolts. Starts left of vertical seam. At 2nd bolt move right to ledge then flakes to roof, move left then continue to top.

313. **Cerveza Verde** ✹ 5.8 *Sport,* 5 bolts. Starts left of high roof. Thin face move up to bulge then anchors.

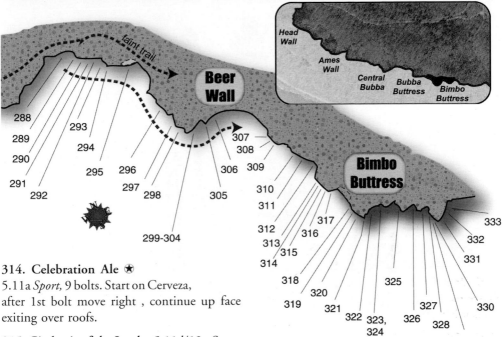

314. Celebration Ale ✪
5.11a *Sport*, 9 bolts. Start on Cerveza, after 1st bolt move right , continue up face exiting over roofs.

315. Cirrhosis of the Leader 5.11d/12a *Sport*, 2 bolts. Short route under high roof.

316. Delirium Tremors 5.11a *Sport*, 5 bolts. Starts on right side of high roof.

317. Eating Bimbo Pie 5.7 *Trad.* Starts at right side of high roof. Follow dihedrals to top.

318. Beer Wench 5.8 *Sport*, 4 bolts. Short crack to bulge and finish in dihedral to anchors.

Bimbo Buttress

319. Peanut Bubba and Jam 5.8 *Trad.* Finger and handcrack to top.

320. The Icon of Control 5.10c *Mixed*, 1 bolt. Face to small roof.

321. Learning Curve 5.8 *Sport*, 4 bolts. Start right of wide crack, move up to arete. Finish up arete and face.

322. The Wong Woute 5.7 *Trad.* Corner to crack system.

323. Bugerschnatz ✪ 5.10d *Sport*, 5 bolts. Start at left facing corner then left to face and overhang to top.

324. The Wang Way 5.6 *Trad.* Left facing corner and cracks to top.

325. Crank to Power ✪ 5.11d *Sport*, 4 bolts. Overhanging orange face.

326. Bubbalissima ✪ 5.11c *Sport*, 4 bolts. Starts on right side of high roof.

327. The Power Line 5.11c *Mixed*, 1 pin. Follow thin crack, move left past pin near top.

328. Airwaves 5.10c *Sport*, 4 bolts. Left facing corner to moving right at roof then up to top.

329. The Innocence Mission 5.12d R *Mixed*, 1 bolt. Traverse left out low roof, then up and left past bolt, continue to roof moving right.

330. It Comes in Spurts 5.7 *Trad.* Corner.

331. Taming of the Shrewd 5.10c *Trad.* Left facing corner up to left leaning flake.

332. Direct Aretection 5.10a *Sport*, 4 bolts. Overhanging arete.

333. Gunpowder 5.12a *Toprope or highball*. Overhanging face to anchors.

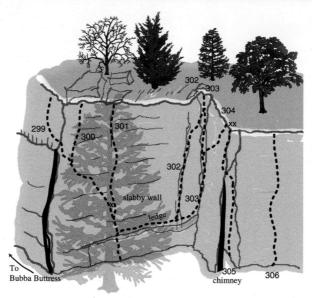

large tree

Lisa Horst on St. Pauli Girl (5.10c), Bubba City.
Photo: Eric Horst Collection

Pace on Michelin Man (5.12a), Bubba City.
Photo: Dan Brayack

Eric Horst on Logotherapy (5.13a/b), Bubba City.
Photo: Eric McCallister

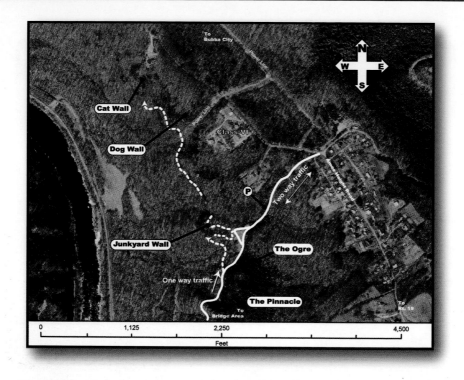

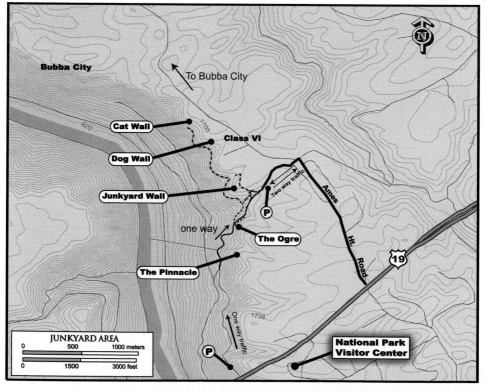

3

J u n k y a r d   W a l l

101 routes • 2 sport • 99 trad / mixed

At one time, Junkyard Wall was just that, an overflowing hillside of rusted refrigerators, washing machines and household garbage that was tossed over the hill in typical Appalachian fashion. To reach the crag, you had to pick your way through this refuse carefully stepping over the thick layer of our cultures debris that had accumulated over the years. Recent efforts have removed a majority of the rubbish but some still remains. Be careful of broken glass and sharp objects while hiking to the cliff. Junkyard has an excellent selection of easy to moderate traditional style climbs. The cliff varies in height from 35' to 60' with many classic crack climbs in the 5.9 to 5.10 range. A standard rack of camming units and stoppers is recommended. Easy access to the top of the cliff makes Junkyard a popular top-roping area. Since the cliff faces southwest, it is shaded during the mornings and receives sun in the afternoon. Junkyard Wall receives the most traffic but Dog Wall and Cat Cliff contain

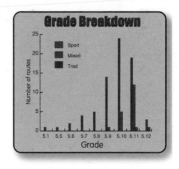

a number of quality rock climbs. To reach Dog Wall, continue following the trail at the base of Junkyard Wall. Pass through the powerline cut and the next section of wall is Dog Wall. Continue following this trail for 10 minutes to reach the Cat Cliff. These areas are less traveled but have a good selection of climbs and should not be overlooked if you arrive at Junkyard and find it overcrowded.

Access

Junkyard Wall is easily accessed from either the North Bridge Wall or from the parking area below Ames Height Road. At the four-way intersection on Ames Height Road, turn left and drive down the dirt road 150 yards, pull off to the left and park, continue walking another 100 yards to a sharp left turn in the road. The trail begins here by stepping over the stone gabions at the right end of the guard rail. This new trail winds down to the base of Rapscallions Blues. If you hike in from the North Bridge Area, turn left at the iron stained overhang (The Ogre) and follow the trail to the base of the wall. It is also possible to drive from the Bridge Buttress. At the first hairpin turn after driving downhill past the Bridge Buttress, continue straight up the narrow steep road, this passes The Pinnacle and The Ogre climbing areas. Do not park on this road. Continue up to the top and park at the designated parking areas on the right just after the short steep section and small hairpin turn.

Notes

Please try to limit your impact at this climbing area by using the fixed anchors at the top of climbs. This cliff receives a great deal of weekend traffic so be prepared for a crowd if you show up on Saturday or Sunday. The road that you drive down from Ames Height is two way until the parking area and then becomes one way with traffic direction moving uphill.

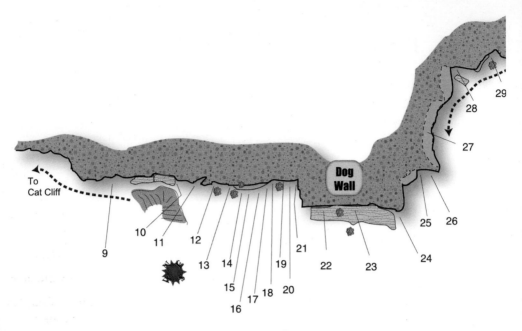

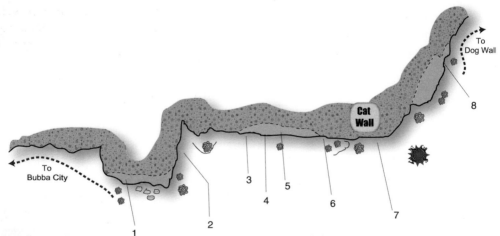

Cat Cliff

1. Amarillo Dawn ✪✪ 5.11a *Trad.* Corner to ledge, then follow crack and pull roof to finish.

2. The Good Life 5.10c *Trad.* Crack.

3. Neuva Vida 5.11b *Trad.* Roof and crack.

4. Kentucky Whore ✪ 5.11c *Trad.* Roof to corner and finish on face.

5. Australian Whore 5.11a *Trad.* Roof to crack then pull second roof.

6. Labrador Reliever ✪✪ 5.8 *Trad.* Crack to roof, move left and follow crack to top. Good 5.8!

7. Morning Glory 5.11a *Trad.* Crack to roof.

8. More Bum, More Fun 5.10d *Trad.* Corner to roof, move right and then pull second roof.

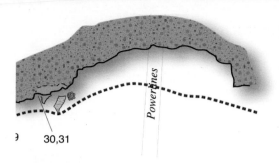

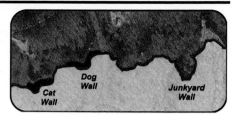

30,31

Dog Wall

9. Mongrels 5.10a *Trad*. Face to roof then continue to the top.

10. Underdog 5.11a *Mixed*, 1 pin. Corner.

11. Doggy Style 5.11c R *Trad*. Seam to horizontal, move left to flakes.

12. Bitch in Heat 5.11a R *Trad*. Seam.

13. Dingo ✪ 5.10d *Trad*. Face to crack.

14. A Dog Always Returns to It's Vomit 5.10c R *Trad*. Face to roof and finish on ledge.

15. Call of the Wild 5.11c *Mixed*, 1 pin. Up to bulge, move left 10 feet and finish on ledge.

16. Dog Day Afternoon 5.11a *Trad*. Crack.

17. Point the Bone 5.11a *Trad*. Face to corner and finish on *Dog Day*.

18. Hangdog 5.11c *Trad*. Crack, traverse right and finish on *Pit Bull*.

19. Pit Bull Terror ✪ 5.10b *Mixed*, 1 pin. Crack to ledge, up face to short crack then left under roof and finish at tree.

20. Puppy Love 5.10d *Trad*. Face.

21. Nasty Poodle Chew ✪ 5.6 *Trad*. Dihedral. Sometimes this can be dirty.

22. Born Under A Bad Smell 5.10c *Trad*. Crack to face.

23. Black Dog 5.8 *Trad*. Crack and flakes.

24. One-Eyed Viper 5.10b *Trad*. Corner to crack.

25. Unnamed JW #1 5.9 *Trad*. Short dihedral to ledge trend up and right following corner.

26. Unnamed JW #1 5.9 *Trad*. Top-rope. Start at low roof, follow flake system up and left to horizontal, traverse right then pull through roof and con't up and left to top.

27. Dreamtime ✪ 5.9 *Trad*. Follow crack system on the left through three roofs.

28. Themetime ✪ 5.6 *Trad*. Follow crack system to ledge, pull small roof and continue to top.

29. Poodle with A Mohawk 5.1 *Trad*. Wide crack up to ledge, move left and pull through small roof into corner and continue to top.

30. Unnamed JW #3 5.6 *Trad*. Start as above straight up corner to anchor under roof.

31. Unnamed JW #4 5.7 *Trad*. Short left-facing corner to ledge, move right and up face to small corner and anchor.

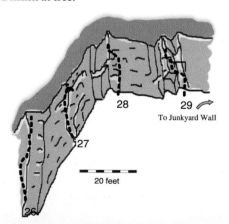

28   29 ↗

To Junkyard Wall

27

26

20 feet

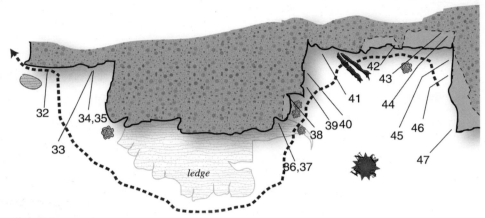

ledge

Junkyard North

32. Spoon Fed 5.9 R *Trad*. Crack and flakes to ledge move right and finish on crack.

33. Commuter Flight 5.11a *Mixed*, 1 pin.

34. Direct Deviation 5.11a *Trad*. Corner to first roof of *Deviated Septum*.

35. Deviated Septum 5.11a *Mixed*, 1 pin. Crack to roof moving right then continue up face.

36. Chased By Spiders to the Left ✪ 5.9 R *Trad*. Same as above except traverse left at roof.

37. Chasing Spiders to the Right ✪ 5.7 *Trad*. Start at low overhang and follow orange dihedral to roof, traverse right at roof.

38. Never Alone 5.8 *Trad*. Jugs to corner and traverse right below roof.

39. Brother Sun 5.12b/c *Mixed*, 2 pins. Corner, roof, crack.

40. I Just Eight 5.8 *Trad*. Small corner through small overhang.

41. Poison Ivy 5.10c R *Trad*. Corner to crack.

42. Pilots of Bekaa 5.12a *Mixed*, 1 pin. Corner, roof.

43. Faith Crack 5.10c *Trad*. Crack.

44. Squids in Bondage 5.9 *Trad*. Wide crack. Rap from slings.

44a. Link-up 5.11b R *Trad*. Continue right from slings of *Squids* onto *Childbirth*.

45. Childbirth ✪ 5.11b *Trad*. Crack/corner system, finishing out roof crack.

46. Lap Child ✪ 5.12a/b *Mixed*, 4 bolts. Face climb in middle of wall.

47. Name It and Claim It ✪ 5.11 *Mixed*, 1 pin. Arete.

48. Aimless Wanderers 5.10d *Mixed*, 1 bolt. Wanders up face.

49. Brown Dirt Cowboy ✪ 5.10c *Trad*. Face up and left. Nice face climbing. Can be dirty at times.

50. Emotional Barbecue 5.10d *Trad*. Flakes to ledge then crack, traversing 20 feet right around blunt arete or finish straight up.

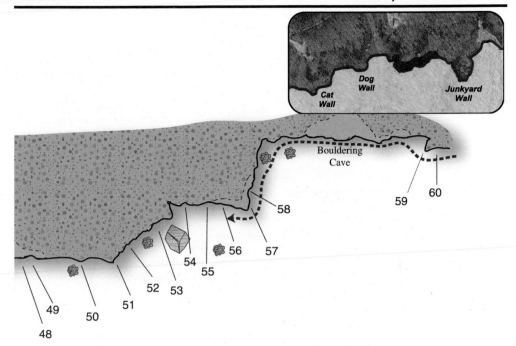

58

54
55
56   57

52   53
51
49   50
48

59   60

Bouldering
Cave

Cat
Wall

Dog
Wall

Junkyard
Wall

51. Enemy Line 5.10c X *Trad.* Face up to shallow dihedral, move right to smaller roof then move back left at second roof and con't to top.

52. Five-Eight 5.11b *Mixed*, 1 bolt. Thin crack to face.

53. Modern Lovers 5.11c *Trad.* Right leaning crack then move left to other crack system and up.

54. Recreation 5.9 R *Trad.* Face to top.

55. Suck Face 5.11a *Trad.* Straight up face

56. Zealous ✪✪ 5.10d *Trad.* Begin at low roof crack, follow crack up to horizontal, move right to obvious left leaning crack/flake system and continue to anchor. Classic line!

57. Kansas Shitty 5.10c *Mixed*, 1 pin. Arete, roof and crack.

58. Redemption 5.11c *Trad.* Roof crack finishing right of leaning crack.

59. Beware of Euro-Dog 5.11d *Mixed*, 1 pin. Shallow left-facing corner, overhang then arete to top.

60. Anomalous Propagation 5.10a R *Mixed*, 1 pin. Face to small roof finishing on face.

61. Walk in the Park 5.8 *Mixed*, 2 pins. Start 50' left of ladder. Excellent moves over moss and lichen

Dave Heinbach on the classic Entertainer (5.10a), Junkyard Wall. Photo: Cater.

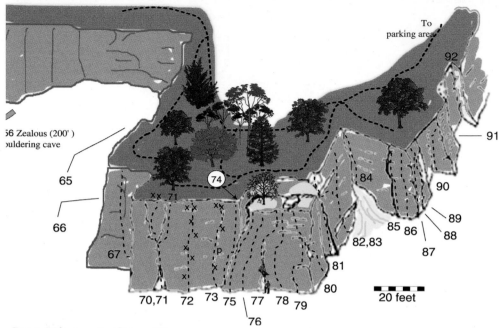

Junkyard South

62. Churning in the Huecos 5.10d *Mixed*, 3 pins.

63. Anxiety Neurosis 5.11b R *Mixed*, 1 bolt. Crack and face.

64. Who Knows? 5.7 *Trad*. Corner.

65. V-Slot ✪✪5.9 *Trad*. Left hand crack finishing left below roof.

66. Stuck in Another Dimension ✪✪5.11a *Trad*. Right hand crack to roof. Great fun!

67. Rhododenema 5.9 *Mixed*, 1 pin. Face then move left to upper dihedral. Move left up and over small roof.

68. Mr. Ed 5.8 *Trad*. Crack to corner.

69. Slip Trip 5.11c R *Mixed*, 1 bolt. Face.

70. The Entertainer ✪✪ 5.10a *Trad*. Crack to small roof then follow left trending cracks and flakes to shuts.

71. Realignment ✪✪5.10d *Trad*. Start on *Entertainer* and after pulling small roof, follow the right crack system to the top.

72. Mystery Dance ✪5.12a *Sport*, 4 bolts, 1 pin.

73. Reachers of Habit ✪ 5.11b *Sport*, 2 bolts, 1 pin.

74. The Contortionist ✪5.9 *Trad*. Wide Crack.

75. The Distortionist ✪5.6 *Trad*. Wide crack to right leaning arete. Finish at shuts.

76. Bubba Meets Jesus 5.11a R *Trad*. Face left of *Team Jesus*.

77. Team Jesus ✪✪5.10b *Trad*. Follow thin crack until it ends then move right on face and continue to shuts. Technical face climbing.

78. New River Gunks Direct 5.11b *Trad*. Face between *New River Gunks* and *Team Jesus*. Good top-rope problem.

79. New River Gunks ✪✪5.7 *Trad*. Start on face, move up then traverse right to crack. Up crack then follow ledge system to small roof. Take short crack straight up (5.7) or traverse right to arete or pull roof 5 feet left of short crack. Shuts at top. Great route and popular.

80. J.Y.D. 5.11c *Mixed*, 2 pins. Overhanging crack moving left to arete then up to *NRG* anchor.

81. Frigidator 5.10b *Trad*. Crack on right wall inside chimney.

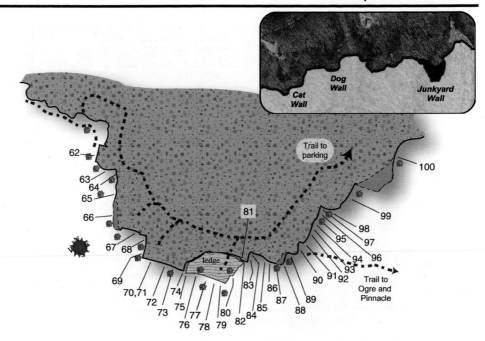

82. Andropov's Cold ✪ 5.11c *Trad.* Short, over-hanging finger crack.

83. Keep It Tight But Don't Give Me AIDS 5.6 *Trad.* Flake or slab to ledge then move up and left to chimney. **Variation Finish** 5.10a. Move up and right at middle ledge.

84. Jumpin' Jack Flash 5.7 *Trad.* Dirty corner. Not bad, but always dirty.

85. New Yosemite ✪✪ 5.9 *Trad.* Splitter handcrack to shuts.

86. Yew Nosemite 5.12b *Mixed*, 1 pin. Face.

87. Just Say No 5.11a R *Trad.* Arete.

88. Scott's Turf Builder 5.10b *Trad.* Crack to corner up to roof then finish on *Enteruptus*.

89. Enteruptus 5.10a *Trad.* Crack to flakes and roof then finish to the right. Straight over roof it's 5.11d.

90. Four Sheets to the Wind ✪✪ 5.9 *Trad.* Starts at overhanging dihedral move up and right and pass through two upper roofs. Finish by moving left into alcove near top or moving right up low angle corner. Shuts at top. One of the classics!

91. Rapscallion's Blues ✪✪ 5.10c *Trad.* Slightly overhanging dihedral and corner, pull roof and move left and up to top.

92. Rock Rash 5.11a *Trad.* Right wall face up to crack, undercling right at roof then ledge.

93. Whales in Drag 5.10a *Trad.* Corner to roof, traversing right then back left 15 feet finishing straight up face.

94. Princess Diana 5.9 R *Trad.* Up face moving right above roof.

95. Danger in Paradise 5.10b *Mixed*, 1 pin. Crack and flakes to ledge.

96. Crack Sap 5.9 *Trad.* Corner to roof, moving left to ledge.

97. The Hornet 5.9 *Trad.* Start left of *Lapping the Sap*, angle up and right on flakes and connect with above route.

98. Lapping the Sap 5.10 *Trad.* Corner to roof, then move right.

99. Nine Lives 5.11c *Mixed*, 3 bolts. Arete and face.

100. Ann's Revenge 5.8 *Trad.* Left facing corner to crack.

101. Long Reach 5.9 *Trad.* Crack.

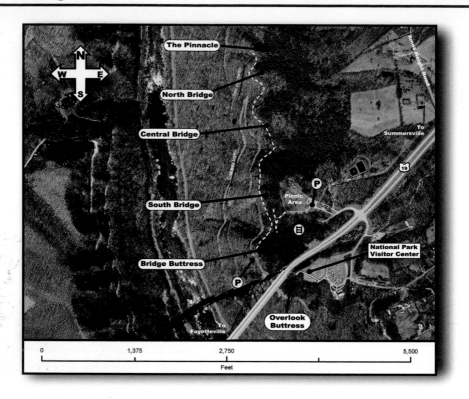

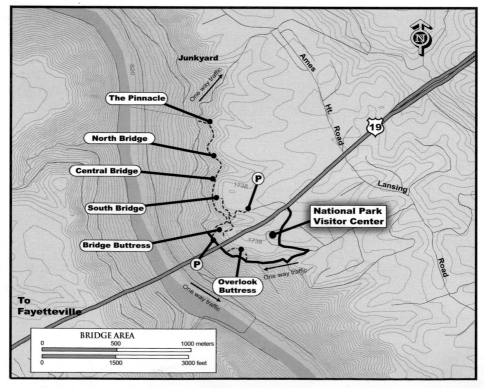

4

B r i d g e   A r e a

193 routes • 30 sport • 163 trad/mixed

The Bridge Area is one of the most popular climbing areas at the New River Gorge. The easy access and large number of moderate routes attracts many of the first timers who visit the New. The main buttress is only a few feet away from the parking area and the excellent cracks and faces are a good sampling of the climbing throughout the New River Gorge. Historically, the Bridge Area was the first cliff at the New to be developed as a rock climbing area. Local climbers Rick Skidmore and Hobart Parks made early ascents of *Zag* (5.8), *The Mayfly* (5.9), and *Chockstone* (5.9) in the mid 70's. For many years climbing activity was centered around the Bridge Area. Today, the heavy climbing and tourist traffic has contributed to a great deal of erosion at the Bridge Buttress, please attempt to lessen your impact at the cliff by not destroying vegetation, placing gear anchors instead of tying off trees, picking up trash and cigarette butts and using established trails. In spring 1998, volunteers with the help of the Access Fund and Park Service installed steps under Zag, placed gravel on trails, created a new trail from Bridge Buttress to South Bridge Area, and installed support on the embankment under Angels Arete to reduce the rate of erosion. The cliff is very crowded on weekends and should be avoided.

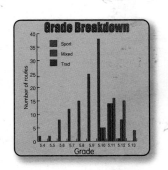

The cliff varies from 30' to 90' in height and offers a good selection of crack and face climbing. The majority of climbs are trad routes in the moderate range.

Access

The Bridge Area stretches from the main bridge down to Junkyard Wall. Access is gained from the parking area under the bridge or from the Junkyard Parking Area. The Bridge Parking Area is the most popular access point and allows an easy approach to the Overlook Buttress, Bridge Buttress, South Bridge Wall and Central Bridge Wall. The North Bridge Wall and Pinnacle area may be easily accessed from the pull-off located 3/4 mile down from the main bridge parking area.

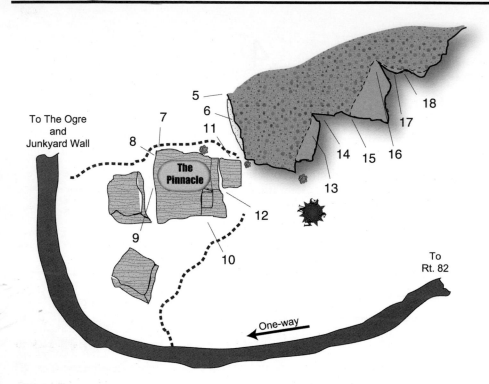

The Ogre

The Ogre is a small cliff located between Junkyard and The Pinnacle. From the Pinnacle, continue walking up the road another 100 yds. An overhanging cliff appears on the right with an orange leachate puddle at its base.

1. Food for Thought 5.8 Trad. Dirty crack.

2. Leachate 5.12a *Sport*, 4 bolts.

3. Roadcutt Manner 5.11d *Sport*, 6 bolts.

4. The Best Little Roadcut Out of Texas 5.12c *Sport*, 6 bolts.

The Pinnacle

5. The Spamling 5.7 *Trad*. Dihedral.

6. Spams Across America 5.6 *Trad*. Corner.

7. Destination Unknown 5.11a *Trad*. Up face 25 feet then move right to arete, pull roof then face and crack to top.

8. Texas Bolt Massacre 5.12a *Mixed*, 3 bolts. Arete.

9. The Reverse Traverse 5.9 *Trad*. Offwidth to roof, move left to ledge.

10. The Vertex 5.10c/d R *Trad*.

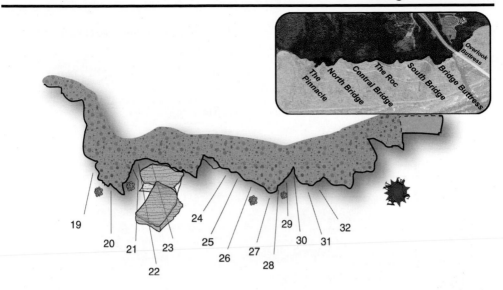

North Bridge Wall

11. Pinnacle Flats 5.9 *Trad*. Wide crack to ledge, finish on *Afternoon Delight*.

12. Afternoon Delight ✪ 5.5 *Trad*. Offwidth crack to large ledge, move left to corner and traverse right or left at roof. Continue on easy ground to top. Wide gear for bottom.

13. Jams Across America 5.10b *Trad*. Thin crack to ledge and rappel.

14. Mr. Peanut Head 5.9 *Trad*. Wide crack to roof and corner.

15. Fat Cat ✪✪ 5.13a *Sport*, 4 bolts. Obvious overhanging arete. Lots of fun!

16. Porcupine Crack 5.8 *Trad*. Corner to roof and belay on ledge.

17. Ode To Stoat 5.10b *Mixed*, 1 bolt. Up to roof, traverse left then over roof to top. **Direct Start** 5.10d- Starts to the right of regular route.

18. Meto Power 5.10c *Trad*. Roof to crack.

19. The Gloom Index 5.10a *Trad*. Crack to arete and finish on crack.

20. The Artful Dreamer 5.9 *Trad*. Up to roof, then move left and angle right to cracks.

21. Chattasuga Choo-Choo 5.9 *Trad*. Start just right of rotten looking overhang, move up and left pulling a roof and continue to top.

22. The Gospel Trek 5.5 *Trad*.

23. Gaye Belayed 5.8 *Trad*. Crack to ledge.

24. Orange Blossom Special ✪ 5.6 *Trad*. Follow flake system up and left to the top.

25. The Eggman 5.11b *Mixed*, 1 pin. Pull roof to pin, con't up face to top.

26. Unnamed BA #1 (Unknown) *Mixed*, 1 bolt, 1 pin. Face.

27. Ook Ook Kachook 5.11a R *Trad*. Start on arete then move right onto face and then back left to arete, continue to top on left side of arete.

28. The Walrus 5.10 *Trad*. Pocketed face to ledge, con't up face to top.

40. Sphagnum Dopus 5.8 *Trad.* Left-leaning right facing corner.

41. Bhopal West 5.10a R *Trad.* Offwidth crack.

42. Slave to the Past 5.11c *Mixed*, 2 bolts.

43. Le Brief 5.10c *Trad.* Face to ledge then rap.

44. First Strike ✪✪ 5.10a *Trad.* Obvious left leaning crack to top.

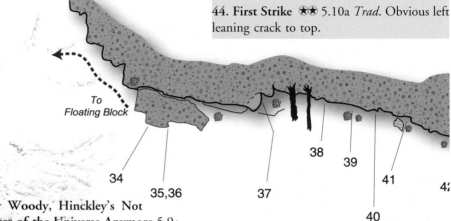

To Floating Block

34

35,36

37

38

39

41

4:

40

29. Hey Woody, Hinckley's Not the Center of the Universe Anymore 5.9+ *Trad.* Face left of *Midway.*

30. Midway 5.8 *Trad.* Dihedral to dirty corner.

31. Dr. Rosenbud's Nose ✪ 5.10b *Mixed*, 1 bolt. Climb face up to below small roof and arete, gain arete and continue to top.

32. Share the Faith 5.9 *Trad.* Thin crack.

Central Bridge Wall

33. Impaled 5.10b *Trad.* This climb is located on the "Floating Block" 50 yds. along the trail. Face to ledge then finger crack to top.

34. Needful Things 5.11c *Sport,* 4 bolts.

35. Joey's Face 5.10b *Trad.* First 10' of *Dark Hollow* then right and up.

36. Dark Hollow 5.8 *Trad.* Corner.

37. Throw in the Rack 5.7 *Trad.* Dihedral.

38. M.I.C. 5.10a *Trad.* Short finger crack.

39. Magnum Gropus 5.10d *Trad.* Crack.

45. Big Al's 5.9 *Trad.* Crack to corner.

46. The Hopfenperle Special ✪ 5.7 *Trad.* Corner.

47. Lichen Illusion 5.11d *Mixed*, 1 bolt, 1 pin. Face.

48. Burning Bungee 5.11c *Mixed*, 1 bolt. Bulging arete.

49. Akron Motor Speedway 5.12a/b *Mixed*, 5 bolts. *Midnight Moonlight* to ledge, step right to bolted line.

50. Midnight Moonlight ✪ 5.7 *Trad.* Left trending ramp and dihedral to small roof.

50a. Diver Down 5.10d *Trad.* Up face left of *Midnight Moonlight.* Big holds and steep. Step right at the big ledge to avoid the final 5.6 R section at the top.

51. Rockin' Robyn ✪ 5.11d *Mixed*, 3 bolts, 1 pin. Begin 5' right of ramp, straight up following pin and bolts.

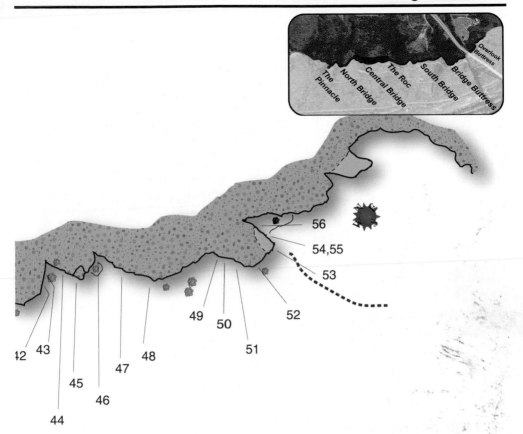

The Pinnacle
North Bridge
Central Bridge
The Roc
South Bridge
Bridge Buttress
Overlook Buttress

56

54,55

53

49 50

52

42 43

48

51

47

45

46

44

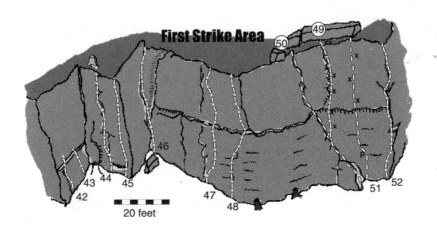

First Strike Area   50   49

46

43   44   45

42

47

48

51   52

p

20 feet

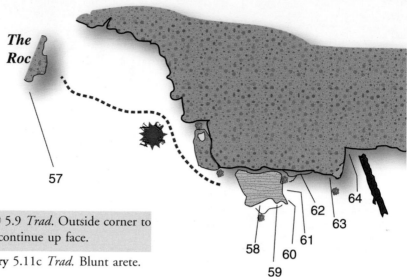

The Roc

57

52. Milk Run ✪ 5.9 *Trad.* Outside corner to roof and crack, continue up face.

53. Hairy Canary 5.11c *Trad.* Blunt arete.

54. Quantum Meruit 5.4 *Trad.* Climb *Dairy Area*, continue left after traverse then move straight up face. Same finish as *Milk Run*.

55. Dairy Area ✪ 5.4 *Trad.* Climb up and left to roof, continue traversing left around corner and then angle back up and right.

56. 'Til The Cows Come Home 5.10b *Trad.* Roof to corner.

The Roc

57. Ducks Unlimited 5.7 *Trad.* Corner.

58. Big Mac Attack 5.11a *Mixed*, 1 bolt. Corner, crack to arete.

59. Pancake Ledge 5.9 *Trad.* Start on right side of block, climb up and left passing just right of the bulge. Continue to top.

60. Jimmy's Swagger 5.10b *Mixed*, 1 bolt. Right side of arete.

61. Salvation Salesman 5.11d *Mixed*, 1 bolt and 1 pin. Face to right angling flake.

62. Strongly Stationary 5.12a *Mixed*, 2 bolts. Face.

63. Welcome to Huecool ✪ 5.12a R/X *Mixed*, 1 bolt, 1 pin. Start left of blunt arete, move up and right staying left of arete.

64. Synaptic Lapse 5.10a *Trad.* Corner to roof, move left and finish on corner.

65. Sultans of Swing 5.12a *Trad.* Layback flake then face to top.

66. Esse Crack ✪ 5.10c *Trad.* Roof to crack.

67. Eyes of Mind 5.12b *Mixed*, 2 bolts, 2 pins. Roof to groove.

68. Mind Shaft ✪ 5.12a/b *Sport*, 5 bolts.

69. Chinese Style 5.8 R *Trad.* Offwidth.

70. Highlander 5.10a *Trad.* Same start as above at ledge, straight up face finishing slightly left.

71. Happy Head 5.8 *Trad.* Chimney to ledge, step left, face to crack then arete to top.

72. Promised ✪✪ 5.10b *Trad.* Start on face and climb up and left towards the crack in the middle of the face, gain the crack and continue to top.

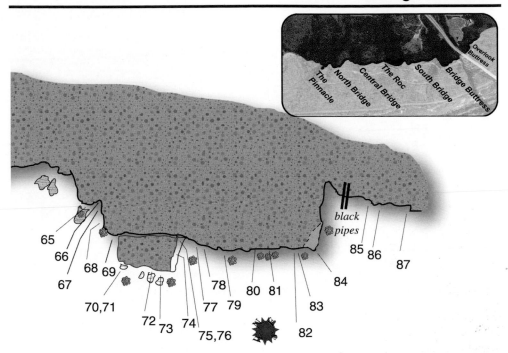

65
66
67
68 69
70,71
72 73 74
75,76
77
78
79
80 81
82
83
84
85 86
87

black pipes

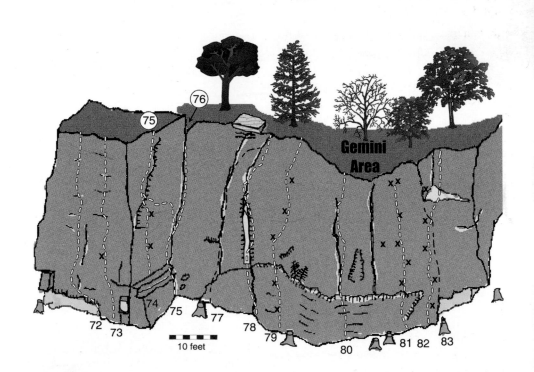

Gemini Area

75
76

74
75
77
72 73
78
79
80 81 82 83

10 feet

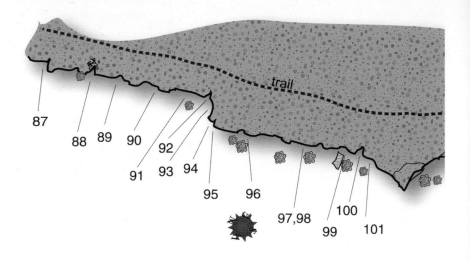

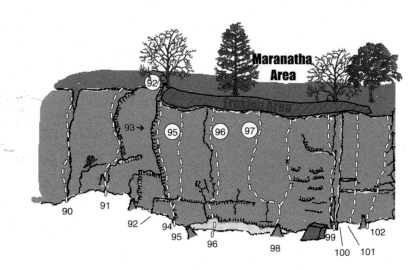

73. My Wife Is A Dog ✪ 5.10b *Mixed*, 1 bolt. Face.

74. Reunification 5.12b *Mixed*, 2 bolts. Face.

75. Berlin Wall 5.10a *Trad.* Start as *Lollipop*, move left at ledge then traverse to flake.

76. Lollipop ✪ 5.7 *Trad.* Crack.

77. Gemini Crack - Left ✪✪ 5.10c *Trad.* Left hand crack. Nice line except it gets dirty after rain.

78. Gemini Crack - Right ✪✪ 5.10a *Trad.* Right hand crack. Nice line but again, dirty after rain.

79. Turan Route 5.11c *Sport*, 5 bolts. Face.

80. The Third Dimension 5.9 *Trad.* Left hand crack and finish on face.

81. Catatonic Conflicts 5.10b *Mixed*, 1 bolt. Face.

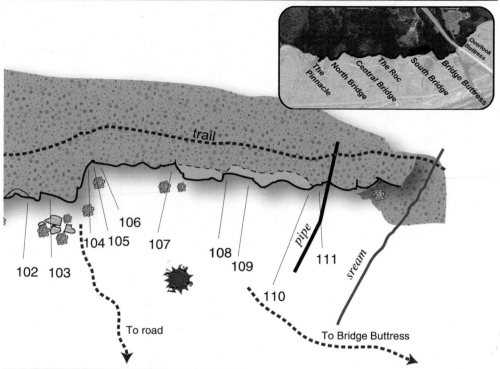

82. Blackberrry Blossom ✪ 5.9 *Trad.* Outside corner to ledge, move right to right facing corner.

83. The Last Tango 5.11b *Sport*, 5 bolts.

South Bridge Wall

84. Fast Asleep in A Dangerous World 5.12a *Mixed*, 2 bolts. Traverse in from the right, then arete to top.

85. Junk Food 5.10b X *Trad.* Boulder problem

86. The Force ✪ 5.11c *Trad.* Thin crack up through bulge.

87. Square Pegs 5.9 *Trad.* Corner.

88. In Tribute to Skid 5.7 *Trad.* Flake to wide crack.

89. Kiss Your Fingers 5.12c *Sport*, 2 bolts, 1 pin. Slab.

90. Sundowner 5.10b *Trad.* Dirty crack.

91. Mossy Groove 5.6 *Trad.* Flake system to top.

92. Beginners Only ✪ 5.7 *Trad.* Low angle corner that is often dirty.

93. Unnamed BA #2 5.11c *Sport*, 4 bolts.

94. Min-Arete 5.11a *Mixed*, 2 bolts. Small roof to arete.

95. Bye Bye Bow Wow 5.10d *Trad.* Seam to ledge then face.

96. Maranatha ✪✪ 5.10c *Trad.* Start at low roof below small left facing corner, climb up passing another small roof then move right towards the crack system and continue to top.

97. Little Head Logic 5.11d *Mixed*, 1 bolt. Same start as Ledge Lips. Move left and up face past bolt.

98. Ledge Lip ✪ 5.11a/b *Mixed*, 2 bolts. Crack to face, angling right to top.

99. Are You Asparagus? 5.11a *Mixed*, 1 bolt. Just left of arete, face.

100. Where Real Men Dare ✪ 5.8 *Trad.* Start at low roof and follow obvious corner to top.

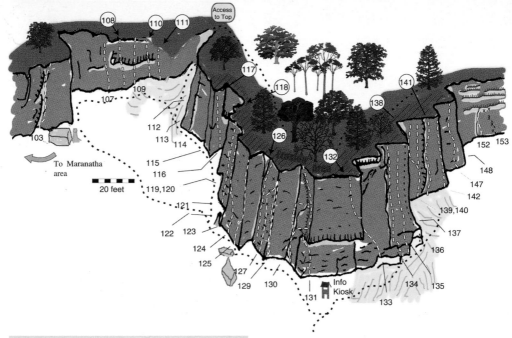

101. Not Bosched Up 5.11a *Trad*. Face and crack.

102. Can't Find My Way Home 5.11a *Mixed*, 1 pin. Face.

103. Agent Orange ✪✪5.11d *Trad*. Overhanging orange flake. One of the best routes at the Bridge Area.

104. Your Mother ✪✪ 5.9 *Trad*. Crack to corner.

105. Trick or Treat ✪ 5.11a *Trad*. Chimney to roof then follow crack to top.

106. Dynamite Crack 5.10d *Trad*. Thin flake to crack above roof on *Trick or Treat*.

107. Unnamed BA #3 5.11d *Sport*. 4 bolts.

108. Two-Edged Sword ✪ 5.10d *Trad*. Start at overhanging corner, and follow crack system to top.

109. Unnamed BA #4 5.12a/b *Sport,* 7 bolts.

110. Desperados Under the Eaves 5.11a *Sport*, 6 bolts. Start 20' left of pipe. Bulge and roof to slab. Tree anchor.

111. Pipe Dreams 5.10c *Trad*.

Bridge Buttress

112. Monkey See, Monkey Do 5.5 *Trad*. Low angle face with sparse protection.

113. Grapefruit Wine 5.11b *Trad*. Face.

114. Butterbeans ✪ 5.10a *Trad*. Offwidth crack to top.

115. Let's Get Physical ✪✪ 5.12a *Trad*. Wide crack that starts at a small overhang.

116. Locked on Target ✪ 5.12d *Sport*, 3 bolts.

117. Underfling ✪✪ 5.10b *Trad*. Start in left corner under the trash compactor roof. Follow corner to roof traversing out left and continue to top.

118. Chockstone ✪✪ 5.9 *Trad*. Thin crack system up to right facing corner.

119. Dresden Corner ✪✪ 5.11d R *Mixed* 1 bolt. Start at arete and climb up and right into dihedral. Follow dihedral to top.

120. A Touch of Tango 5.11c *Mixed*, 1 bolt. Starts on *Dresden Corner*, traverse right to face and arete.

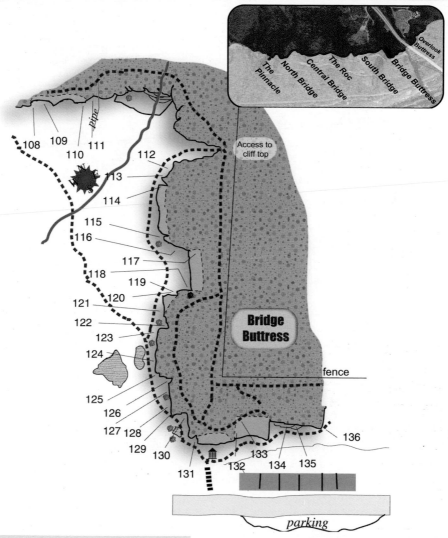

121. Marionette ✪✪5.11c *Trad.* Crack to roof then follow obvious crack to top.

122. Tree Route ✪✪ 5.10a *Trad.* Left facing corner. The famous tree fell down in 1/98.

123. Preferred Dynamics ✪ 5.11d *Mixed*, 1 bolt. Start a few feet right of corner, up to bolt then straight up face to small left facing corner.

124. Tentative Decision 5.10d *Mixed*, 1 bolt. Face to bolt, traverse left 15' and follow flake system to small roof. Finish on *Preferred Dynamics*.

125. Are You Experienced? ✪ 5.12a *Mixed*, 1 bolt. Start left of arete, move up and right to bolt then straight up arete.

126. Jaws ✪5.9 *Trad.* Corner, crack to top.

127. Raptured 5.11a *Trad.* Corner to face, traverse right 20 feet and continue to top.

128. Ruptured (aka Stretch Armstrong) 5.11d/12a *Sport*, 5 bolts.

129. Team Machine ✪ 5.12a *Sport*, 5 bolts, 1 pin. Blunt arete and face.

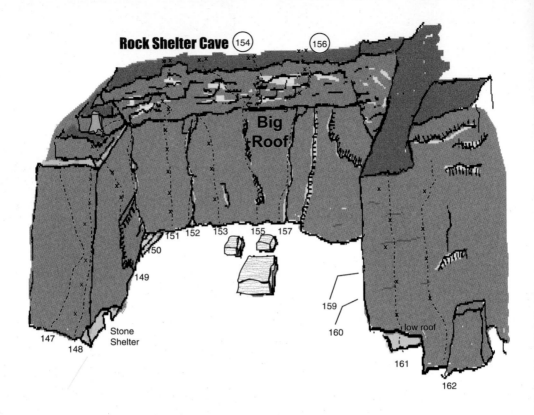

130. Easily Flakey ✹✹ 5.6 R *Trad*. Start in shallow corner and move up and left at small overhang. Traverse 20' right at tree passing a bolt to gain the wide flake system or continue straight up at tree and traverse right at the end of the shallow crack to gain the wide flake.

131. Englishman's Crack ✹✹ 5.11b *Trad*. Overhanging crack. Finish on *Easily Flakey*. first 5.11 at the New!

132. Gag Reflex 5.12d *Trad*. Start on *Handsome and Well Hung*, move out left to arete and onto face then right facing flake to top..

133. Handsome and Well Hung ✹✹ 5.11a *Mixed*, 2 bolts. Orange dihedral that starts from ledge. Dihedral up to roof and then traverse out right under roof to finish.

133a. Bio-Diesel 5.13- *Trad*. Obvious roof crack above *Handsome and Well Hung*. Finally freed spring 2005 after many attempts throughout the years.

134. Zag ✹✹ 5.8 *Trad*. Wide handcrack that starts from ledge.

135. Pearly Gates 5.11b *Trad*. Face between *Angels Arete* and *Zag*.

136. Angel's Arete ✹✹ 5.10b *Mixed*, 1 pin. Obvious white arete with sparse gear placements. (Pin missing as of 10/2005)

137. Mega Magic ✹ 5.12b *Sport*, 4 bolts. Slightly overhanging face.

138. Penalty Situation 5.8 *Trad*. Wide crack.

139. Blunder and Frightening ✹ 5.10b *Trad*. Start on low angle face and climb up to flake system, move up and left.

140. Frenzyed 5.12a *Mixed*, 1 bolt, 1 pin. Start right of *Blunder* and move up and right on face, continue to top passing a bolt and pin.

141. The Layback ✹✹ 5.9+ *Trad*. Start at polished low angle flake and follow to top.

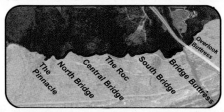

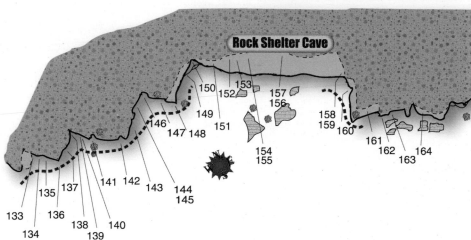

Rock Shelter Cave

142. Pirouette 5.12d *Sport*, 6 bolts. Missing hangers.

143. The Stratagem ✸ 5.12a *Sport*, 6 bolts. No anchors.

144. The Midas Touch 5.11a *Trad*. Starts left of *Mayfly* and finishes on *Gayfly*.

145. The Gayfly 5.9 *Trad*. Variation. Traverses left into flake system.

146. The Mayfly 5.9- *Trad*. Dihedral.

147. Lotus Land 5.10b *Trad*. Face to flakes.

Rock Shelter Cave

148. Love Shack ✸ 5.12c *Sport*, 6 bolts. Starts above stone shelter.

149. Whammy 5.13a *Sport*, 4 bolts. Starts right of stone shelter.

150. Labor Day ✸ 5.10c *Trad*. Dihedral to sling anchor, continue traversing left to ledge and belay.

151. Coal Miner's Daughter 5.12b *Sport*, 9 bolts. Climb face then roof to top.

152. High Times ✸ 5.10c *Trad*. Short finger crack to bolt anchor.

153. Let the Wind Blow ✸ 5.12a *Sport*, 3 bolts. First 5.12 at the New (top-roped). Bolts were added later.

154. Love Jugs 5.12c *Sport*, 8 bolts. Starts on *Fat Factor* then moves right.

155. The Fat Factor 5.10b R *Trad*. Flake to horizontal then move left to bolts on *High Times*.

156. Mean Old Mr. Gravity ✸ 5.12b *Sport*, 5 bolts. Continue from anchors of *Horton's Tree*. Up to last bolt it is 5.11a.

157. Horton's Tree 5.7 *Trad*. Short right leaning crack to anchors.

158. Bailing Wire 5.11 *Sport*, 4 bolts. Continues from anchors of Dog Fight.

159. Dog Fight 5.10b *Trad*. Left-hand crack.

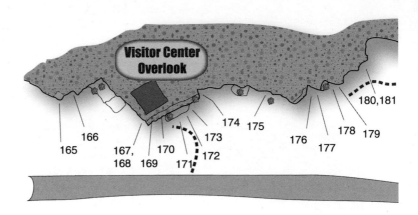

160. **Macho Man** 5.9 *Trad*. Right hand crack on right side of cave.

161. **Wicca** 5.13 *Sport*, 8 bolts. Missing hangers.

162. **Golden Summer** ✪ 5.11b *Sport*, 4 bolts. Missing hangers.

163. **Scarey** 5.9 *Trad*. Face to notch in roof, finish on face.

164. **Gaye's Gaze** 5.9 *Trad*. Flake to roof then corner.

Overlook Buttress

165. **Cheap Thrill** 5.7 *Trad*. Dihedral to roof move left and finish on face.

166. **Barefoot Alley** 5.8 *Trad*. Dihedral to face.

167. **House of Cards** 5.10a *Mixed*, 1 bolt. Start on *Sandman*, move up staying left of arete.

168. **The Sandman** 5.10a *Trad*. Corner to roof move right to crack and belay at platform.

169. **C.M.Q.** 5.12a/b *Sport*, 5 bolts. Starts under large roof.

170. **The Hall Effect** 5.8 *Trad*. *Pitch 1*: Corner to roof and belay at ledge. *Pitch 2*: Angle right up face.

171. **The Incredible Overhanging Wall** 5.10d *Trad*. (Top-rope) Face.

172. **Tree in Your Face** 5.9 *Trad*.

173. **Up to Disneyland** 5.7 *Trad*. Face to crack.

174. **Rocky Roads** 5.8 *Trad*. Corner to roof.

175. **Out to Lunch** 5.8 *Trad*. Crack.

176. **Gunky Heaven** ✪ 5.6 *Trad*. Right facing corner thru two small roofs.

177. **Under A Blood Red Sky** 5.10d *Mixed*, 1 bolt and 2 pins.

178. **Ledge City** 5.8 *Trad*. Rotten roof leads to corner.

179. **Be Bold and Be Strong** 5.11b R *Mixed*, 1 pin. Right facing flake to cracks then move right below roof.

180. **The Butler** 5.9 *Trad*. Corner to roof then up arete.

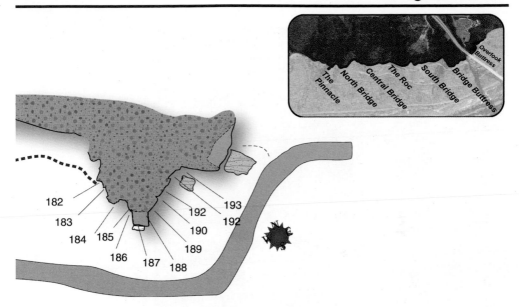

181. **Solitary Hang** 5.6 *Trad.* Left leaning crack at roof of *Butler*.

The Rostrum

182. **Crack'n Clutch** 5.7 *Trad.* Dihedral

183. **Beer Belly Roof** ✪ 5.9 *Trad.* Dihedral to roof then layback.

184. **Mortimer** 5.11a *Sport*, 2 bolts. Arching line up and right to shared anchor.

185. **Kiss of the Spider Woman** 5.10d *Sport*, 2 bolts. Angles up and left.

186. **The Mankey Monkey** 5.9 *Trad.* Corner to offwidth.

187. **Penalty for Early Withdraw** 5.11a *Sport*, 3 bolts. Start from large ledge and follow bolt line to top.

188. **Mounting Madness** ✪ 5.8 R *Trad.* Face.

189. **You Snooze, You Lose** 5.10d R *Trad.* Roof and face.

190. **Rapid View** 5.6 R *Trad.* Offwidth.

191. **Boltus Prohibitus** 5.10c *Trad.* Roof to short facing corner.

192. **Race Among the Ruins** 5.10c *Mixed*, 2 pins and 1 bolt. Face.

193. **Palladium** 5.9 *Trad.* Corner to roof.

Dave Heinbach near the top of Layback Crack (5.9), Bridge Buttress. Photo: Cater

Rachael Babkirk on Channel Zero (5.11c), Endless Wall . Photo: Cater.

Mike Kelly on New Yosemite (5.9), Junkyard.
Photo: Dan Brayack.

Jason Babkirk on Agent Orange (5.11), Bridge Buttress . Photo: Mike Turner.

Roxanna Brock on the classic Zag (5.8), Bridge Buttress . Photo: Cater.

Robert Hutchins on Handsome and Well Hung (5.11a), Bridge Buttress. Photo: Mike Turner

Pat Goodman on
Green Envy (5.12b/c),
Beauty Mountain.
Photo: Mike Turner

5

Ambassador Buttress

26 routes • 1 sport • 25 trad/mixed

One of the first climbers to visit this cliff ran into an old man at the base who said he was the "General Ambassador of the Universe". It's now believed that this man was in fact the world famous "General Ambassador", Donald C. Owens of Kaymoor. Hence the name Ambassador Buttress.

Ambassador is one of the lesser known climbing areas of the New. The small cliff is located between the Bridge Buttress and Fern Buttress and offers a number of quality trad routes. The cliff ranges from 30' to 50' in height with slabby to vertical walls. Access requires a 3-4 minute walk from the Gunpoint pull-off on Rt. 82 or short rappel from the top of the cliff.

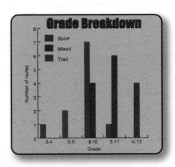

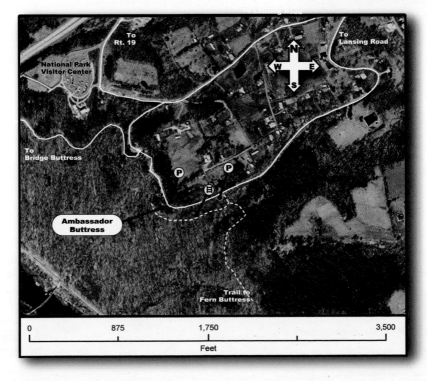

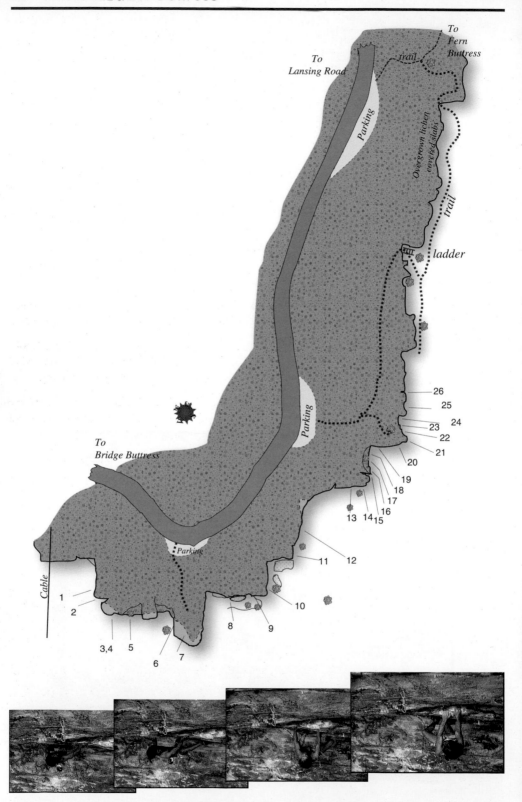

1. **Unnamed** Project. 2 bolts, 1 pin.

2. **Wienie Roast** 5.9 *Trad*. Flake to roof, move right to second flake.

3. **The Happy Hooker** 5.11a R *Trad*. Start on *Consenting Clips*, then left to arete.

4. **Consenting Clips** 5.10b *Trad*. Left side of wall. Face up and right.

5. **Pleasure Principals** 5.11a *Mixed*, 2 bolts, 2 pins. Start at small corner on right side of gray wall.

6. **Liddlebiddanuthin'** 5.10b R/X *Trad*. Flake.

7. **The Geneva Convention** 5.11d *Mixed*, 1 pin. Flake, seam, roof then face.

8. **The Glitch** ✪ 5.4 *Trad*. Crack up and right to flake then straight up to top.

9. **Unnamed** 5.11 *Mixed*, 2 bolts. Starts from ledge move up and right on slab, con't to top.

10. **Reefer Derby** 5.12c *Mixed*, 1 bolt. Face moving right.

11. **Chasing Rainbows** 5.10a *Trad*. Face to flake on arete then right to face.

12. **Auld Lang Syne** 5.12b *Mixed*.

13. **Enter the Dragon** 5.12b *Mixed*. Joins *Dragon in Your Dreams* above the second bolt.

14. **Dragon in Your Dreams** ✪ 5.11c *Mixed*, 2 bolts. Pocketed face.

15. **The Bolting Blowfish** ✪ 5.12b *Sport*, 2 bolts, 2 pins. Face to roof.

16. **The Spineless Perpetrator** 5.10a *Trad*. Face to ledge then white flake.

17. **Unnamed** 5.10d *Mixed*, 2 bolts. Slab up to ledge.

18. **Unnamed** 5.10d *Mixed*, 2 bolts. Slab up to ledge.

19. **Unnamed** 5.11d *Mixed*, 3 bolts, 2 pins, shuts.

20. **Clumsy Club Crack** ✪✪ 5.10b R *Mixed*, 2 bolts. Climb the obvious handcrack which leads to a shallow dihedral.

21. **New-veau Reach** 5.11c *Mixed*, 1 pin, 1 bolt. Starts on prominent arete 8' left of the large flake.

22. **The Underdiddled** 5.10c R *Mixed*, 1 bolt. Start in corner/flake system and climb to roof. Move right and pull roof, continue to top.

23. **Lunar Tunes** ✪ 5.10a *Trad*. Start on easy flake system and climb to roof. Traverse left to arete and continue to top.

24. **Kidspeak** 5.10a *Trad*. Short dihedral.

25. **Comfortably Numb** 5.10d R *Trad*. Face.

26. **Nookie Monster** 5.9 *Trad*. Crack.

Porter Jarrard on Sanctified
(5.12d), Kaymoor.
Video Capture: Cater

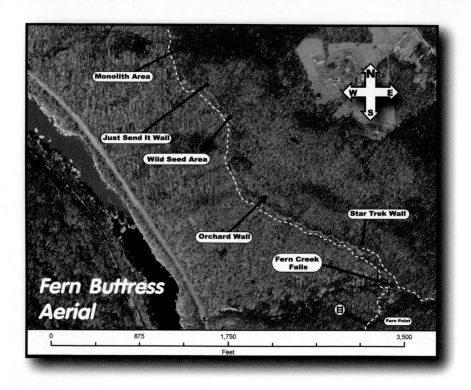

Fern Buttress
Aerial

Monolith Area

Just Send It Wall

Wild Seed Area

Orchard Wall

Star Trek Wall

Fern Creek
Falls

Fern Point

| 0 | 875 | 1,750 | 3,500 |

Feet

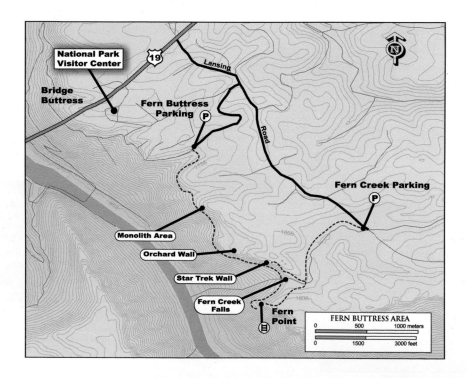

National Park
Visitor Center

Bridge
Buttress

US 19

Lansing

Fern Buttress
Parking P

Road

Fern Creek Parking P

Monolith Area

Orchard Wall

Star Trek Wall

Fern Creek
Falls

Fern
Point

FERN BUTTRESS AREA

| 0 | 500 | 1000 meters |

| 0 | 1500 | 3000 feet |

6
F e r n   B u t t r e s s
171 routes • 42 sport • 129 trad/mixed

One night while sleeping in my car at the Fern Buttress pull-off, I awoke to the soft pitter-patter of combat boots outside my car. When the footsteps retreated and then returned a minute later, I sat up in haste in the back of my little wagon. Peering through the drivers window were two dark figures, who on spying me, hesitantly stepped back a few feet. The full moon cast an eery glow on my unexpected late night visitors and being reluctant to leave I rustled around a bit more and then in shock noticed that one of them was holding a large handgun- the type used to shoot aliens or gun down helicopters. I slipped out of my sleeping bag and was prepared to dive out the door into the woods when they hesitantly started walking away in hushed conversation. They stopped 40 yards up the road and I jumped into the drivers seat, hit the high beams, spun the car around and drove off, all the while, expecting to receive a few rounds. Be careful if you plan on car camping at Fern Buttress pull-off.

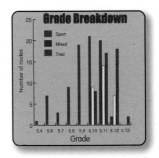

Climbers first started establishing new routes at Fern Buttress in the mid 80's. The cliff ranges from slabby to vertical and averages about 40' to 80' in height. There is an excellent variety of crack and corner climbs in the lower to moderate grades plus a good selection of sport routes. The cliff faces southwest and should be avoided during hot days. On crowded weekends Fern Buttress remains relatively uncrowded and is a good choice if you want to get away from the masses.

Access

The most popular access to Fern Buttress is from the Rt. 82 road in Lansing. Turn off of Rt. 19 onto Lansing Road, take an Immediate right after the gear shop and then take an immediate left. Drive about .65 miles and park at the Parking Area on the left side of the road. Be sure that your vehicle is 5' off the paved road. Rafting buses regularly drive on this road and require lots of space. The steep trail heads down the embankment and crosses a waterfall. Continue following this trail for several hundred feet to where it eventually drops down to the cliff line and emerges at the first small buttress. It is also possible to reach Upper Fern Buttress from Fern Point. This approach is longer and should only be used if you are interested in the Fern Creek Falls routes or routes located upstream at Fern Buttress.

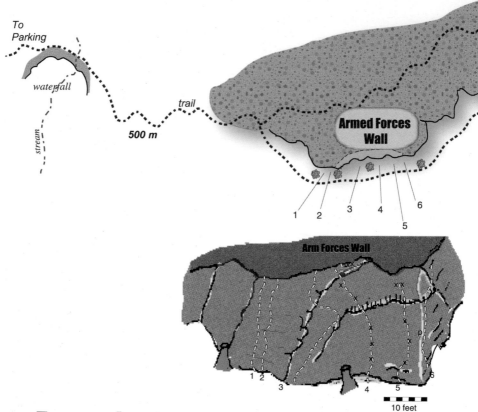

Arm Forces Area

1. Cow in A China Shop 5.8 *Trad.*

2. The No-Zone 5.10a *Trad.* Face to right facing corner.

3. Naked Potatoes 5.10b *Trad.* Right leaning dihedral to roof, traverse left and then move straight up.

4. Ron Kauk Gets A Perm 5.11c *Sport,* 5 bolts.

5. Arm Forces 5.11c *Sport,* 4 bolts.

6. Dead Beat Club 5.11d *Mixed,* 1 pin. Start 5' right of *Arm Forces*, pull small roof climb past pin and continue on face up and right.

7. Mega-jug ✹ 5.11b *Sport,* 4 bolts.

8. October Surprise 5.10d *Sport,* 4 bolts. Starts left of low roof.

Monolith Buttress

9. Dog Day Afternoon 5.12a *Sport,* 4 bolts.

10. Teleconnections ✹ 5.11c *Sport,* 6 bolts.

11. Power Talk ✹ 5.12a *Sport,* 6 bolts.

12. Wings and A Prayer 5.11d *Mixed,* 2 bolts. Start 5' right of *Power Talk*.

13. Dixie Chicken 5.11c *Trad.* Flake on right side of arete, continue following blunt arete to top.

14. First Person ✹ 5.10c *Sport,* 4 bolts. Shallow corner to face.

15. Close to the Edge ✹ 5.12b *Sport,* 5 bolts.

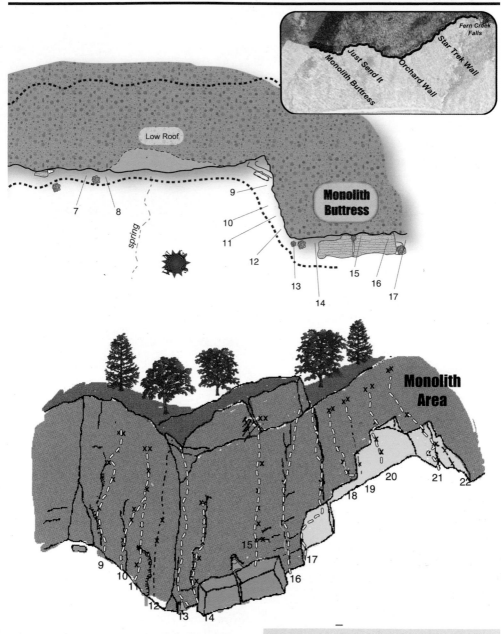

16. Spiderwalk ✹✹ 5.10c *Trad*. Right leaning crack system to roof, traverse right at roof.

17. Hummingbird ✹ 5.10c *Trad*. Climb dihedral to roof, move right 8' and pull roof, continue up face and crack to top.

18. My Stinking Brain ✹ 5.13a Sport, 6 bolts.

19. Unnamed FB #1 Project.

20. The Monolith 5.11d A1 *Mixed*, 3 bolts. Follow crack out large roof.

21. Air Apparent ✹ 5.11a *Sport*, 5 bolts. Begin on inside, left of arete.

22. Over the Edge 5.11c *Sport*, 6 bolts. Start on outside face, joins *Air Apparent* at 3rd bolt.

23. Fried Mush 5.8 *Trad*. Broken crack up lichen covered slab.

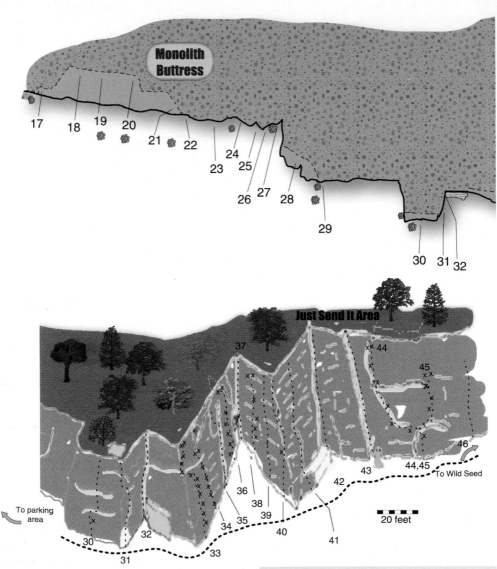

24. **Chew Electric Death You Snarling Cur** 5.8 *Trad.* Face.

25. **McStumpy's Sandwich Crack** 5.6 *Trad.*

26. **Devils Arete** 5.10a R *Mixed*, 1 pin.

27. **The Puddy System** 5.11a *Trad.*

28. **The Yert Yak Crack** 5.9 *Trad.* 2 Pitches

29. **Unnamed** FB #2 5.10c *Trad.*

30. **Preservation of the Wildlife** ✪✪ 5.11d *Mixed*, 1 bolt. Face up to roof, pull roof, con't to top. Interesting climbing but not done very often.

31. **Two Bag Face** ✪✪ 5.9 R *Trad.* Begin below arete and move left onto face.

32. **The Lichen in Me** 5.10d *Trad.* Corner.

33. **Bosnian Vacation** ✪ 5.12d Sport, 10 bolts. Start right of arete, up to horizontal, moving to left of arete near top.

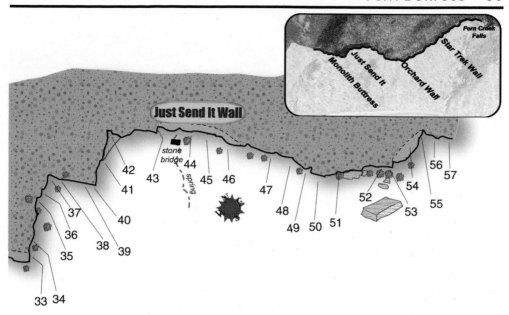

34. Wall Drug ✹ 5.12c *Sport*, 7 bolts.

35. Mr. Workman's Crack ✹ 5.11b *Trad*. Start on crack, moving left to thinner crack at small roof and finish on *Workmen's Comp* anchor.

36. Workmen's Comp ✹ 5.10d *Sport*, 5 bolts.

37. Mrs. Workman's Corner ✹ 5.9 *Trad*. Climb left side of flake/crack past small roof to top.

38. Climb-max ✹ 5.11d *Sport*, 5 bolts.

39. Graceland 5.11a *Trad*. Face, crack, arete.

40. Toss that Beat in the Garbage Can 5.10d *Mixed*, 1 bolt. Arete.

41. Hole in the Wall 5.11a *Trad*. Dihedral to heuco, pull through roof and con't to top.

42. Beat Me Daddy, Eight to the Bar 5.8 *Trad*.

43. Mud and Guts 5.10b *Trad*. Right facing dihedral to the top.

44. Just Send It ✹✹ 5.13a/b *Sport*, 7 bolts. Angles up and left.

45. Welcome to Conditioning ✹✹ 5.12d *Sport*, 6 bolts.

46. Stab Me I Don't Matter 5.12d *Sport*, 4 bolts.

47. Hold the Dog 5.11d *Sport*, 3 bolts, 1 pin. Ends at tree.

48. Party Out of Bounds 5.11d *Trad*. Left hand crack.

49. The Udderling 5.12a *Trad*. Right hand crack to ledge. Rap.

50. Toxic Waste 5.7 *Trad*.

51. One of Many Smells 5.9- *Trad*. Right facing flake and face.

52. Quickie in the Molar 5.12a *Sport*, 4 bolts. Pitch #1- Up and right to ledge. Pitch #2- Traverse left 20' on ledge then climb through roofs.

52a. Quickie Direct Finish- 5.12a *Trad*. Finish straight up through roofs. One fixed wire.

53. Muscle Belly 5.11c *Sport*, 5 bolts. Arete.

54. Wild Seed ✹✹ 5.11a *Sport*, 6 bolts. Start in broken corner, up and right and pull through roof near top.

55. Lies and Propaganda 5.9+ *Trad*. Obvious open book. Finish on last 20' of face right of corner.

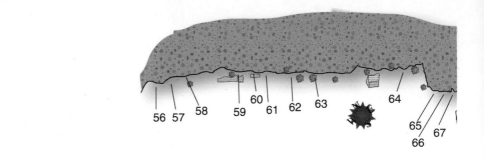

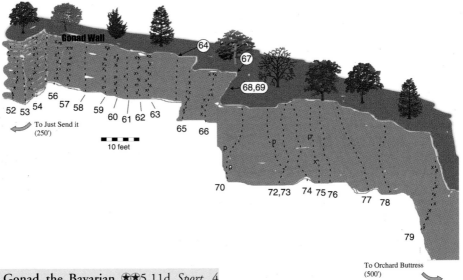

To Just Send it (250')

10 feet

To Orchard Buttress (500')

56. Gonad the Bavarian ✹✹5.11d *Sport*, 4 bolts. Starts 10 feet right of corner, up through shallow crack system to anchors.

57. Foutre a la Doigts 5.12a *Sport*, 4 bolts.

58. No Kiss, No Lubrication 5.11d *Trad*. Crack.

59. The Chameleon ✹ 5.10b *Sport*, 5 bolts. Juggy face.

60. Salvador Dali's Car 5.12b *Sport*, 4 bolts.

61. Old and In the Way 5.11b *Mixed*, 2 bolts, 1 fixed wire.

62. Fly Girls ✹✹ 5.12a *Sport*, 5 bolts. Starts left of tree.

63. Doer Not a Critic ✹ 5.11c *Sport*, 6 bolts. Starts right of tree.

64. Aquatic Ecstasy 5.11b *Trad*. Start on face, up left into crack. Follow to the top.

65. Arbor Day ✹ 5.12a *Mixed*, 4 bolts, 1 pin.

66. Fragile Ego System ✹ 5.10a *Sport*, 5 bolts.

67. Stoat Goes to Joshua Tree and Tears A Flapper on Baby Apes 5.7 *Trad*. Dirty vegetated crack with small tree growing in it.

68. Use Your Power 5.12d *Sport*, 6 bolts.

69. Unnamed FB #3 Project.

70. The Brawn Wall ✹ 5.12a *Mixed*, 2 pins. Pitch #1- Overhanging white corner to face, traverse right at roof and belay on face below crack. Pitch #2- **Brawn Wall Direct Finish** 5.10c *Mixed*, 1 pin. Climb *Brawn Wall*, belay

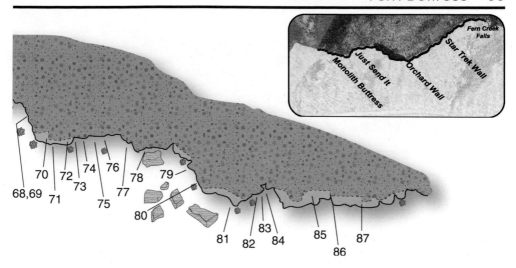

and then finish straight up on finger crack.

71. Brawn Wall Direct Start Project , *Sport*, 3 bolts. Starts around corner from white dihedral. Straight up and connect with direct finish.

72. Pop Top 5.11c *Mixed*, 1 pin. Pull roof then left thru roof and onto face.

73. Eye of Zen 5.10b *Mixed*, 1 bolt. Same start as *Pop Top*, straight up

74. Rolling Rock 5.9 *Trad*. Pull low roof then pass on right side of second small roof, continue on featured face to top.

75. Bolt Rookies 5.11a *Mixed*, 1 bolt, 1 pin. Face, small roof.

76. Prepare to Succeed 5.11c/d *Trad*. Inverted V to dirty thin groove.

77. Baptism by Fire 5.9 *Trad*. Flake and corner.

78. Mean, Mean Girl 5.11d *Trad*. Follow flake system moving right at roof.

79. Two-Tone Arete ✪✪ 5.10b *Sport*, 6 bolts. Right of arete.

80. Emerald Dance ✪ 5.9 *Trad*. Follow crack system up to small roof, continue on face up to top.

81. Thieves In the Temple ✪✪ 5.12a *Sport*, 8 bolts.

82. Grand Larceny 5.11d *Mixed*, 3 bolts.

83. Wounded in Action 5.12b *Mixed*, 2 bolts.

84. Presto 5.10a *Trad*. Offwidth and chimney.

85. Unnamed FB #4 (Unknown) *Mixed*, 2 bolts.

86. The Fourgasm ✪ 5.9 *Trad*. Crack and corner through two roofs.

87. Bushong 5.9 *Trad*. Wide crack up to roof, then move left.

88. Tongue in Groove ✪✪ 5.12a *Sport*, 5 bolts. Sport route up orange face.

Orchard Buttress

89. Sometimes A Great Notion 5.11a *Trad*. Dihedral and roofs.

90. Portly Gentleman's Route ✪✪ 5.12c *Trad*. Start in dihedral, climb up to roof crack, pull roof and finish on thin crack. Hard climbing at crux.

91. Beowolf 5.12b *Mixed*, 3 bolts and 1 pin. Thin face climbing on suspect edges.

92. Sun Viking ✪✪ 5.11d R *Mixed*, 1 bolt, 2 pins. Thin face, moving right to crack.

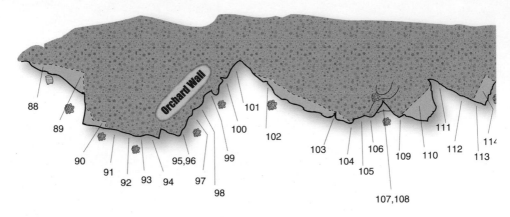

93. Thor 5.12d *Mixed*, 2 bolts. Face straight up to crack.

94. Loki ✱ 5.12b *Sport*, 5 bolts.

95. White-Out 5.11d *Mixed*, 2 pins and 3 bolts.

96. God of Fire 5.11b/c *Mixed*, 2 pins and 2 bolts. Same start as *White-Out*, move left at 2nd pin.

97. Bisect ✱ 5.10b *Trad*. Start under low roof crack, pull roof and continue following crack to anchors.

98. Anal Clenching Adventures ✱ 5.10a *Trad*. Low angle flared crack to ledge and belay (same as *Bisect* belay).

99. Triple Treat ✱✱ 5.10a *Trad*. Through low roof, nice corner then past roofs to top.

100. Springboard ✱✱ 5.10a *Trad*. Very nice hand crack to the top.

101. Lewd Operator 5.10b *Trad*. Crack, flake, corner.

102. The Mighty Stoat 5.11c *Trad*. Hand crack through roof.

103. Shiney Faces 5.10d *Trad*. Offwidth into fingers.

104. Hysteria 5.8 *Trad*. Begins at right hand end of roof. Continue up face to top

105. Mello Drama 5.9 *Trad*. Face to right facing dihedral.

106. Furry Nerd 5.10c R *Trad*. Arete then move right onto face.

107. Wishbone Left 5.10b *Trad*. Corner to roof, move left and continue to top.

108. Wishbone Right 5.9 *Trad*. Traverse right at roof then follow groove and face to top.

109. Total Sex Package ✱ 5.12a *Sport*, 7 bolts. Blunt arete off ground. Fingery.

110. Give Me the Strap-On ✱ 5.12a *Sport*, 8 bolts. Up steep face and out big roof. Originally bolted by Kenny Parker, this route sat idle for four years until a hold broke in the roof revealing a jug.

111. No Static at All 5.10a *Trad*. Crack to tree, traverse right and follow crack to top.

112. Parsimony 5.10c R *Trad*. Face to right crack finish on *No Static*.

113. Really Gotta Boogie 5.11d *Mixed*, 1 bolt.

114. Rumor of War 5.12d *Sport*, 2 bolts, pin.

115. The Undulator 5.8 *Trad*. Offwidth

116. Optical Illusion 5.11c *Trad*. Handcrack out low roof.

117. Grand Space ✱✱ 5.11b *Trad*. Follow short crack to dihedral. Continue up right facing corner passing thru roofs to finish on short crack.

118. Nervous Bachelor 5.11d *Mixed*, 6 bolts.

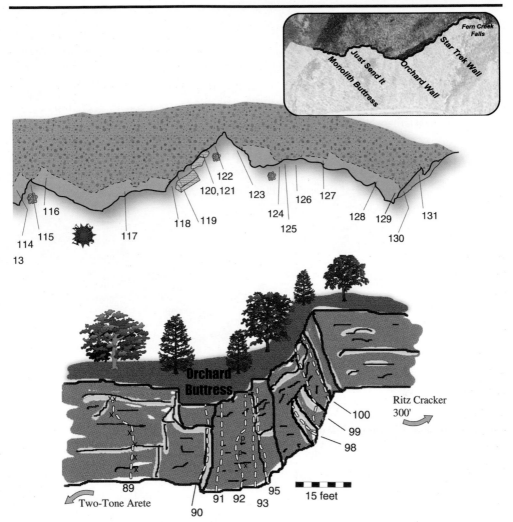

119. **Bill and Ken's Excellent Adventure** 5.11b *Mixed*, 3 bolts.

120. **Goofer's Retreat** 5.9 *Trad*. Same start as *Ritz Cracker* but move left at first ledge and continue up crack or dihedral to obvious ledge. Continue following the wide crack to the top.

121. **Ritz Cracker** ❀❀ 5.9 *Trad*. Pitch #1: Splitter crack to ledge, belay. Pitch #2: Move right and continue up left facing dihedral and roof.

122. **Jacuzzi Bop** 5.10d *Mixed*, 2 bolts. Face right of *Ritz Cracker*.

123. **Contemplation** 5.10a *Trad*. Obvious crack to top.

124. **Morning Dew** ❀ 5.12a/b *Sport*, 6 bolts.

125. **New Tricks for the Old Dog** ❀ 5.10c *Sport*, 7 bolts.

126. **Sandy's Sweet Bottom** 5.9 *Trad*. Face to dihedral.

127. **Anticipation** 5.9 *Trad*. Overhanging face to crack.

128. **Intimidation** 5.10c *Trad*. Corner to roof, pull roof and follow crack to finish.

129. **Breach Birth** 5.10c *Trad*. Pitch #1: Corner to roof and belay at ledge. Pitch #2: Follow dihedral to ledge. Rap or continue to top.

130. C-Section 5.11c/d *Sport*, 6 bolts. Face left of pitch #2 of *Breach Birth*. Starts at bolt right of *Breach Birth* then crosses it.

131. Constant Velocity 5.10b *Trad*. Left facing flake to overhanging wall.

132. Constant Velocity Variation 5.11a *Trad*. Up and right through bulges.

133. Attach of Eddie Munster 5.12a *Mixed*, 3 bolts.

134. The Monster 5.11a *Trad*. Thin flake, move left 30' then up face to top.

145. Sweet Dreams 5.11b *Trad*. Start right of arete moving onto arete at good horizontal.

146. Pleasure and Pain 5.11b *Mixed*, 2 pins. Follow cracks and corner to the top.

147. S&M 5.9 *Trad*. Orange dihedral.

148. Berserker 5.11c *Trad*. Crack to ledge, move right to crack then move back left to crack.

135. Cowabunga 5.6 *Trad*. Dirty corner.

136. Look, Me, Awesome 5.9 *Trad*.

137. Wumpus Cat Blues 5.10d *Mixed*, 1 bolt.

138. A Wild Hair 5.6 *Trad*. Starts in dihedral, move into wide flake.

139. Fire and Waste 5.10b *Mixed*, 1 pin. Direct start to *Crescenta*.

140. Crescenta ✪ 5.10a *Trad*. Follow arch and flake then angle right to ledge. Climb straight up to left facing corner and finish.

141. The Scoop 5.11a *Mixed*, 1 bolt.

142. The Weight 5.11d *Mixed*, 4 bolts.

143. Beech, Beeech, Beeeech! 5.6 *Trad*. Dihedral to top.

144. Surge Complex ✪ 5.11a *Trad*. Follow left leaning hand crack, pull roof then follow flake past roof to top.

Star Trek Wall

149. Panama (Abandoned Project) 5.13? *Mixed*, 2 bolts. Crack out large low roof.

150. Transporter Crack ✪ 5.6 *Trad*. Short wide crack which leads to a ledge where routes 152,153,154,155 and 156 start .

151. Three Dimensional Chess ✪ 5.8+ *Trad*. Traverse left at tree on *Transporter Crack*. Follow crack to ledge and belay.

152. Crack of the Klingons ✪ 5.6 *Trad*. Left hand crack to short roof.

153. The Wrath of Kahn 5.8 *Trad*. Start on *Crack of Klingons*, move up and left to crack and face left of arete.

154. Beam Me Up, Scotty ✪ 5.6 *Trad*. Middle crack.

155. Impulse Power 5.4 *Trad*. Follow crack to top.

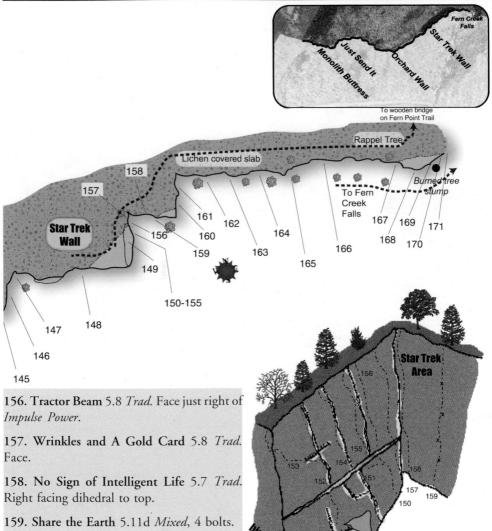

156. Tractor Beam 5.8 *Trad.* Face just right of *Impulse Power*.

157. Wrinkles and A Gold Card 5.8 *Trad.* Face.

158. No Sign of Intelligent Life 5.7 *Trad.* Right facing dihedral to top.

159. Share the Earth 5.11d *Mixed*, 4 bolts.

160. Holey Trinity 5.11a *Mixed*, 2 bolts.

161. Subsidized Development 5.119 *Mixed*, 4 bolts.

162. Daughter of Dracula 5.10b *Mixed*, 3 bolts. Face. Take small TCU's.

163. Night Moves 5.9 *Trad.* Crack.

164. Just Another Obscurity 5.12a *Mixed*, 1 bolt. Face climb with bolt 20' up.

165. Common Ground 5.10c *Mixed*, 2 bolts.

166. Stop the Presses, Mr. Thompson 5.11b *Trad.* Flakes to crack, move left then back right continue to top passing small roof.

167. Rap-N-Go 5.9+ *Trad.* Face passing small roof.

168. Lethargical Lion 5.8 *Trad.* Flake to right leaning roof then to the top.

169. Blues Brothers 5.9 R *Trad.* Face, starts 10' left of charred tree.

170. Smoke on the Water 5.8 *Trad.* Pull overhang and continue up face to the top.

171. Levitation 5.10d *Trad.* Climbs through two overhangs

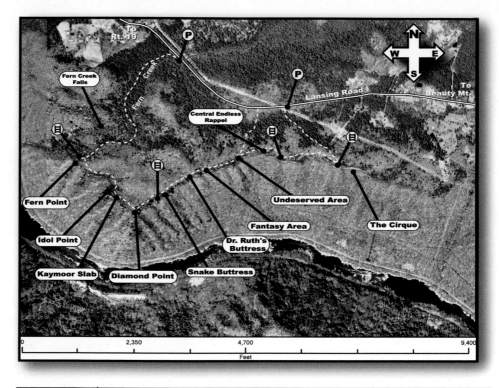

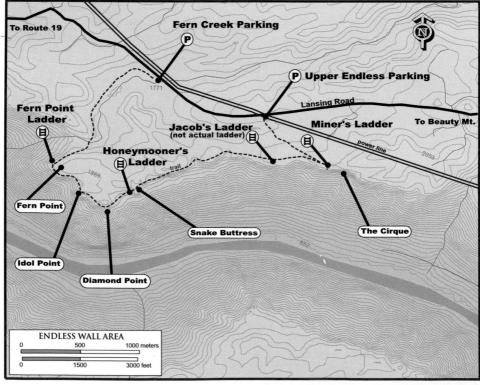

7
E n d l e s s   W a l l

477 routes • 217 sport • 256 trad/mixed

Endless Wall actually stretches from Fern Point to Beauty Mountain. This is an extensive section of wall and contains a high concentration of excellent rock climbs at various grades, both sport and trad style. The numerous corners, aretes and faces yield some of the New's most notable lines. Classic routes such as *Remission* (5.10a), *Jesus and Tequila* (5.12b), *Leave It To Jesus* (5.11c) and *Quinsana Plus* (5.13a) are located at this section of wall. The cliff line varies from 60' to 150' in height and ranges from slab to slightly overhanging.

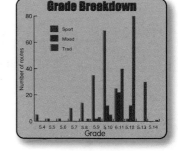

Access

Access to Endless is from the Central Endless parking area on Lansing Road or from the Fern Creek parking area on Lansing Road. To reach the Fern Point ladders from Fern Creek parking area, follow the trail out to Fern Point. Near the cliff top look for a trail that goes down and right towards a cleft in the rock. A series of ropes and ladders will put you at the base of the cliff. Turning left near the cliff top and following the top trail upstream for another 10-15 minutes will put you at the top of the Honeymooner's Ladder. The cliff top trail passes over Diamond Point (it is possible to rappel in from any point along the trail) and then continues to the Honeymooners' Ladders. The ladders are located at the back of a small cirque inside a wide chimney and are impossible to see from the trail. Look for a large dip in the trail with a three way intersection at the bottom. To access the cliff from the Central Endless parking area, follow the trail out the back of the parking area. At the first intersection, take a right and continue following the trail. After several hundred feet, the trail merges with the main cliff top trail. Continue walking for 10-15 minutes. Look for a dip in the trail and a three way intersection. The Honeymooners' Ladders are located here. The Cirque area is best accessed from the Central Endless parking. From the parking area follow the trail and turn left at the intersection at the cliff top. The trail eventually drops down into a gully where the Miners' Ladder is located. The Miner's Ladder is located between the main cliff and a large block and is approximately 20' high. Many people also rappel in at the Central Endless Rappel station. This is a large tree perched on th edge of the cliff above a huge overhang that used to have a cable wrapped around it. Rappeling in here will put you near the base of Suspended Sentence and very close to the Undeserved Area.

Please note that the only nontechnical climbing escape routes are Fern Point Ladders, Honeymooner's Ladders, Jacobs Ladder (5.0) and Miners' Ladder.

Note: Jacobs Ladder is a scramble up rock ledges and could be dangerous in wet conditions. There are no wooden ladders here despite the name.

Climber near the top of Discombobulated (5.11a) on Snake Buttress. Photo: Cater.

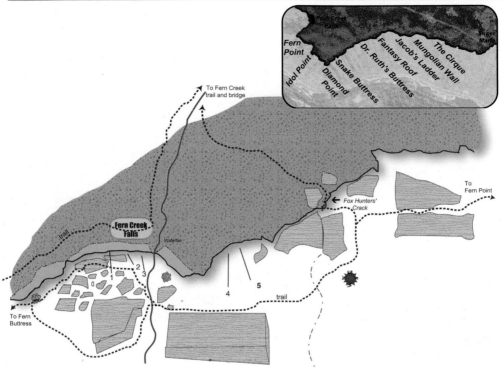

Fern Creek Falls

The easiest and shortest access to Fern Creek Falls is from Fern Point. At the base of the Fern Point Ladders, turn right and continue following the trail through a beautiful fern forest and boulderfield. Routes 1 thru 3 are just left of a waterfall.

1. Colors ✪ 5.13a *Sport*, 5 bolts

2. The Land That Time Forgot ✪✪ 5.12d *Sport*, 5 bolts. Step off right from boulder to gain the first holds.

3. Fall Line (a.k.a. Just Plain Fun) ✪✪ 5.12b *Sport*, 7 bolts. First climb left of the waterfall. Fun route in a cool setting. Overhanging and pumpy!

4. Fern Creek Direct 5.11a *Trad*. Crack, face and arete to top.

5. Water Power 5.11c *Trad*. Flake, face and finish on flake.

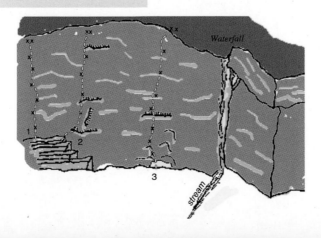

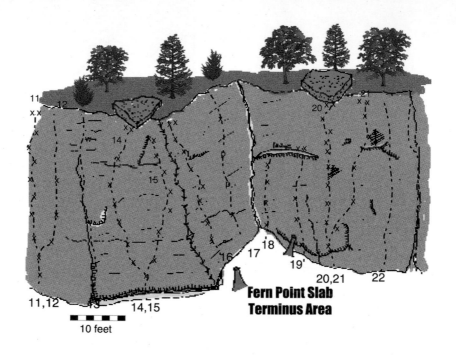

**Fern Point Slab
Terminus Area**

10 feet

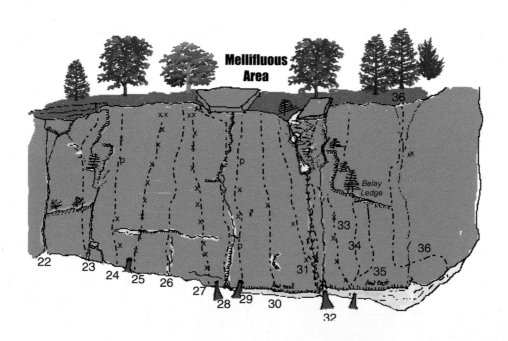

**Mellifluous
Area**

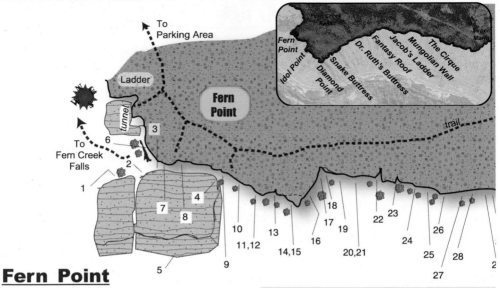

Fern Point

1. Standing Up in the Big Tent ✵ 5.12c *Sport,* 3 bolts, 1 pin. Start right of tree.

2. Whip It 5.12b *Sport,* 5 bolts. Arete.

3. Salvador Raleigh's Blow Up Dolly 5.12b *Sport,* 6 bolts. Face route on block inside corridor.

4. The Ribbon 5.12a *Mixed,* 1 bolt, 2 pins. Arete.

5. Express Yourself ✵✵ 5.12d *Sport,* 6 bolts. Back of boulder.

6a. Seeing Stars ✵ 5.11d *Sport,* 4? bolts. Starts just right of Fern Point Ladders. Stick clip first bolt then follow blunt arete to top.

6. George of the Gorge 5.9 *Sport,* 5 bolts. Slabby arete.

7. Positron 5.12a *Sport,* 5 bolts.

8. Civilizing Missions 5.12a/b *Sport,* 5 bolts.

9. New Age Equippers ✵✵ 5.11c *Sport,* 6 bolts. Starts just outside of the corridor on the left.

10. Dangerous Liaisons ✵ 5.12a *Sport,* 8 bolts.

11. The Exqueetion 5.12b *Sport,* 9 bolts.

12. Texas Wine 5.11c *Mixed,* 3 bolts. Same start as *Exqueetion.* Right hand bolt line.

13. Linear Encounters ✵✵ 5.11a R *Trad.* Crack and left facing corner to top. The fixed gear is an old bashie.

14. Eurobics 5.12d *Sport,* 8 bolts. Start at low roof and follow left bolt line to anchors.

15. La Futuriste ✵ 5.12a/b *Sport,* 7 bolts. Same start as above but move right and follow left side of white arete.

16. Be-attitudes 5.12c *Sport,* 7 bolts.

17. The Wetterbox 5.11d *Mixed,* 2 bolts and 2 pins.

18. Terminus 5.9 *Sport,* 4 bolts. Short slab climb to ledge. Move right to shuts on *Wench.*

19. The Vertical Wench 5.12d *Mixed,* 3 bolts. Small TCU's.

20. Is It Safe? 5.11d/12a *Sport,* 8 bolts.

21. Defunked 5.12b *Sport,* 6 bolts. Same start as *Is It Safe,* moves right.

22. The Reception 5.8 *Trad.* Left hand chimney.

23. Seventh Sign ✵ 5.7 *Trad.* Right hand chimney.

24. Slabbers of Habit 5.11b/c *Mixed,* 3 bolts, 1 pin. A bit run-out!

25. Dead Painters' Society ✵ 5.12a *Sport,* 8 bolts.

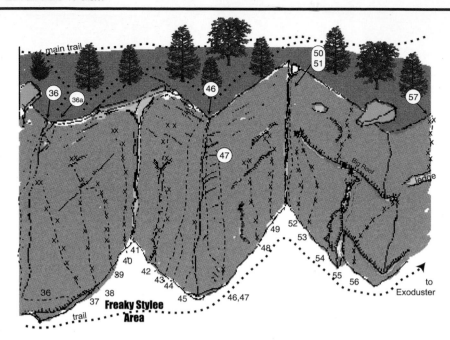

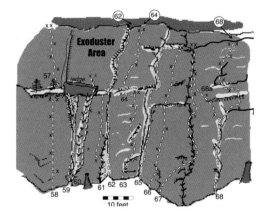

26. Son of Frankenstein 5.11d *Mixed*, 1 pin.

27. The Magnificent Pudcasso ✿ 5.12a *Sport*, 9 bolts.

28. Mellifluous ✿✿ 5.11a *Trad*. Follow hand and finger crack to right facing flake and top. Exit to the left at the top and use *Magnificent Pudcasso* anchors. Classic route, need small wires (RP's)!

29. Roll It Over in Your Mind 5.11d *Mixed*, 2 bolts, 2 pins.

30. Slick Olives 5.10d *Mixed*, 1 bolt.

31. Driven to the Edge 5.11d *Mixed*, 2 bolts.

32. Nasty Groove 5.9 *Trad*. Right facing corner with handcrack. Finish at pine tree or continue to top.

33. Acid Atomizer 5.11d *Sport*, 4 bolts. Finish on ledge.

34. Live Wire 5.10d *Trad*. Face climb.

35. The Flyin' Hawaiian 5.9 *Mixed*, 1 pin. Face to left side of arete. Finish on ledge.

36. The Prowess ✿✿ 5.9 R *Trad*. Start 20' right of arete and traverse left out to and around arete, continue up slab to top. This route has sparse protection placements. May be done in one or

two pitches. Belay at *Stim-O-Stam* anchors (or ledge) and/or continue to top.

36a. The Repossessed 5.8+ R *Trad*. Variation finish on *Prowess*. Right side of arete.

37. Stim-o-Stam ✿5.11c *Sport*, 6 bolts. Stay right of arete until possible to move left onto arete.

38. Freaky Stylee ✿✿ 5.12a *Sport*, 5 bolts. One of the first 5.12a sport routes in the Gorge. A must do for the aspiring 5.12 climber!

39. Techman ✿✿ 5.12c *Sport*, 8 bolts. Just right of *Feaky*. Nice face climb.

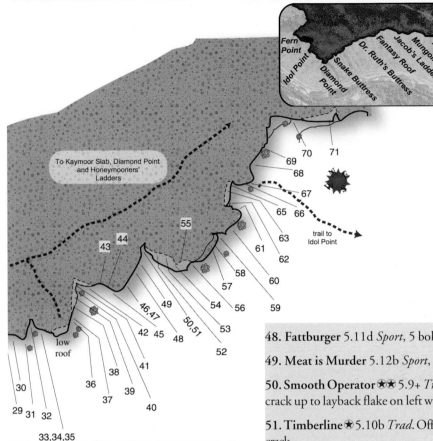

40. **Stealth'n'Magic** ✱✱ 5.12c *Sport*, 7 bolts.

41. **Biohazard** ✱ 5.10a *Trad. Corner*, traverse right across face at roof. It is possible to stop under roof at fixed anchor and not do the travers.

42. **Fascist Architecture** ✱ 5.12b/c *Sport*, 5 bolts.

43. **Inexorably Delicious** 5.10d R *Trad.*

44. **Exquisite Lace** 5.10b *Trad.* Variation start to above route. Corner to ledge, move left and finish on *Inexorably*.

45. **Party Till Yer Blind** ✱ 5.10b *Mixed,* 1 bolt. Arete. Starts 10' left of arete. Moves right. Technical climbing finishes as 46 and 47.

46. **Party in My Mind** ✱ 5.10b *Mixed,* 1 bolt. Start as below, left at 15', up to top right of arete.

47. **Party All the Time** ✱✱ 5.10b *Mixed,* 1 bolt. Face. Start below bolt. Classic route straight up nice face, moving left to arete near ledge 25' below top. Up short corner to top.

48. **Fattburger** 5.11d *Sport*, 5 bolts.

49. **Meat is Murder** 5.12b *Sport*, 4 bolts.

50. **Smooth Operator** ✱✱ 5.9+ *Trad.* Left hand crack up to layback flake on left wall.

51. **Timberline** ✱ 5.10b *Trad.* Offwidth corner, crack.

52. **Modern Primitive** ✱✱ 5.12b *Sport*, 4 bolts.

53. **Plyometrics** 5.12d *Mixed*, 4 bolts. Small TCU's.

54. **Harbinger Scarab** ✱✱ 5.12c *Mixed*, 10 bolts. Use double ropes, and bring a few wires for the beginning moves, no anchor.

55. **Back in the Saddle** 5.10c *Trad.* Right facing corner to rap anchor under roof.

56. **The Sweetest Taboo** ✱✱ 5.13a/b *Sport*, 5 bolts. Starts 10" left of corner.

57. **Crimes of Flashin'** ✱ 5.12a *Sport*, 5 bolts. Starts from upper ledge.

58. **'Bout Time** ✱ 5.13a/b *Sport*, 4 bolts.

59. **Diversity in Microcosm** 5.9 *Trad.* Obvious corner crack up to chimney. Finish at 'Bout Time anchors or continue to top from ledge above anchors.

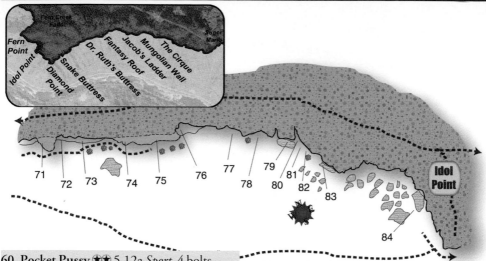

60. Pocket Pussy ★★ 5.12a *Sport*, 4 bolts.

61. The Plug 5.12a *Sport*, 3 bolts. Start on right of arete. Direct start on left is 5.12d

62. Autumn Fire ★★ 5.9 *Trad*. Corner crack to ledge. Then follow flake/crack to top. Tree anchor.

63. Exoduster ★★ 5.10b *Sport*, 4 bolts. Popular sport route up to anchors under roof.

64. Eat My Dust 5.11b *Sport*, 4 bolts. Continuation of *Exoduster*. Move out left around roof then up to anchor.

65. Premarital Bliss ★★ 5.9+ *Trad*. Start at twin crack up to roof, move right and up corner, traverse right (5.10) to *Through the Never* anchor or move left to top of cliff.

66. Through the Never ★ 5.12b *Sport*, 6 bolts. Up orange face to anchors.

67. Mental Wings ★ 5.12c *Sport*, 8 bolts.

68. S'more Energy ★★ 5.11c *Sport*, 8 bolts. Starts in orange dihedral, up to ledge, move left and up to anchors passing 1 pin up high.

68a. Chouinard-Steck Variation 5.11d *Sport*, 8 bolts. Link-up between *S'more Energy* and *Mental Wings*.

69. Manute Bol 5.10d *Trad*. Overhanging crack and corner.

70. Hooked on Bionics 5.11d *Sport*, 3 bolts.

71. Idols of the Tribe ★ 5.13a *Sport*, 9 bolts.

Fern Cirque

72. Life's a Bitch And Then You Climb 5.10b *Trad*. *Pitch #1*: Start from ledge, follow corner past roof and belay on right at ledge. *Pitch #2*: Corner to top. Same finish as Fist Fodder.

73. Fist Fodder 5.9 *Trad*. *Pitch #1:* Start in corner and follow crack up to ledge *Pitch #2:* Move left, follow corner to top.

74. Aquarian Conspiracy 5.10c *Trad*. Face to crack. Right facing flake on face.

75. Guns of Sassoun 5.10 *Mixed*, 1 bolt. Crack thru roof to ledge, step right, easy face to top.

76. Jane 5.9 *Trad*. Corner.

77. Grin Reaper 5.10b R/X *Trad*. Roof to ledge then top.

78. Tarzan 5.10a *Trad*. Orange and white corner to crack. Belay at ledge.

79. Golden Olympics 5.10a *Mixed*. Thin left leaning crack to right facing corner and ledge. Then straight up past bolt to top. (#2 friend)

80. Video Waves 5.9 *Trad*. Thin crack to ledge then dihedral to top.

81. Soft Torture 5.11d *Mixed*, 5 bolts. Needs TCU's up high and nut to go to first bolt.

82. Radford Rockers 5.11d *Sport*, 4 bolts.

83. Dead Animal Crackers 5.9 *Trad*. Flake and crack.

Bill Chouinard, Mississippi Burning (5.12b), Endless Wall. Photo: Cater

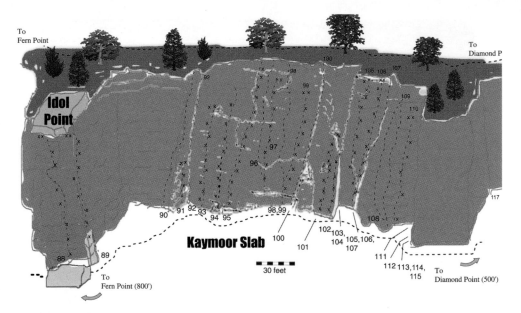

84. **Unnamed** EW #1 *Trad.* Easy climb-out to top. Starts just left of wide cave/crack. Up to small ledge move out left to face avoiding wide crack and then up face to top.

Idol Point

85. **Unnamed** EW #2 5.8 *Trad.* Wide crack.

86. **French Tickler** 5.12b/c *Sport*, 8 bolts.

87. **The Saint** ★★ 5.12d *Sport*, 7 bolts.

88. **The Spectre** ★★ 5.11a *Sport*, 7 bolts. Take a few small cams for the top.

89. **Idol Point Arete** ★★ 5.12a *Sport*, 8 bolts. Start at wide crack on right side of arete.

90. **Riding The Crest of the Wave** ★★ 5.9 *Trad.* *Pitch #1*: Face to left facing corner, cross face to belay ledge. *Pitch #2*: Arete to flakes and corner finishing right of roof.

91. **Meniscus Burning** ★ 5.11c *Sport*, 3 bolts.

92. **Command Performance** ★ 5.11a *Trad.* Flared corner/chimney/crack.

Kaymoor Slab

93. **What Will People Think?** 5.12c *Sport*, 8 bolts. Shuts at ledge.

94. **Slab O'Meat** 5.11d *Sport*, 9 bolts.

95. **Fool Effect** ★★ 5.9 *Sport*, 13 bolts. Requires double rope rappel from top. No anchor.

96. **Paralleling** 5.11a R *Trad.*

97. **A Date With Disappointment** 5.12b *Sport*, 8 bolts.

98. **New Wave** 5.11a *Mixed*, 1 bolt.

99. **The Upheaval** ★★ 5.9 *Sport*, 8 bolts. Slabby face left of vegetated corner system. Belay from ledge. Several climbers have been dropped while being lowered. Make sure your rope is 50+m.

100. **Newd Scientist** 5.4 *Trad.* *Pitch #1*: Begins in chimney and moves right across face then up towards tree. Belay on ledge. *Pitch #2*: Follow corner to the top.

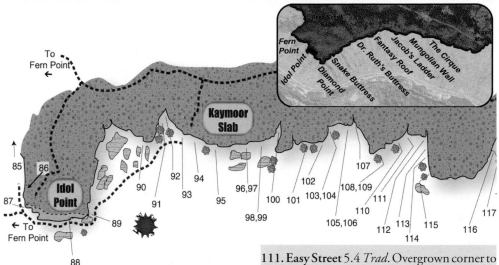

101. Little Help From My Friends ❋5.10a *Sport*, 8 bolts.

102. Unnamed EW #3 5.11b Sport, 4 bolts. Start at small overhang. Finish on *Pocket Pool* or *Wimpy*.

103. Pocket Pool ❋5.12c *Mixed*, 1 bolt. Start on Wimpy, move right to face then up arete.

104. Wimpy, Wimpy, Wimpy ❋5.9 *Trad*. Right facing corner/crack and chimney. Rap at ledge.

105. Pudd's Pretty Dress ❋❋5.12c/d *Sport*, 10 bolts. Overhanging orange wall. Awesome route!

106. Villain's Course ❋5.13a *Sport*, 9 bolts. Same start as *Pudd's*. Stay right. Tweaky!

107. Hefty, Hefty, Hefty 5.10a *Trad*. Right facing corner/crack to flaring chimney.

Nuttall Slab

108. Rotating Heads 5.10a R *Trad*. Start as below, after 30' angle left then up left hand clean streak.

109. Walking In Your Footsteps 5.10a R *Trad*. Flakes and face to top.

110. Total-E-Clips ❋❋5.8 *Sport*, 5 bolts. Slabby face to anchors.

111. Easy Street 5.4 *Trad*. Overgrown corner to ledge. Rap from ledge.

112. Rat's Alley ❋ 5.7 *Trad*. Corner to ledge and tree. Rap from tree.

113. The Meaty Urologist ❋ 5.12b *Sport*, 4 bolts.

114. Rhythm of Movement ❋ 5.12a *Mixed*, 3 bolts. Same start as *Fat*. Continue underclinging right to arete then up.

115. Fat 'n' Happy 5.11c *Mixed*, 3 bolts. Right facing corner, undercling right then straight up.

116. The Americans, Baby 5.10c X R *Trad*. Face and flakes.

117. Ambiance 5.8 *Trad*. Offwidth.

118. Stop Or I'll Shoot 5.11b *Sport*, 6 bolts.

119. Lisa's Lunge Time 5.12b *Sport*, 6 bolts.

120. Jazz Rock Confusion Open project. Shuts at top of thin crack.

121. Flash Point ❋❋ 5.11d *Sport*, 12 bolts. Starts on right side of smooth orange concave face right of bolted seam. Use last two bolts as anchor or continue to top. 60m rope required.

122. Euro-Nation ❋❋5.11c *Sport*, 8 bolts. This route is 5.10b if you stem off the tree to bypass the crux starting moves.

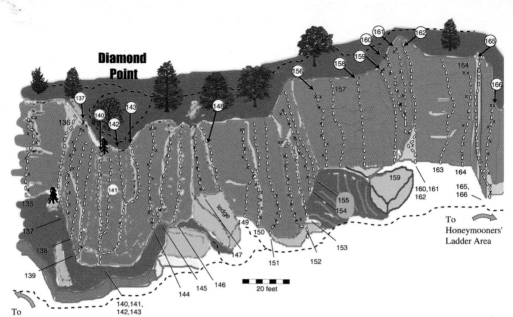

Diamond Point

Diamond Point

133. The Diving Swan ✪✪ 5.11a *Trad.* Follow the shallow corner, crack system to the top.

134. Bodyphobic 5.11c *Mixed,* 2 bolts. Technical face climbing up to small roof.

135. This Sport Needs an Enema ✪✪ 5.12b *Sport,* 6 bolts. Slab to slightly overhanging orange flake and crack.

136. Carcus Tunnel Syndrome ✪ 5.8 *Trad.* Chimney and crack system to top. Exit out to the right. Normal rack.

137. Homer Erectus ✪✪ 5.11b *Sport,* 9 bolts. Bolt line right of wide corner. Fun climbing on technical face.

138. The Weatherman's Thumb ✪ 5.12d/13a *Sport,* 11 bolts. Tall climbers will find this about 5.12c.

139. Zygomatic ✪✪ 5.11c *Trad.* Face to orange dihedral and small roof. Great route!

140. Remission ✪✪ 5.10b *Trad.* Broken crack system trending up and left to the top.

141. Durometer 64 5.10b *Trad.* Climb first 15 feet of *Remission* then continue directly up face.

123. The Stratowienie ✪ 5.11a *Mixed,* 1 bolt. Past 1st bolt then left and up to large flake. Up flake and face to top.

124. Ed Sullivan Show 5.11c *Sport,* 7 bolts. Same start as *Stratowienie*, bolts up and right.

Finial Point

125. April Fools 5.11c *Mixed,* 2 welded shuts. Scramble into corner up to a small pad, then face to top.

126. Shudder Bugger ✪ 5.12b/c *Sport,* 7 bolts.

127. Thilly Puddy 5.10d *Trad.* Crack.

128. Flying Sideways 5.9 *Trad.* Begin in corner at left side of Finial.

129. Stoke Victim 5.8 *Trad.* Start on *Thought Crime*, continue up arete.

130. Thought Crime ✪ 5.7 *Trad.* Arete, traversing right to crack. Shuts on top of Finial.

131. The Nutcrafter Suite 5.10c *Trad.* Thin cracks.

132. Ex-pudd-ition 5.11c *Sport,* 5 bolts.

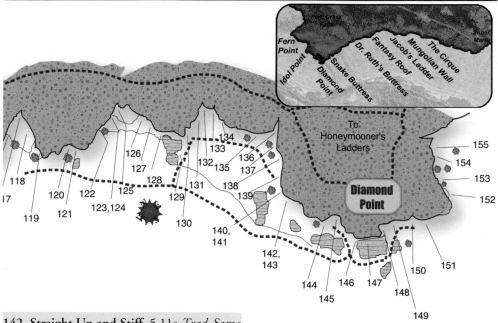

142. Straight Up and Stiff 5.11a *Trad*. Same start as below but continue straight up crack and face, trending left avoiding the easy traverse out right.

143. Can I Do It Till I Need Glasses? ✪✪ 5.10c *Trad*. Follow crack until it is possible to traverse right to corner and belay or continue following small corner to top.

144. Fine Motor Control ✪ 5.12a *Sport*, 7 bolts. Starts at blunt arete 5' left of *Raging Waters*.

145. Raging Waters ✪✪ 5.11a *Trad*. Start below flake in shallow corner. Follow flake to top.

146. Crack A Smile ✪✪ 5.10a *Trad*. Offwidth crack that starts from ground.

147. Strike a Scowl ✪✪ 5.10b *Sport*, 7 bolts. Starts from top of large block. Original route was all trad and given an R rating.

148. Supersymmetry 5.7 *Trad*. Right side of flake which starts on ground behind large block.

148a. The Apprentice 5.11a *Sport*, 9 bolts. Starts 6 feet right of *Strike a Scowl*. Leaves big flake after third bolt and continues diagonally right to the top. (Bolts removed due to proximity infraction)

148b. Three Exams 5.12c *Sport*, 9 bolts. Starts 10 feet left of *Ovine Seduction*. Move left after 4th

bolt. Joins *The Apprentice* at the last bolt.

148c. The Beauty of Innocence 5.13b *Sport*, 10 bolts. Same start as *Three Exams*. Move right at 4th bolt. Finish at anchors 15' below top of cliff.

149. Ovine Seduction ✪ 5.11a *Trad*. Hand/finger crack thru bulges then traverse right to ledge and up finger crack to top.

150. How Hard Is That Thang 5.12b/c *Sport*, 10 bolts. Shallow corner/face to arete. Crosses *Ovine Seduction* at ledge.

151. Stupendid Animation 5.11c *Mixed*, 5 bolts.

152. The Gift of Grace ✪✪ 5.12b *Sport*, 8 bolts. Start under roof and traverse left to arete.

153. Leave it to Jesus ✪✪ 5.11c/d *Trad*. Obvious crack in center of face. Finish at anchors of *The Gift of Grace* or continue around left side of arete then up face (original finish 5.9). Doug Reed free soloed this in 1996. **Direct Finish** 5.11b *Trad*. From horizontal after crux continue up short corner to top.

154. The Dark Side 5.11b *Sport*, 7 bolts.

155. Strange Duck 5.11c *Mixed*, 2 pins and 1 bolt. Face to small corner, continue to top.

156. Luck of the Draw 5.11c *Sport*, 5 bolts. Face right of major corner. Shares some moves with *Hog Woller*.

157. Hog Woller 5.10d *Trad*. Face up to corner/ crack, pull small roof and move up and left on flake to top.

158. Pulling on Porcelain ✱ 5.13a *Sport*, 13 bolts. Starts 7' left of *Maximum Leader*. Follow blunt arete and then move left onto white face. Finish at anchor at top of cliff

159. Maximum Leader ✱✱ 5.12c *Sport*, 9 bolts. Starts from top of huge block. Up overhanging corner to roof. Pull out roof and continue up arete/ face to top.

160. Clean Sweep ✱ 5.12c *Sport*, 9 bolts. Start as *Hell Bound* and traverse left at third bolt.

161. Hell Bound for Glory ✱✱ 5.12a *Sport*, 8 bolts. Same start as *Frictional Heat Experiment* but move left at roof.

162. The Frictional Heat Experiment ✱ 5.10a *Trad*. Start under roof in wide crack, move right and continue following corner to top.

163. Dust Bowl 5.9+ R *Trad*. Crack and face.

164. Glass Onion ✱✱ 5.10b *Sport*, 5 bolts. Starts left of wide crack. Blunt arete/face to anchors.

165. Voyeur Variation ✱✱ 5.10a, *Mixed*, 2 bolts. Up face two bolts then continue straight up dihedral to top.

166. Voyeur's Hand ✱ 5.12c *Sport*, 7 bolts. Start as above but continue following bolt line up and right.

167. Nestle Crunch Roof ✱ 5.10b *Trad*. *Pitch #1*: Starts in left facing corner and traverses left out the large roof to belay. *Pitch #2*: Follow dihedral to the top. Crosses *Voyeur's Hand*.

168. Can't Find My Guernsey Cow 5.12b *Mixed*, 5 bolts and 1 pin. Start right of large roof, up arete then right onto face.

169. The Height of Flashin' 5.11b *Sport*, 8 bolts. Slab with ledges.

170. Brass Monkey 5.10a R/X *Mixed*, 1 bolt, 1 pin. Corner to ledge then corner to top.

171. Struck By Lichening 5.11d *Mixed*, 3 bolts. Begin on *Brass Monkey* and traverse right at first bolt. Traverse right edge of face to easy crack.

172. Southern Hospitality 5.10a *Trad*.

173. Open Mouths 5.11a *Trad*. Corner to flake then face to top.

174. Static Line 5.11d *Mixed*, 3 bolts, 1 pin. Blunt arete and finish on *Open Mouths*.

175. Harlequin ✱✱ 5.12b *Sport*, 5 bolts, 3 pins. Starts 15' left of *Libertine*.

176. Oblivion ✱✱ 5.12d *Sport*, 6 bolts. Begin on *Libertine* and move left at third bolt.

177. Libertine ✱✱ 5.12d *Sport*, 7 bolts. Right hand bolt line. Shares start with *Oblivion*.

178. Sacrilege ✱✱ 5.12b *Sport*, 8 bolts. Start off large block. Climbs featured face.

179. Jesus and Tequila ✱✱ 5.12b *Sport*, 9 bolts. Arete. Stick clip first bolt on arete. Most people step off block to arete. Follow arete then move right out on face then straight up shallow corner moving out left at small roof near top.

180. Get Thee Behind Me, Satan ✱ 5.13a *Sport*. Begin on *Jesus and Tequila* arete and move right at fourth bolt to arete. Links-up with *Satanic Verses* at arete.

181. Satanic Verses ✱✱ 5.13b/c *Sport*, 11 bolts. Face up to small roof and flared corner. Then arete to top.

182. Noelle 5.12c R *Mixed*, 3 bolts, 1 pin. Starts in shallow corner and moves out right onto face.

183. Quinsana Plus ✱✱ 5.13a *Sport*, 8 bolts. Obvious line up orange colored wall. Ends under small roof.

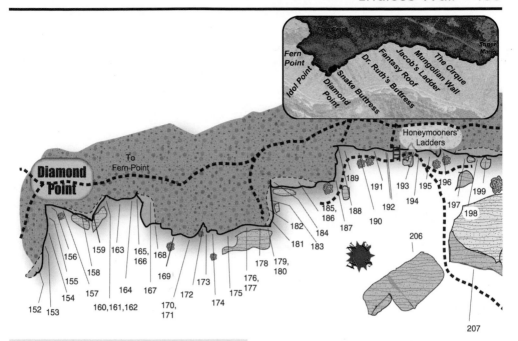

184. Crimes of Fashion ✪✪ 5.10a *Trad.* Wide corner to undercling, left at roof then up corner.

185. Rainy Day Route ✪ 5.12b *Sport*, 8 bolts. Shallow corner to roof, traverse left under roof then pull roof and finish on tricky moves up to the anchor.

186. Big Boss Man ✪ 5.12d *Sport*, 7 bolts. Start on *Rainy Day Route* and continue straight up at bolt 5. Lower off last two bolts.

187. The Rabbit Almost Died ✪ 5.12a *Mixed*, 3 bolts. Start on arete then move onto right face. Continue up face until it is possible to move back left to arete. Good climb but rarely done.

188. Lunar Debris ✪✪ 5.9 *Trad.* Offwidth corner.

189. Crescent Moon ✪✪ 5.7 *Trad.* Follow the wide, left arching crack to top. Lots of small horizontals for small cams.

190. Double Feature 5.11d *Sport*, 7 bolts.

191. The Bonemaster Gear Fling ✪ 5.11b/c *Sport*, 8 bolts. Slab to blunt arete

192. Sooner or Ladder 5.11b *Sport*, 5 bolts. Starts from the ledge at top of main ladder.

Honeymooner's Ladders

193. Unnamed EW #5 5.9 *Trad.* Right leaning corner and flake system.

194. Muck Raker ✪ 5.10d *Sport*, 8 bolts. Starts 20' right of ladder. Angle up and right on blunt arete.

195. Perserverence 5.10a *Mixed*, 2 bolts. Concave face trending up and right.

196. Wire Train ✪✪ 5.10c *Trad.* Corner and flake that angles up and right.

197. Stink Bug ✪ 5.12b *Sport*, 7 bolts. Start at overhang.

198. Free Flow ✪ 5.11b *Sport*, 7 bolts. Overhanging start.

199. Channel Zero ✪✪ 5.11c *Sport*, 6 bolts. Fourth sport route right of ladder. Overhanging start.

200. Motor King ✪ 5.11c/d *Sport*, 7 bolts. Dihedral to roof traverse left, con't on face to top.

201. I Feel Like A Wog 5.12b *Mixed*, 2 bolts, 1 pin. Face to roof, pull roof to lichen face.

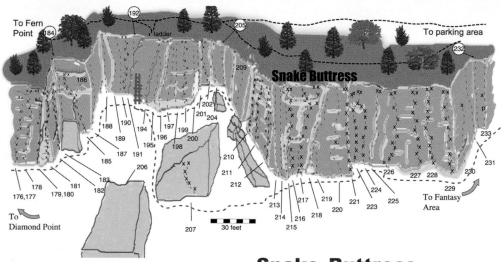

Snake Buttress

202. Double Flat ✱ 5.9 *Sport*, 6 bolts. Start from ledge. Move up and left following bolt line.

203. Walking on the Moon 5.11a *Trad*. Corner to roof then right to *Moonraker* crack.

204. Moonraker ✱ 5.7 *Trad*. Crack and flake system to the top.

205. Off Like A Prom Dress 5.10 *Mixed*, 2 bolts. Face climb 5' right of *Moonraker*. Face.

The next two routes are located on giant boulders in the middle of the cirque.

206. Bouldergiest 5.12b *Sport*, 4 bolts. Route on boulder.

207. I Advance Masked ✱ 5.12b *Sport*, 4 bolts. Short overhanging route on boulder.

208. Harvest 5.11c/d *Sport*, 7 bolts.

209. Sugar Bubbas ✱ 5.11a *Sport*, 4 bolts, 1 pin. Slabby arete to tree anchor.

210. Mississippi Burning ✱✱ 5.12b *Sport*, 7 bolts. Technical arete climbing. Hard 2nd clip.

211. Dial 9-1-1 ✱✱ 5.13a *Sport*, 8 bolts. Bolt line on left side of overhanging white wall.

212. The Racist ✱✱ 5.13b *Sport*, 9 bolts. Bolt line on right side of overhanging white wall.

213. Favorite Challenge ✱ 5.11d *Mixed*, 1 pin, 1 bolt. Follows right side of arete.

214. Snake Patrol 5.10c *Trad*. Starts on face, move up and right to arete (*Razor Sharp*). Up arete then left to short corner, continue up to a seam then up and finish left to other arete on left side of face

215. Razor Sharp 5.11b *Trad*. Start left of blunt arete and work your way up to small ledge. Follow thin flake traversing near the top. Finishes left of *Discombobulated*.

216. Discombobulated ✱✱ 5.11a *Sport*, 8 bolts. Bolted line left of big tree. Thin move at bottom followed by fun climbing and an exciting exposed finish. 55m rope.

217. Legacy ✱✱ 5.11a *Sport*, 10 bolts. Bolt line that starts behind big tree. After pulling the last roof, traverse left and finish (5.11d) or climb

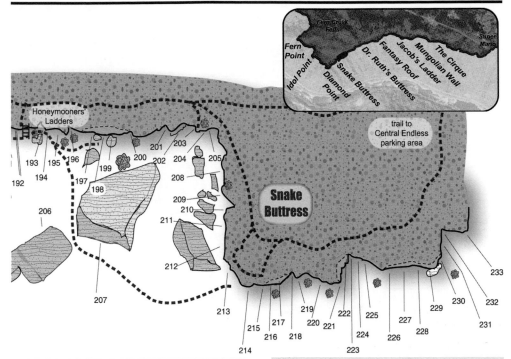

straight up and finish at anchors (5.11a finish). 55+ meter rope required for lowering.

218. Stolen Kisses ✹5.9+ *Trad.* Start left of large flake system. Climb up and right following flakes and large corner to top.

219. Adam Ant 5.11a *Trad.* Direct start to *Stolen Kisses.* Start right of flake system, finish on *Stolen Kisses.*

220. Rock Lobster ✹5.10c *Mixed,* 1 bolt. Start at right-facing flake left of arete. Work your way up the face passing one bolt. Double ropes recommended. Good top-rope.

221. Bullet the New Sky ✹✹5.12a *Sport,* 8 bolts. Arete.

222. S.T.A.N.C. ✹5.10b *Trad.* Offwidth corner.

223. Bloodshot ✹5.13a *Sport,* 8 bolts.

224. Pocket Route (a.k.a. Black Rider) ✹✹ 5.13a *Sport,* 9 bolts. Slab up to corner, move right then pull small roof. Continue up past second roof then traverse left and up.

225. Silent But Deadly 5.13a *Sport,* 9 bolts.

226. Raw Deal (a.k.a. Vulcan Block) ✹✹5.12c *Sport,* 9 bolts. Start off blocks, thin right arching flake up to face, straight up passing thru roof. 90' to anchors.

227. Shoveljerk ✹ 5.13b *Sport,* 8 bolts.

228. Dissonance ✹✹5.13a *Sport,* 9 bolts, 1 pin. Overhanging start to vertical face climbing. One of the first 5.13s at the Gorge.

229. New World Order ✹✹ 5.12a/b *Sport,* 7 bolts. Starts left of overhanging arete.

230. One-Eyed Willy ✹11c *Sport,* 5 bolts. 1 bolt anchor. Short and pumpy.

231. New Speedway Boogie 5.10c *Trad.* Flake to corner and crack and finish up face.

232. Gang Bang 5.9 *Trad.* Wide corner crack.

233. Do the Funky Evan ✹✹5.10d R *Mixed,* 1 bolt, 1 pin. Excellent climbing on this arete. Good top-rope problem for the timid.

234. Martini Face ✹✹ 5.12c *Sport,* 8 bolts. Zig zag bolt line, lower off last two bolts or use tree at top.

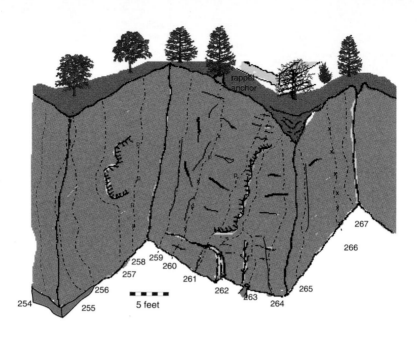

235. Translate Slowly 5.10c R *Trad*. Face to ledge, then crack to top.

236. Translate Slowly Direct Start 5.11a R *Trad*. Begin left of normal start, straight up to ledge.

237. What A Jam 5.9+ *Trad*. Crack up left side of large flake. Belay at small tree at top of *Pink Eye* or continue to top.

238. Lobster in Cleavage Probe ✪ 5.10a *Trad*. Follow the center flake until it is possible to move right and finish on *Pink Eye* or move left and finish on *What a Jam*.

239. Pink Eye 5.8 *Trad*. Right side of flake (rap from tree).

240. Night Gallery 5.9+ *Trad*. Crack.

241. Ray-Hall's Redemption Round 5.10a R *Trad*. Face to ledge, finish on *Sneak Preview*.

242. Sneak Preview 5.10a *Trad*. Face and crack to flake, then face to top.

243. Drug Virgin ✪ 5.11d *Sport*, 3 bolts. Short bouldery route.

244. Cosmic Thing ✪ 5.13a/b *Sport*, 4 bolts. Angles up and right to anchors.

245. Scream Seam ✪ 5.11a *Trad*. Short corner to ledge. Move left to anchor.

246. Two Fish Limit ✪ 5.12a/b *Sport*, 5 bolts.

247. Monster in My Pants 5.10a *Mixed*, 1 bolt.

248. The Separator 5.10a *Trad*. Corner and crack.

249. In Real Life 5.12a *Mixed*, 3 bolts. Begin as *Amigo Bandito* and move left to arete.

250. Amigo Bandito 5.10a *Trad*. Corner to crack.

251. Leave Me Bee 5.11c *Mixed*.

252. Sufficiently Wasted ✪ 5.10d *Trad*. Crack to roof, move left and follow wide crack to top.

253. The Wasted Weeblewobble 5.10b *Trad*. Crack and face to top.

254. Black Noise 5.10a *Trad. Face* left of arete.

255. Technarete ✪✪ 5.10b *Trad*. Up and left to corner and ledge, move left around arete, con't on flakes to top.

256. Arms Control 5.11b *Mixed*, 1 bolt.

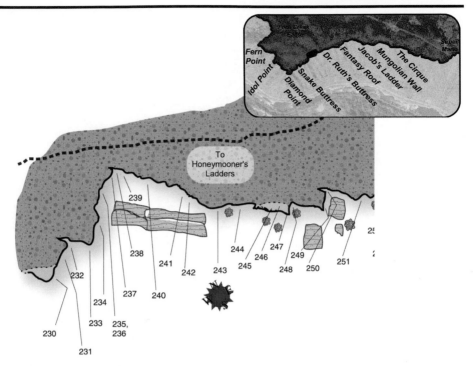

To
Honeymooner's
Ladders

239

238
241
242 243
232 244 247
246 249
245 248 250 251
237 240
234
233 235,
236
230
231

Dr. Ruth's Big Buttress

257. Recondite 5.11b *Trad*. Face to left-facing corner then continue to top.

258. Power Source 5.12b *Mixed*, 3 pins, 1 bolt.

259. Pride of Cucamunga 5.10d R *Trad*.

260. Idiotsyncracies 5.11b *Mixed*, 3 bolts and 1 pin.

261. The Diddler 5.10a *Mixed*, 1 pin.

262. The Grafenberg Crack ✪✪ 5.9- *Trad*. Follow 25' handcrack to ledge, move right into layback flake and continue to top. Finish by moving left onto slabby face or angle up and right on easier ground.

263. Dr. Ruth's Variation 5.8 *Trad*. Start just right of the handcrack in a small dihedral, join up with the normal route where the layback flake starts. Finish on normal route.

264. Between Coming and Going 5.10c *Trad*.

265. Insertum Outcome 5.10b *Trad*. Start on right side of arete. Follow cracks and layback to top passing a small roof.

266. Giant Steps 5.11d *Sport*, 6 bolts.

267. Crystal Vision 5.10a R *Trad*. Face.

268. Bad Head of Lettuce 5.10a *Mixed*, 2 bolts.

269. Closer to the Heart 5.9+ *Trad*. Up face staying right of right arching small corner, con't to top following arete.

270. The Growing Hole ✪✪ 5.12a *Sport*, 8 bolts. Up face to blunt arete.

271. Celluloid Vipers 5.9+ *Trad*. Corner to roof, move left and follow wide crack to top.

272. Titan's Dice ✪✪ 5.13a *Sport*, 9 bolts. Overhanging crack and corner. Strenuous and tricky!

273. Permission Granted 5.10a *Trad*. *Pitch #1*: Start at back of giant roof and climb dihedral, move right at roof and belay at lip. *Pitch #2*: Follow crack to small roof and move left to old rap anchors (2 pins).

274. Unnamed EW #7 5.10 *Mixed*, 1 bolt.

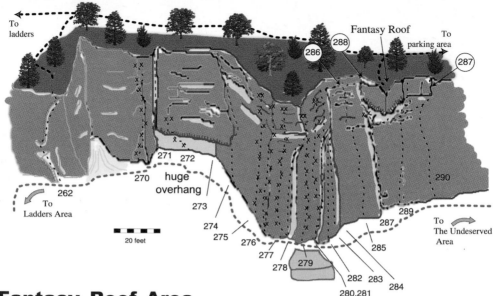

Fantasy Roof Area

275. Virgin Thing✪5.12a *Sport,* 7 bolts. Slab to roof crack.

276. The Stick ✪✪ 5.11d *Sport,* 8 bolts. Start at small overhang at arete and finish through roof at top. 55m rope required.

277. Blackhappy✪✪5.12a/b *Sport,* 9 bolts. Start on *Black and Tan,* move left to first bolt.

278. Black and Tan ✪✪ 5.10a *Trad.* Obvious dihedral to roof, move right and finish on *Aesthetica* anchors or continue to top.

279. Aesthetica✪✪5.11c *Sport,* 8 bolts. Bolt line that starts at broken crack and moves up orange bulge. One of the classics at the New.

280. Erotica ✪✪ 5.12a *Sport,* 6 bolts. Scramble up ramp (*Doce Doe*) and move left at ledge to first bolt. Continue straight up face passing through high roof.

281. Doce Doe ✪ 5.9 *Trad.* Start on ramp and follow dihedral to belay station (5.6). Rap from fixed gear or continue to top (5.9).

282. Veil of Addiction 5.10d *Mixed,* 2 bolts. Starts right of arete. Finish on *Doce Doe* rap station or continue to top.

283. Men Under Water 5.10a *Mixed,* 1 bolt. Climb left side of thin flake to its end then move up and left past bolt to ledge. Finish at *Doce Doe* anchor.

284. Pinka Pooka Party 5.9+ *Trad.* Dirty corners to roof, finish up and left on *Doce Doe* roof or move right to anchors.

285. Fantasy Face 5.12a *Sport,* 6 bolts.

286. Mr. Fantasy 5.11c Sport, 5 bolts. Starts at fixed anchors 15' left of belay ledge of *Fantasy.* Climb up and left through roof to chain anchors.

287. Fantasy ✪✪ 5.8 *Trad. Pitch #1:* Follow obvious left leaning hand crack to ledge under roof and belay. Pitch #2: Traverse right 25' on easy ground and then angle up and right and finish on small corner to top (5.5).

288. Fantasy Roof Direct Finish✪5.10a *Trad.* Variation on pitch two. Climb up and left through juggy roof and finish on top.

289. Dreams of White Toilet Paper 5.11a *Mixed,* 1 bolt.

290. Super Face 5.11c *Mixed,* 3 bolts. Finishes up and right of *Fantasy Roof.*

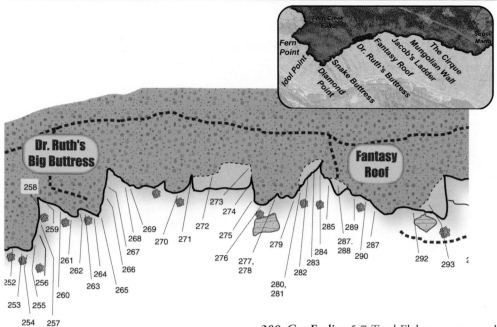

291. **Progresso** 5.11d *Mixed*, 3 bolts. Use double ropes. Up face to ledge then right and up finishing on easy ground.

292. **Vidassana** ✪✪ 5.11d *Sport*, 6 bolts. Angles up and right to large hueco.

293. **Wu Wei** ✪✪ 5.12c *Sport*, 4 bolts. Climbs out steep roof finishes on *Vidassana*.

294. **The Orgasmatron** 5.10d *Trad*. Begins behind large block in chimney. Left-angling crack.

295. **Riddle** ✪ 5.10c *Sport*, 7 bolts. Face and bulge up to ledge then face to anchors. Tricky face moves up high. Hidden pocket above first bolt.

296. **Two-Step Arete** ✪✪ 5.8+ *Trad*. Wanders up the arete. Gear placments can be tricky.

297. **The One-Step** 5.8+ R *Trad*. Right side of arete then follow corner, traverse right 10' and continue to top.

298. **Steppin' Out** 5.7 *Trad*. Traverses right at horizontal near the top of *Two-Step Arete* and follows left facing corner to top.

299. **Statistical Reminder** 5.9+ R *Trad*. Face, finish on *One Step*.

300. **Gut Feeling** 5.7 *Trad*. Flake to corner and finish on above route.

301. **Liddlebiddariddum** 5.10d *Trad*. Corner and crack.

302. **Jet Cap** ✪5.12a *Sport,* 6 bolts.

303. **The Beach** 5.10b *Trad*. *Mixed*, 1 bolt (no hanger). Crack and face, finishes on *The Tide*.

304. **The Tide** 5.8 *Trad*. *Pitch #1*: Dihedral and move left at roof, belay. *Pitch #2*: Move left and finish.

305. **Sequential Butt Pirates** 5.12a/b *Sport,* 6 bolts. Bolted face climb. Starts in small left facing corner between *The Tide* and *Four Star*.

306. **Four Star** 5.11b *Trad*. Corner and crack to roof. Crack out roof.

307. **Unnamed** EW #8 5.12a, 6 bolts.

308. **Flirting with VMC** 5.9 *Trad*. *Pitch #1*: Flake and corner. *Pitch #2*: Flake and chimney.

309. **Old Duffer's Route** 5.12b *Sport*, 3 bolts, 1 pin. Boulder problem-like crack out low roof.

310. **Unnamed** EW #9 Project. Roof right of *Old Duffer's Route*.

311. **Rebel Spade** ✪✪ 5.12b *Sport*, 9 bolts. Pull low roof to blunt arete.

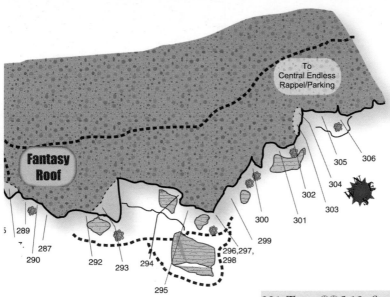

312. **New Fangled Dangle** ★★ 5.11a *Trad*. Arching dihedral with overhanging start.

313. **Sparks** ★ 5.12c *Sport*, 7 bolts.

314. **Caption** ★ 5.12b/c *Mixed*, 7 bolts. Start as *Erogenous Zone* and move left to first bolt.

315. **The Erogenous Zone** 5.10c *Trad*.

The Undeserved Area

316. **Back with My Kind** ★ 5.11c/d *Mixed*, 4 bolts. Blunt arete to ledge and fixed anchor.

317. **Mig Squadron** ★ 5.10d *Trad*. Begin on *The Undeserved*, move left after 30" to left facing dihedral and continue to anchors.

318. **The Undeserved** ★★ 5.10b *Trad*. Obvious flake and crack. Traversing left to left-facing dihedral at second horizontal break. Loose block in crack. Belay at ledge w/shuts.

319. **Young Whippersnapper's Route** 5.11b X *Mixed*, 1 pin. Face to flake and move right towards tree.

320. **Unnamed** EW #10 5.11 *Trad*. Top-rope.

321. **Tatoo** ★★ 5.12a *Sport*, 7 bolts. Starts on *No Mas* and follow bolt line to the left.

322. **No Mas** 5.12b *Mixed*, 2 bolts. Start on ledge, move up and right.

323. **Roy's Lament** ★★ 5.9 *Trad*. Flakes to ledge, move right at roof and finish at fixed anchors.

324. **Roy's Lament Direct Start** 5.9 *Trad*. Begins in crack fifteen feet left of regular start.

325. **Roy's Lament Direct Finish** 5.9+ *Trad*. Pull directly over roof at the top.

326. **Celibate Mallard** ★★ 5.10c *Trad*. Handcrack. Pull small roof and follow corner and crack system to top. Very Yosemite-like. Finish at fixed anchors.

327. **Something Fierce** 5.10d *Sport*, 5 bolts. Short route below large roof.

328. **Tuna Fish Roof** 5.11d *Trad*. *Pitch #1*: Dihedral to roof, move right at roof and belay. *Pitch #2*: Corner to top.

329. **Hot Tuna** ★★ 5.12b *Mixed*, 3 bolts. Shallow corner up to horizontals. Move left 15' then up to bolts, after second bolt move right to arete.

330. **Never Cry Tuna** 5.11c *Mixed*, 1 bolt.

331. **Give a Boy a Gun** 5.11c *Trad*.

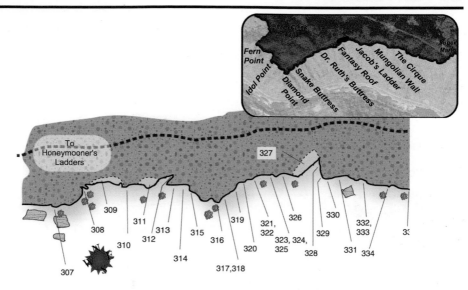

Kline Wall

332. Fun with Jello 5.11a *Mixed*, 1 pin.

333. Brain Death 5.10c *Trad*.

334. Wad Cutter 5.12a/b *Mixed*, 3 bolts, 1 pin.

335. Alcan Highway 5.6 R *Trad*. Clean streak on left finishes on *Double Negative*.

336. Double Negative 5.9 X *Trad*. Face up clean streak.

337. Dab Hand 5.10b *Trad*. Face.

338. Purity Made 5.7 *Trad*. Corner.

339. Bubbas at Arapiles ✪ 5.12b *Sport*, 3 bolts, 1 pin.

340. Oyster Cracker ✪ 5.10a *Trad*. Right arching flake and corner. Great route but is often wet.

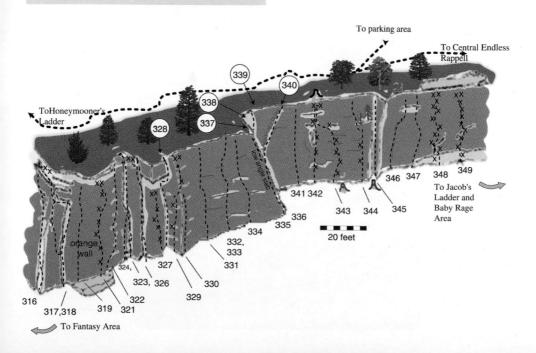

341. Man O'War 5.12b *Mixed*, 3 bolts.

342. Kline the Billy Goat ✸✸ 5.11c *Sport* (almost), 5 bolts. Excellent route. Needs a small cam between the last two bolts.

343. New Reed Route ✸ 5.11b *Sport*, 6 bolts. Start 10' right of *Kline* and follow bolt line up and left finishing on *Kline* at the last bolt.

344. Lying Egyptian 5.10b/c *Mixed*, 2 bolts.

345. Imperial Strut 5.10b AO *Trad*. Corner and flake. The AO is use of the tree.

346. Unnamed EW #11 Project *Sport*, 6 bolts.

347. Golden Years ✸ 5.12a *Mixed*, 2 pins, 1 bolt.

348. Gin and Bulls ✸ 5.12c/d *Sport*, 9 bolts.

349. Pearl River ✸ 5.12b *Sport*, 8 bolts.

350. River Heart ✸ 5.11d *Sport*, 8 bolts.

351. The Centurian ✸ 5.11b *Sport*, 4 bolts. Gear needed for first moves. Same start as *Android* then move left.

352. Android 5.10d *Trad*. Left corner then up and right past flakes to face and roof.

353. Suspended Sentence ✸✸ 5.12c/d *Sport*, 5 bolts. Overhanging left-leaning corner three routes left of rappel tree. No shuts.

354. Unnamed EW #12 5.13a *Sport*, 6 bolts.

355. Unnamed EW #13 Project. 7 bolts.

356. The Good Book 5.9 *Trad*. *Pitch #1*: Corner to roof. *Pitch #2*: Traverse left, then up.

357. Unnamed EW #14 Project. Steep prow.

358. Endangered Species 5.10c/d *Mixed*, 3 bolts and 2 pins. Camming units to #1 Friend.

359. Cheez Boys 5.10d *Sport*, 5 bolts. Shuts at top.

Climber on the classic
Fantasy Crack (5.8),
Endless Wall.
Photo: Cater.

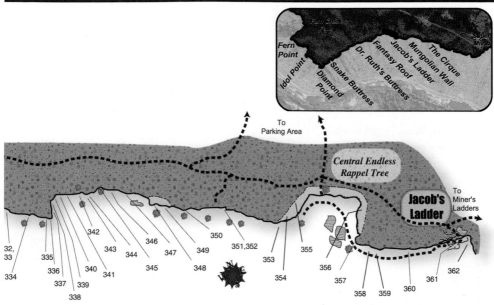

360. Motivation 5.12b *Mixed*, 3 bolts.

360a. Skin the Thief 5.9+ *Trad*. Starts 25' right of *Motivation*. Up and left then straight up and right to small roof. Finish at anchors on tree. Bring #00 Metolius - #1 Camalot.

361. Jacob's Ladder 5.0 *Trad*. Ledge system. May be used as a climb-out or climb-in.

362. Save the Human Race 5.5 *Trad*. Right-facing corner.

363. Just Forget It 5.12b/c *Sport*, 4 bolts.

364. Senility 5.11a *Trad*. Corner to finger crack.

365. Captain Chaos 5.10a *Trad*. Start on *Senility*, traverse left and up flakes to top.

366. Route 66 5.11b R *Trad*. Face to corner.

367 Stubble 5.12b/c *Sport*, 5 bolts.

368. Almost Heaven 5.10a *Trad*. Juggy roof up and right to slab. Then up and right past short crack.

369. Churning in the Butter ★★ 5.11b *Sport*, 9 bolts. 55+m rope required. Up and right then slab to overhangs.

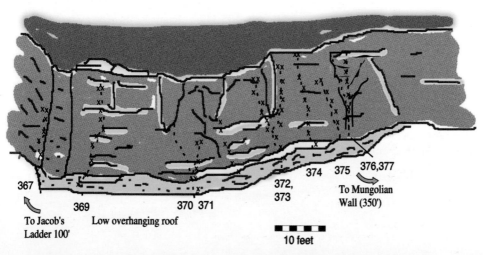

To Jacob's Ladder 100' Low overhanging roof

10 feet

370. The Alpha and the Omega 5.11b *Mixed*. *Pitch #1*: Roof crack to flake, con't up and left and belay in heuco. *Pitch #2*: Traverse left then straight up face to small roof crack and top.

379. Solitaire 5.10d *Trad*. Start at undercut crack, then follow crack up and left to ledge, con't up to roof, pull roof and con't to top.

380. Petrified Pink Puke 5.10c *Trad. Pitch #1*: Flake system up to roof, thru roof on left and belay in corner. *Pitch #2*: Follow corner traversing right and continue to top.

381. Big Gulp 5.9+ *Trad*. Flake and crack to roof, hand traverse right to ledge.

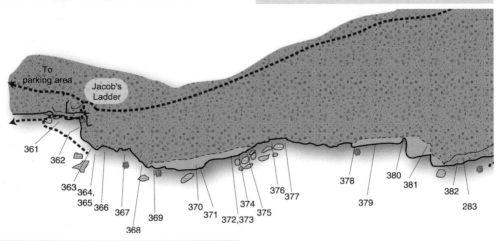

371. Baby Rage ✪✪ 5.12a *Sport*, 4 bolts. Out juggy roof then up to anchors in alcove.

372. Mechanical Bull ✪5.13a *Sport*, 8 bolts. Left hand bolt line.

373. Fat Back ✪5.12c *Sport*, 8 bolts. Same start as above, but follow right hand line.

374. Unnamed EW#15 5.12b *Sport*, 7 bolts.

375. Shotgun ✪✪ 5.12d *Sport*, 5 bolts. Left leaning crack.

376. Fearful Symmetry ✪✪ 5.12b *Trad*. Start at heuco move up and left through roofs con't following thin crack to top.

377. The Gram Delusion Project. *Sport*, 7 bolts. At heuco bolt line up and right.

378. Unnamed EW#16 5.10d *Sport*.

382. Caffeine Free 5.9 *Trad*. Crack to top. Starts from ledge.

383. Nutrasweet 5.10d *Trad*. Crack right of *Caffeine Free*, finish on *Caffine Free*.

384. Weenie Roast 5.8 *Trad*. Face left of arete then up and right to ledge

385. High Octane 5.10c *Mixed*, 2 bolts. Starts on upper ledge, right of arete.

386. Blue Angel 5.10c/d *Sport*, 4 bolts.

387. Blind Sight 5.10b *Trad*. Small left facing corner crack to ledge.

388. Blood Donors 5.10d *Trad*. Continuation to *Blind Sight*. At ledge, walk left 20' and climb orange left facing dihedral.

389. Sunshine Daydream 5.10a *Mixed*, 1 pin. Clean right facing flake traversing left then right facing flakes to top.

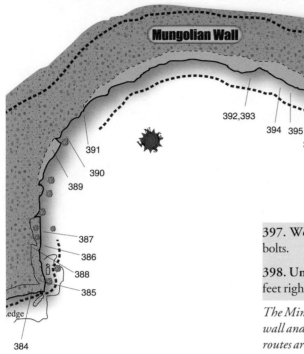

390. French Roast ✪ 5.12c *Sport*, 7 bolts.

391. Expresso Yourself ✪ 5.12a *Sport*, 7 bolts. Orange face to left-facing dihedral.

392. Overkill 5.12d *Sport*, 6 bolts.

393. Future Proof 5.12b *Sport*, 10 bolts. Same start as above move right.

394. Pigtail ✪ 5.12b *Sport*, 6 bolts.

395. Slide Rule ✪ 5.12a *Sport*, 6 bolts.

396. Unnamed EW#17 5.12c. *Sport*. Starts behind stalactite that is stuck in the ground.

397. Welcome to Mungolia ✪ 5.11b *Sport*, 8 bolts.

398. Unnamed EW#18 Project, 7 bolts. A few feet right of above route.

The Miner's Ladder are located between the main wall and a huge free standing pillar. The next two routes are located on the river side of the pillar.

399. Spree ✪ 5.11a *Sport*, 6 bolts. Starts on left side of pillar at short arete.

400. Topiary ✪5.12a *Sport*, Bolted line on right side. Up broken crack system on orange face.

401. Belly Up 5.12c *Mixed*, 2 bolts. Up arete to thin right leaning crack.

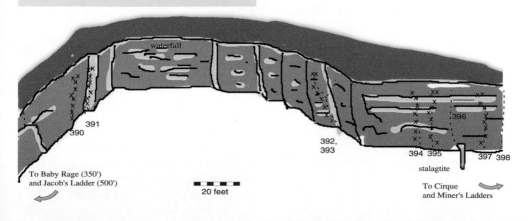

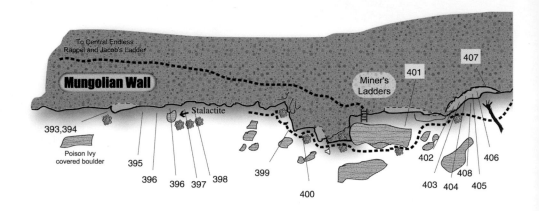

The Block

The following routes all start from a ledge partway up the cliff face. Rappel in from the top or climb Access Fun to reach the middle set of anchors. Rappel access is 75' upstream of the Miner's Ladder.

402. Block Head✪5.11a *Sport*, 6 bolts. Starts on left side of ledge.

403. Mental Block✪ 5.12d *Sport*, 7 bolts.

404. Block Party✪5.12a *Sport*, 6 bolts.

405. Chip off the Ole' Block ✪5.12c *Sport*, 6 bolts.

406. Blockade 5.12b *Sport*, 5 bolts. Same finish as above route.

407. Cell Block✪5.10b *Sport*, 5 bolts.

408. Access Fun 5.12a *Sport*, 7 bolts. This route starts from the ground and finishes at the middle set of anchors for the Block Routes. Start about 100' right of ladders. Up to small roof, then move right and up.

The Cirque

From the base of the Miner's Ladders walk upstream about 350 feet. The Cirque is a huge overhanging wall that averages about 120' high.

409. Hourglass✪5.12a *Sport*, 7 bolts. Starts at obvious flake on left side of Cirque. After last bolt move up and right. Straight up variation is 5.12b.

410. Nag 5.11b *Sport*, 4 bolts. Move left at first bolt then up through roof to anchor.

411. The Warm Up✪✪5.11a *Sport*, 6 bolts. Up and right then back left to anchors after roof.

412. Old Testament ✪ 5.11b *Sport*, 7 bolts. Move up then traverse right to anchors.

413. Satanic Traverses✪✪5.12c *Sport*, 19 bolts. Start on *Old Testament* then continue traversing, and traversing and traversing until you reach the final anchors.

414. Unnamed EW#19 5.11c *Sport*, 11 bolts. Climb first two bolts then move left traversing to anchors of *The Warm up*.

415. Unnamed EW#20 Project *Sport*, 4 bolts.

416. Proper Soul ✪✪ 5.14a *Sport*, 10 bolts. Obvious line up through large corner. The first 5.14 at the New. This route was originally bolted and attempted by Porter Jarrard many years ago. It was reequipped and red pointed by Brian McCray in the fall of 1997.

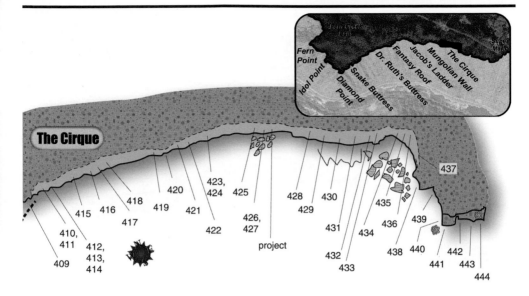

The Cirque

416a. Lord Voldemort ★★ 5.14a *Sport*, 10 bolts. Climb Proper Soul through the dihedral, to the 7th bolt (but don't clip it). Move left onto the line of "home-made" hangers. Finesse your way through a tenuous face crux to gain a good rest stance just below the upper headwall. Up you go to the finishing dyno off of a couple of crimps. If you top it out above the anchors...there is a nice ledge with grass and pine trees. 60meter rope required!

417. New Testament ★ 5.12d *Sport*, 10 bolts. Up three bolts then traverse right to anchor.

418. Norse Code 5.12d *Sport*, 6 bolts.

419. Graffiti ★★ 5.12a/b *Sport*, 5 bolts.

420. Superstition ★ 5.12d *Sport*, 11 bolts. Pitch #1- 5 bolts up to ledge and anchors. Pitch #2- Traverse right 10' then 6 bolts to bolt anchor.

421. Sloth 5.12c *Sport*, 6 bolts.

422. Xanth ★★ 5.13b *Sport*, 8 bolts/open shuts.

423. Unnamed EW#21 Projects. Start at small corner straight up and through high roof.

424. Unnamed EW#22 Project. Moves right.

425. High Yeller ★ 5.13a *Sport*, 8 bolts.

426. Finders Keepers ★★ 5.12b/c *Sport*, 9 bolts/open shuts.

427. Losers Weepers ★★ 5.13b/c *Sport*, 8 bolts/open shuts.

428. Ride the Lightning ★★ 5.13b *Sport*, 10 bolts. Moves out left through bombay chimney near the top.

429. Ragnarock ★★ 5.13b *Sport*, 10 bolts. Up face to roof then move left and finish on *Ride the Lightning*.

430. The Woody Project *Sport*, 9 bolts. The top of this route has not been free climbed as of this date, but the first 2/3 is climbing at 5.12b.

431. Mr. McGoo ★ 5.12c *Sport*, 7 bolts.

432. Brian's House of Cards ★★ 5.13c/d *Sport*, 8 bolts.

433. Hasta la Vista ★★ 5.12c *Sport*, 8 bolts.

434. New Life ★★ 5.11c *Sport*, 9 bolts. Grungy flakes up to corner, traverse right out nice flake then up and left to avoid wet section.

435. Live and Let Live ★★ 5.12b *Sport*, 9 bolts. Move right at first bolt then up passing small overlaps.

436. Holier Than Thou ★ 5.12d *Sport*, 9 bolts.

437. The Blacklist ★ 5.12d *Sport*, 10 bolts. Starts at small corner/crack system, up to roof, pull roof then crack/flake to anchors.

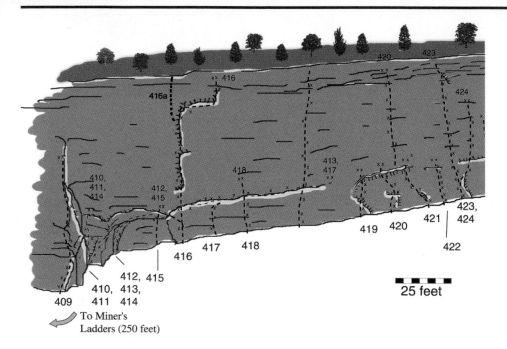

25 feet

To Miner's
Ladders (250 feet)

Mark Stevenson on Hourglass (5.12a), Endless Wall.
Photo: Cater

Tom Clancey on Welcome to Mungolia (5.11b),
Endless Wall. Photo: Cater

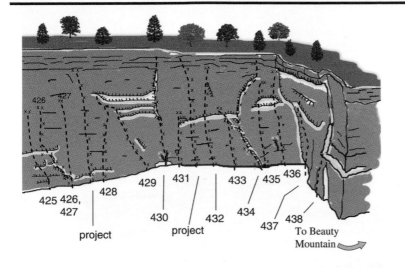

425 426,   428   429   431   433   435   436
     427
                         430   project   432   434   437   438
     project   To Beauty
                                                                 Mountain

Jim Suffecoool on Finders Keepers (5.12b/c), Endless Wall. Photo: John Burcham

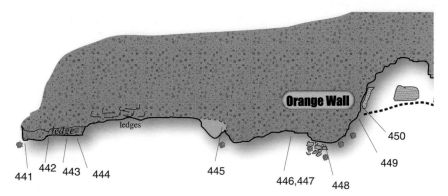

438. Unnamed EW #23 Project *Sport*, 5 bolts.

439. High and Lively 5.10b *Trad*. Right facing corner to ledge, move left to crack/corner system.

440. Out Of Hand 5.11b *Trad*. Variation start to *Wedgie*. Short finger crack to ledge.

441. Wedgie ✪ 5.10a *Trad*. Easy right facing corner to ledge then arete to top.

442. Fish Out of Water 5.12b *Mixed*, 2 bolts and 1 pin. Shallow right facing corner.

443. Even Cowgirls Get the Blues 5.11b *Mixed*, 3 bolts. Up to ledge.

444. Unnamed EW#24 5.11b *Mixed*, 3 bolts. Arete past bolt to ledge. Up right edge of face past 2 more bolts.

445. Bat Cave 5.8 *Trad*. Left facing corner to cave, squeeze to orange dihedral. Traverse right to finish.

446. Unnamed EW #25 5.10a *Trad*. Same start as *Skiggle* but move left.

447. Skiggle Van Wiggle 5.10b *Trad*. Up face to left facing flake, move right and follow flake to top.

448. Fiesta Grande ✪✪ 5.12c *Sport*, 8 bolts. Start off rock pile to reach first holds.

449. Basket Case 5.11b *Mixed*, 2 bolts. Starts on thin flake system, follow to top.

450. Garden Weasel 5.7 *Trad*. Dirty right facing flake and crack to ledge.

451. Lactic Weekend 5.11c *Mixed*, 1 bolt. Start as Spurtin', up to roof, then traverse left and up past bolt, face and orange scoop.

452. Spurtin' Fer Certain 5.12a *Mixed*, 2 bolts. Open book to small roof, traverse right then up past bolts.

453. Barbecued Babies 5.12b/c *Mixed*, 2 bolts. Overhanging crack.

454. Unnamed EW #26 Project *Mixed*, 3 bolts. Flake to first bolt, up to roof and then slab to top.

455. Sheena Is A Punk Rocker 5.11a *Mixed*, 2 bolts. Slab up clean streak.

456. The Zee Crack 5.10a *Trad*. Handcrack, traversing left to crack and then ledge.

457. Sweet Potato 5.9 *Trad*. Face to ledge, then left facing corner to right facing dihedral, out roof and chimney to top.

458. Tip Terror 5.12c *Mixed*, 2 bolts. Face to ledge.

459. Long John Jamb 5.9+ *Trad*. Thin left-leaning crack up to ledge, then obvious crack out short roof. Follow crack to top.

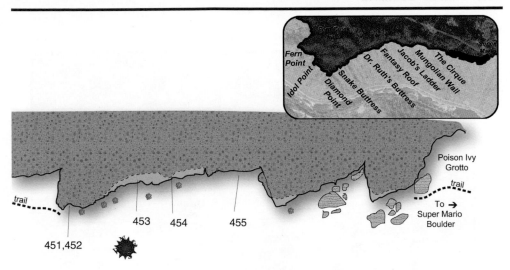

460. Unnamed EW #27 5.8 *Trad.* Left facing flake to ledge, then rap.

461. Unnamed EW #28 5.9 *Trad.* Thin crack to ledge.

462. Ramrod ✪ 5.12c *Sport,* 6 bolts. Start from ledge.

463. Quake ✪ 5.13b *Sport,* 7 bolts.

464. White Powderete 5.11a R *Trad.* Boulder up to ledge then arete to top.

465. She's to Fat for Me 5.10d *Trad.* Face to left facing corner.

466. I Don't Want Her 5.11a *Trad.* Face to small left facing corner.

467. Jack the Tripper 5.12a *Mixed,* 2 bolts. Blunt arete finishing up and right.

468. Unnamed EW #29 5.10c *Sport,* 4 bolts. Starts at blunt arete left of wide chimney crack.

469. The Bunny Hop of Death 5.11b R *Trad.* Low roof right of arete to left facing thin flakes.

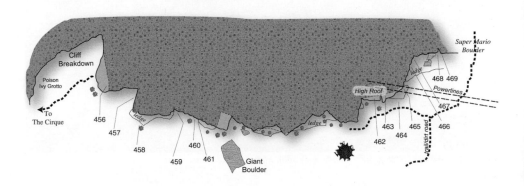

Jason Babkirk getting dialed on 911 (5.13a), Endless Wall. Photo: Cater

Climber on Glass Onion (5.10a), Endless Wall. Photo: Cater

Emma Williams demonstrates the proper technique on Burning Calves (5.10a), Beauty Mountain.
Photo: John Burcham

Climber on Harliquin, Endless Wall. Photo: Cater

Adam Wisthoff on Exoduster, Fern Point Wall. Photo: Daniel Brayack

Author Steve Cater out for a stroll on Air (5.11a), Beauty Mountain. Photo: John Burcham

Chris Carter on Strike a Scowl (5.10a), Endless Wall. Photo: Cater

Climber on Homer Erectus (5.11b), Endless Wall. Photo: Cater

Robert Thomas on Jesus and Tequila (5.12b), Endless Wall. Photo: Mike Turner

Pat Goodman on Sacrelidge (5.12b), Endless Wall.
Photo: Mike Turner

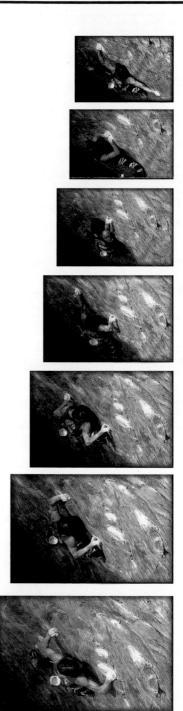

Sean McCauley on Aesthetica (5.11c), Endless Wall.
Photo: Cater

Dan Osman solo on the crux of Gun
Club (5.12c), Beauty Mountain.
Video Capture: Cater

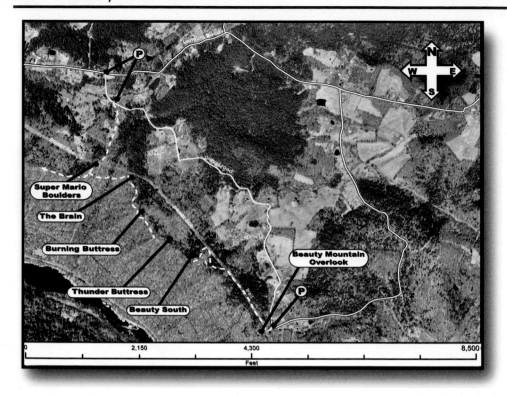

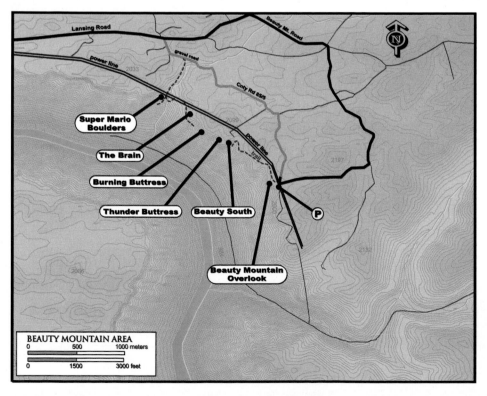

8

B e a u t y   M o u n t a i n

140 routes • 64 sport • 76 trad / mixed

Beauty Mountain is the southern most developed cliff in the New River Gorge. The dramatic overlook and high cliffs attracted the first climbers to the area in the late 70's. Early ascents at Beauty included the routes Screamer Crack (5.8) and Supercrack (5.9) at Thunder Buttress. These two were the first of many excellent moderate crack climbs to grace the walls of Beauty. There is also an excellent selection of sport routes that shouldn't be overlooked. One of the areas hardest routes, The Travisty (5.13c/d), is located near the Brain Wall. Harrison Dekker made the first ascent of this route in 1991. The cliff is about 3/4 mile long and varies from 45' to 100' in height. Beauty faces southwest and in most places is shaded in the morning. The cliff tends to remain wet after a rainy spell due to its orientation and the fact that large trees shade the cliff. Beauty has had several access problems concerning parking areas in the past so please keep this in mind. Be considerate of local traffic and residents.

Access

Beauty Mountain has two access points. The northern access point is located one mile east of the Fern Point Parking Area on Lansing Road. Upper Endless Wall and the Cirque may also be accessed from this point but it is a long walk. Park at the small pull-off on the left by the school bus shed. Do not block the driveway on the left side of the pull-off and park at least 4' off the paved road. If the parking area is full do not park in this area. Walk across Lansing Road and then follow the dirt road for 80 yds. At the intersection, take the middle road and continue walking past two shacks and a vicious, barking dog that is usually chained. The road descends and a large crenulated boulder appears on the right.

To reach the Super Mario Boulder continue walking another 30 yds. and turn right or to reach the Brain Area, turn left at the boulder and follow the trail. It crosses a small stream and then angles up towards the cliff and emerges under the Brain Wall. The second access point is from the Beauty Mountain Overlook. From the Overlook Parking Area, follow the trail under the powerlines for 1/2 mile. Halfway between the fifth and sixth tower turn left onto the trail and follow it down a gully to the base of the cliff. The trail emerges under a large section of overhanging cliff with Welcome to Beauty just around the corner. Do not park overnight at this parking area or leave your vehicle there after sunset. Please obey parking signs.

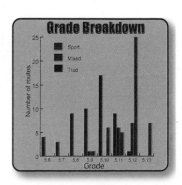

Super Mario Boulder

1. Unnamed BM #1 5.10c *Sport*, 4 bolts. Starts at blunt arete left of wide chimney crack.

2. The Bunny Hop of Death 5.11b R *Trad*. Low roof right of arete to left facing thin flakes.

3. New Route 5.12a *Sport*, 4 bolts.

4. Unnamed BM #2 5.11b *Sport*, 4 bolts.

5. Tubin' Dudes ✪ 5.13b *Sport*, 4 bolts. Short overhanging route on white wall. Variation- **Zelda**, moves out left, 5.13a.

5a. Leap of Faith 5.13c *Sport*, 4 bolts. Starts to the right of *Tubin' Dudes*. Separate line.

6. Rival 5.10a *Sport,* 3 bolts. Starts on face right of wide chimney.

7. Sixteenth Rung 5.10c *Sport*, 4 bolts. Face to small roof.

8. Pinckney Route 5.10d *Sport*, 4 bolts. Face to small roof.

9. Guides Route, Left ✪ 5.5 *Trad*. Start on right facing flake and follow to top passing through a small overhang.

10. Guides Route, Right 5.5 *Trad*. Start 8' right of flake and follow featured face to top passing through small roof at the top.

11. In the Palm of His Hand 5.7+ *Trad*. Face on right side of arete. On seperate boulder acrss from # 10.

12. Super Mario ✪✪ 5.13a *Sport*, 4 bolts. Left bolt line on boulder.

13. European Vacation ✪✪ 5.12a/b *Sport*, 4 bolts. Right bolt line on boulder.

14. Donkey Kong ✪ 5.13a *Sport*, 4 bolts. Left bolt line on overhanging boulder.

Chris Lea on Brain Teasers (5.10a), Beauty Mountain. Photo: Cater

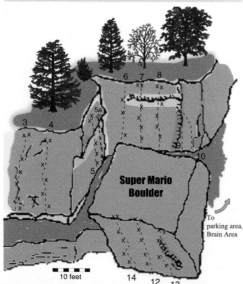

Super Mario Boulder

To parking area, Brain Area

10 feet

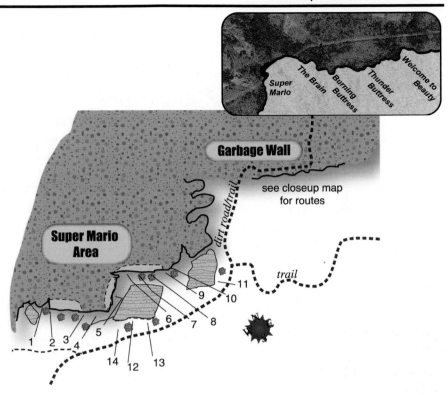

Garbage Wall

see closeup map
for routes

Super Mario
Area

trail

Garbage Wall (Intestinal Wall)

This wall has a couple routes on it that are OK. It is usually seeping and is right below the road .

15. **Batman** 5.9 *Sport*, 3 bolts/1 bolt anchor.

16. **Robin** 5.8 *Sport*, 2 bolts/1 ring bolt anchor.

17. **Aquaman** 5.9+ *Sport*, 2 bolts.

18. **Rubbish** 5.11 *Sport*, 3 bolts/2 bolt anchor.

19. **Shit Can** 5.10 *Sport*, 2 bolts/1 bolt anchor. Angles up and right.

20. **MO** 5.10a *Sport*, 2 bolts and 1 pin. Missing first hanger.

21. **Turan-Acaurus Wrecks** 5.10c *Sport*, 3 bolts.

22. **Dispose of Properly** 5.11c *Sport*, 3 bolts. Angle iron hangers.

23. **Tools for Mutant Women** 5.10c *Sport*, 2 bolts. Angle iron hangers.

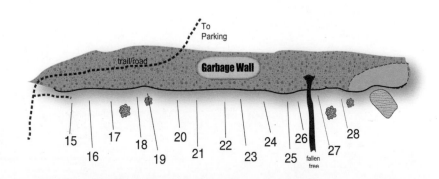

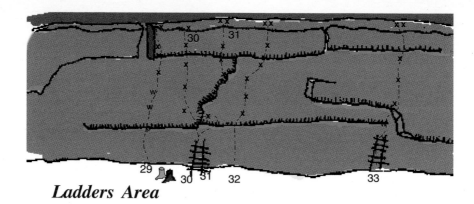

Ladders Area

24. **Pop Top Heaven** Project *Sport*, 3 bolts. Angles up and left.

25. **Dueling Banjos** 5.12a *Sport*, 3 bolts. Angles up and right.

26. **Wonder Women** 5.11d *Sport*, 3 bolts/1 bolt anchor.

27. **Rusty Car** 5.9 *Trad*. Obvious crack to top.

28. **Plastic Man** 5.11a *Sport*, 2 bolts.

Ladders Area

Ladders are helpful if the bottom is wet.

29. **Night Train** ✪ 5.12b *Sport*, 2 fixed wires and 2 bolts.

30. **It's A Fine Line** ✪✪ 5.12d *Sport*, 5 bolts. Same start as *Smokin'*.

31. **Smokin' Guns** ✪✪ 5.12a *Sport*, 5 bolts.

32. **Up, Up and Away** 5.12d *Sport*, 5 bolts.

33. **Heller Route** 5.12d *Sport*, 1 fixed wire, 4 bolts.

The Brain

34. **Way Cerebral** 5.9 *Mixed*, 3 bolts. Start on right side of arete.

35. **Green Thing** 5.9 *Trad*. Thin crack to featured face.

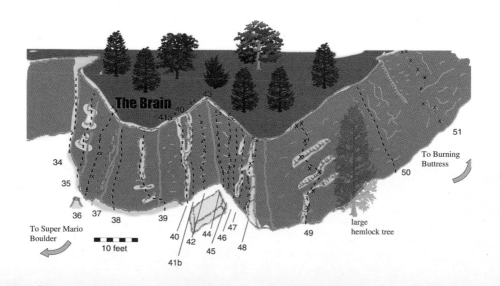

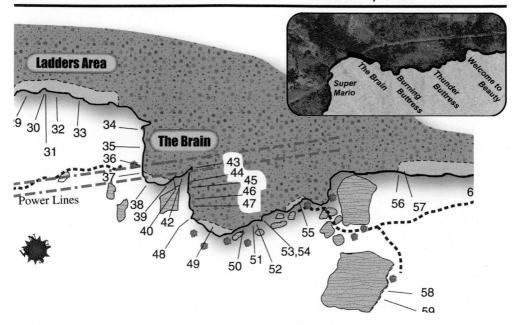

Ladders Area

9 30 32 33 34

31 35

36

37

Power Lines

The Brain

43
44
45
46
47

38
39
42
40

48
49 50 51 52 53,54

55

56 57 6

58
59

Super Mario The Brain Burning Buttress Thunder Buttress Welcome to Beauty

36. You Want It, You Got It ✪✪ 5.9 *Sport*, 5 bolts. Starts 15' left of outside corner.

37. Brain Wave ✪ 5.7 *Trad*. Start on the left side of low roof and follow face staying just left of the arete.

38. Out of Mind ✪ 5.10a *Trad*. Begin at center of low roof. Pull roof at crack and continue up the left edge of the face.

39. Journey to the Center of the Brain ✪✪ 5.7 *Trad*. Start on right side of low roof and move up and left. Follow the obvious line up and through the convoluted featured face.

40. Brain Teasers ✪✪ 5.10a *Trad*. Crack up and right to small right-facing corner and roof. Traverse right past old pin then continue up another corner and small roof, finish on the pocketed face.

41a. Brain Storm 5.8 *Trad*. Direct finish over first roof on *Brain Teasers*. Not much gear.

41b. Brain Child 5.11b *Trad*. Direct start to *Brain Teasers*. Start right of crack and climb face to second small roof.

42. Brain Tweezers ✪✪ 5.10b *Sport*, 5 bolts. Starts left of *Bearpaw Crack*. Enjoyable face climbing.

43. Bearpaw Crack 5.8 *Trad*. Dirty crack.

44. M.E.N.S.A. ✪✪ 5.11d/12a *Sport*, 4 bolts. It's 5.12a if you go straight up at the 3rd bolt and 5.11+ if you move out left.

45. Dancing in the Flesh 5.12a *Sport*, 4 bolts. Second bolt line right of corner. Face.

46. Toadstool 5.8 *Trad*. Dirty flake and crack system up and left.

47. Hot Flash 5.10b *Trad*. Right facing flake system up to right arching flake then left to top.

48. Butta ✪ 5.11c/d *Sport*, 7 bolts. Boulder problem start. Pull past 1st move and climb nice 5.10d

49. Chunky Monkey ✪✪ 5.12b *Sport*, 6 bolts, 2 pins. Start at shallow corner, up and right to stance then move left out roof system up to second roof then right and straight up to anchor. Classic 5.12!

50. Unnamed BM #3 Project. 6 bolts. Overhanging wall.

51. The Travisty ✪✪ 5.13c/d *Sport*, 7 bolts. Technical and hard climbing on nice rock. Originally bolted and then chipped. Porter Jarrard repaired the chip and Harrison Dekker completed the first free ascent.

Mark Stroud betting heavy on Let's Make A Deal (5.11c), Beauty Mountain. Photo: Cater

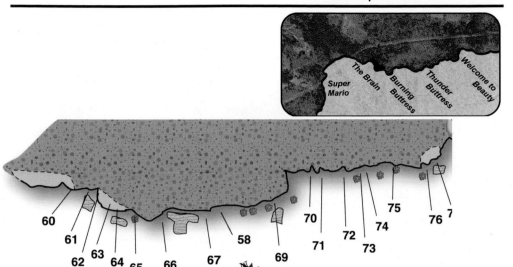

52. Unnamed BM #4 Project.

53. Super Whiny Bugs (Project) Left hand variation of *Whiny Bugs*. Start on right of small slabby arete.

54. Whiny Bugs 5.12b *Sport*, 7 bolts. Same start as above but follow right bolt line.

55. Comatose ✪ 5.12c *Sport*, 4 bolts.

North Beauty

56. Genocide ✪ 5.12a *Mixed*, 1 pin. Climb out roof passing one fixed pin to nice 5.11 handcrack.

57. Unnamed BM #5 Project.

58. Mongoloid ✪✪ 5.12d *Sport*, 4 bolts. Steep face on boulder.

59. Hot Bip ✪ 5.12b *Sport*, 3 bolts. Steep face on boulder.

60. Green Envy ✪✪ 5.12c *Sport*, 7 bolts. First route on right side of huge overhang.

61. Disturbance ✪✪ 5.11d *Sport*, 7 bolts. Obvious bolted crack with pods. Great climbing!

62. Stay Tuned 5.8 *Trad*. Chimney for 10' then step right and up face.

63. Screams in the Woods 5.11b *Mixed*, 1 pin. Pull overhang and up to flake, follow thin crack

to slab, move left and continue to top.

64. Warp Factor III 5.9 *Trad*. Start at right-facing corner under roof. Follow corner to roof and then short crack to top.

64a. Aye, Aye Captain 5.10b *Trad*. Up *Warp Factor* to roof then move right and continue to top.

65. Garden Club 5.12a *Sport*, 7 bolts. Starts behind large tree. Small roof followed by technical slab climbing. Mossy.

66. Baby Cakes 5.12a *Mixed*. Climb thru small roof and follow thin crack passing one pin.

67. Hallaluah Crack ✪ 5.11c *Trad*. Thin crack.

68. Unnamed BM #6 Project. Thin crack with 2 pins, 2 bolts.

69. Unnamed BM #7 Project. Small roof and crack with 2 pins.

70. Happy Hands ✪✪ 5.9 *Trad*. Handcrack up and left to tree anchor.

71. Broken Sling ✪ 5.10a R *Trad*. Right facing flake system then face.

72. Spider Wand ✪✪ 5.10b *Trad*. Flared corner and crack up to roof. Move right out roof.

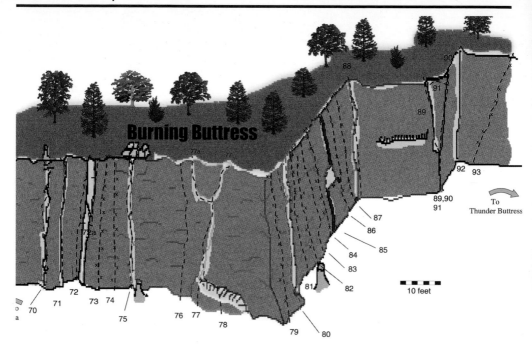

72a. **Wham, Bam, Thanks for the Jam** ✪✪ 5.10b *Trad.* Variation on *Spider Wand.* Start on *Spider Wand* and move right into nice handcrack on the right face after 35'.

73. **The Ruchert Motion** 5.13a *Sport,* 8 bolts.

74. **Fade to Black** ✪ 5.12b *Mixed,* 7 bolts.

75. **Burning Calves** ✪✪ 5.10b *Trad.* Excellent hand and finger crack to top.

76. **Bubbaheads** 5.11c *Trad.* Starts off boulder and moves up right to below a roof, move past roof and follow the crack to the top.

77. **East Meets West** ✪ 5.9 *Trad. Pitch #1*: Climb thin finger crack, traversing right to ledge and belay. *Pitch #2*: Climb corner then follow right leaning ramp to the top.

77a. **Bourbon Street** 5.10d *Trad.* Variation finish to Pitch 2. Moves left at the top out an undercling.

78. **Exposing the Pink** 5.11b *Trad.* Start to the right of *East Meets West* at small roof which has a crack above it. Climb short crack and traverse left to ledge.

Burning Buttress

79. **Sportster** ✪✪ 5.13a *Sport,* 8 bolts.

80. **The Will to Power** ✪✪ 5.11c R *Mixed,* 1 bolt. Follows shallow dihedral on arete and then move right or left near the top.

81. **Chorus Line** ✪✪ 5.12d *Mixed,* 3 bolts, 1 pin. The Direct Start adds a 5.12a move.

82. **Ad Lib** ✪✪ 5.12d *Sport,* 8 bolts.

83. **Steve Martin's Face** ✪✪ 5.11c *Mixed,* 1 bolt, no hanger. Up flake, traversing right to bolt, continue traversing right and then move back left over bolt. Continue up and right to top.

84. **Grace Note** ✪✪ 5.12b *Sport,* 7 bolts.

85. **Rod Serling Crack** ✪✪ 5.10b *Trad.* Left facing dihedral, thru roof to finger crack.

86. **Dark Shadows** ✪ 5.11d *Sport,* 6 bolts.

87. **Broken Dreams** 5.13a *Sport,* 7 bolts. Has not been repeated since a crucial hold broke.

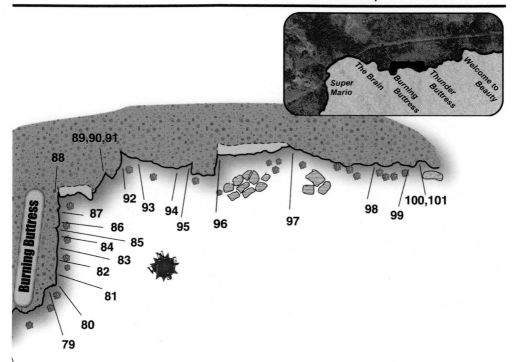

88. Point in Question 5.10a *Trad*. Right-facing dihedral, thru roof to left-hand crack.

89. Hilti as Charged ✪ 5.11d *Sport*, 6 bolts. Start on *Quick Robin* and move left onto face.

90. Quick Robin to the Bat Crack! ✪ 5.10a *Trad*. Corner up to roof move right then up short arete to top.

91. Bat Crack Direct Finish 5.10b R *Trad*. Move out left at small roof. Finish at fixed anchors on *Hilti*.

92. Wild Dogs 5.10c *Trad*.

Middle Beauty

93. Sleeping Beauty 5.12a *Sport*, 7 ring bolts. Vertical wall which is usually wet.

94. West Virginia Water Torture 5.13a *Sport*, 7 bolts.

95. The Zoomin' Human 5.10a *Trad*. Start left of large corner, traverse right and continue following corner to top.

96. Tetelestai ✪ 5.11d *Trad*. Steep corner that used to have a rotten plastic baby dangling in crack.

97. Quaking Flakes 5.8 *Trad*. Crack to flake system. Loose and scary.

98. Mononuclear Knows It 5.8 *Trad*. Right-facing corner-groove.

99. Ewe Can't Touch This 5.12c *Sport*, 10 bolts. Slab.

100. Fat Man's Folly 5.9 *Trad*. Start in corner/chimney then finish up and left on nice hand-crack.

101. Gimme, Gimme Shock Treatment 5.12b *Mixed*, 4 bolts. Pull roof on *Fat Man's Folly* and continue up and right on face making a long traverse to the left.

There are several different ways to gain access to *Chasin' the Wind* Ledge; climb the *Direct Start*, Pitch #1 of *Nazz, Nazz*, or traverse in left from the top of the large block (5.9 1 bolt) or climb the original first pitch.

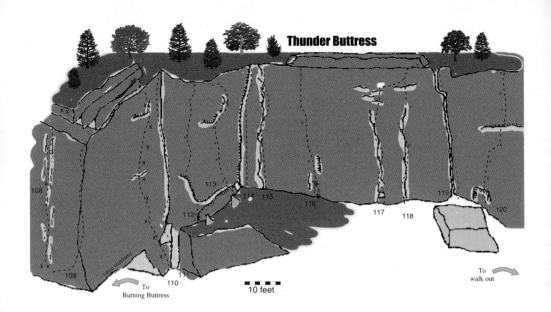

Thunder Buttress

To
Burning Buttress

10 feet

To
walk out

102. Chasin' the Wind Direct Start ✪ 5.12a R *Mixed*, 1 bolt. Starts near left end of ledge. 30' long.

103. Chasin' the Wind ✪✪ 5.11b *Trad*. From Thunder Buttress walk upstream 100 yards to an obvious 10' high boulder. Pitch #1- Start from the top of large boulder. Climb up passing one bolt then traverse right to belay ledge (5.9 with one bolt). Pitch #2- Start at thin crack near left side of upper ledge. Follow crack system to ledge and anchors. Stop at anchors or -original finish- continue to top by traversing left 35 feet on lichen covered rock or by moving straight up and right (5.11c) on thin gear.

104. Nazz, Nazz ✪ 5.12c *Sport*, 10 bolts. *Pitch #1*: Up three bolts to ledge (5.11c). *Pitch #2*: Starts right of *Chasin' the Wind* and continues up past fixed gear to rap anchors.

105. Gone With the Wind 5.12a R *Trad*. Start at far right edge of ledge, up face and right to top.

106. Rainy Daze 5.9 *Trad*. Climb face to roof with fixed rappel anchors.

107. Lone Rhinoceros 5.10c *Trad*. Two pitches up large corner and crack.

108. The Perfect View ✪✪ 5.11d *Mixed*, 1 pin, 1 bolt. Rappel from the top and belay at a 2 bolt anchor at the lip of the gigantic roof. Climb straight up broken crack system and horizontals to top.

109. Air ✪✪ 5.11a *Trad*. Rappel to *The Perfect View* anchors at lip of big roof. Climb up and right towards arete. Follow arete to top.

Thunder Buttress

110. The Gun Club ✪✪ 5.12b/c *Sport*, 9 bolts. Face left of *Supercrack*. 100' to anchors. Soloed by Dan Osman in 1993. Think about that while doing the crux!

111. Supercrack ✪✪ 5.9+ *Trad*. Obvious and excellent crack route up corner. One of the best routes at Beauty!

111a. Photo Finish ✪ 5.9 *Trad*. Variation finish of *Supercrack*. Traverse left out horizontals near the top.

112. The Beast In Me ✪✪ 5.12a *Mixed*, 1 bolt (no hanger), 1 fixed wire. Start from ledge 10' right of *Supercrack*. Good top-rope for the timid.

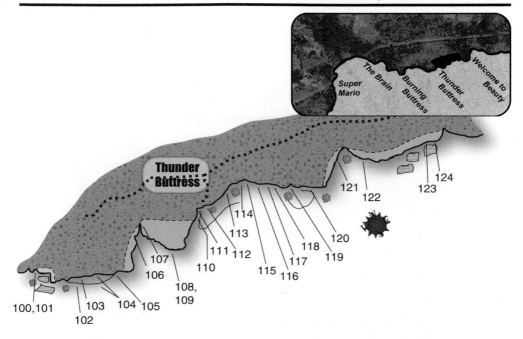

113. **Transcendence** ✪✪ 5.11d *Sport*, 5 bolts. This route was originally a ground up lead, but it was accidently retro-bolted.

114. **Screamer Crack** 5.8 *Trad*. Offwidth.

115. **Mushrooms** ✪ 5.10a *Trad*. Nice crack which may be dirty near the top.

116. **L.S.D.** 5.12a *Mixed*, 1 bolt, 1 pin.

117. **Left Son of Thunder** ✪✪ 5.11d *Trad*. Climb up thin crack until it ends, continue up face then move right to *Right Son of Thunder*.

118. **Right Son of Thunder** ✪✪ 5.11c *Mixed*, 1 pin, 1 bolt. Thin crack, and face to bolt, traverse left and then up to roof.

119. **Momma's Squeeze Box** ✪✪ 5.8 *Trad*. Chimney.

120. **Concertina** ✪✪ 5.12a *Sport*, 7 bolts.

121. **Stabat Mater** 5.13a/b *Sport*, 5 ring bolts to belay and then 6 more ring bolts to the top.

122. **Backlash** ✪✪ 5.12a *Sport*, 4 bolts. Short and steep climb that starts under roof.

123. **Loud Noise** ✪✪ 5.12b *Sport*, 8 bolts. Starts from block.

Bill Saul on Mushrooms, Beauty Mountain.
Photo: Mike Turner

Joe Crocker near the top of Supercrack (5.9), Beauty Mountain. Photo: Cater

124. Let's Make A Deal ✹✹ 5.11c *Sport*, 6 bolts. Starts from top of block at small overhang.

Beauty South

125. Clairvoyance 5.9+ *Trad*. Crack to face.

126. Death of a Salesman 5.9 *Trad*. Flared corner and crack.

127. Beginner's Luck 5.7 *Trad*. Short left facing flake up to ledge.

128. Potato Chip 5.6 *Trad*. Short right facing flake up to ledge.

129. Short 'n Sweet 5.6 *Trad*. Up center of block.

130. Pulp 5.12a *Mixed*, 3 bolts. Scramble up left to ledge, then move right and follow broken crack system to top.

131. Welcome to Beauty ✹✹ 5.11b *Trad*. Obvious crack line that heads up and left under large block. Great line with good climbing.

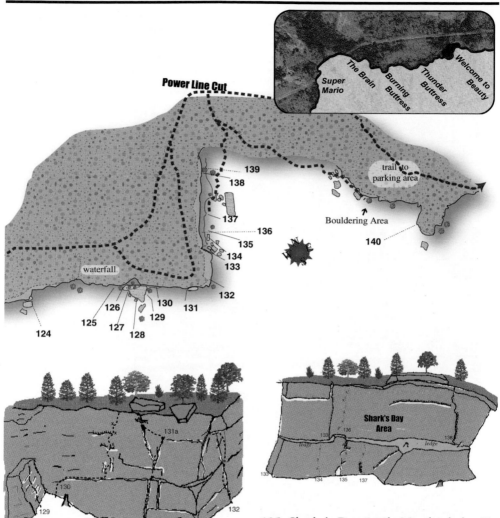

Power Line Cut

Super Mario · The Brain · Burning Buttress · Thunder Buttress · Welcome to Beauty

trail to parking area

139
138
137
136
135
134
133
132

Bouldering Area

140

waterfall

130 131
126
125 129
127
124 128

Welcome to Beauty Area

Shark's Day Area

131a. Right Hand Variation ✪ 5.11c *Trad*. Climb straight up right hand crack after roof then traverse back left.

132. Simple Harmonic Motion 5.10a *Trad*. *Pitch #1*: Up nose to flakes then ledge, belay. *Pitch #2*: Left over roof to overhanging corner.

133. Sojourners 5.10b *Trad*. *Pitch #1*: Climb wide crack up to large ledge. *Pitch #2*: Orange corner 50' right.

134. Plastic Attraction 5.12a *Sport*, 4 bolts.

135. Sharky's Day 5.11b *Mixed*, 2 bolts. Up flakes past two bolts to ledge.

136. Sharky's Night 5.12a *Sport*, 4 bolts, 1 wire.

137. Brook's Route 5.11b *Mixed*, 1 bolt.

138. Ergodicity 5.8 *Trad*. Starts on large ledge left of tree. Right facing corner to roof. Finish off to the right.

139. Throw Down Those Childish Toys 5.7. *Trad*. Climb right curving flake system to large ledge.

140. Unnamed BM #8 5.11a *Trad*. Crack up through roof.

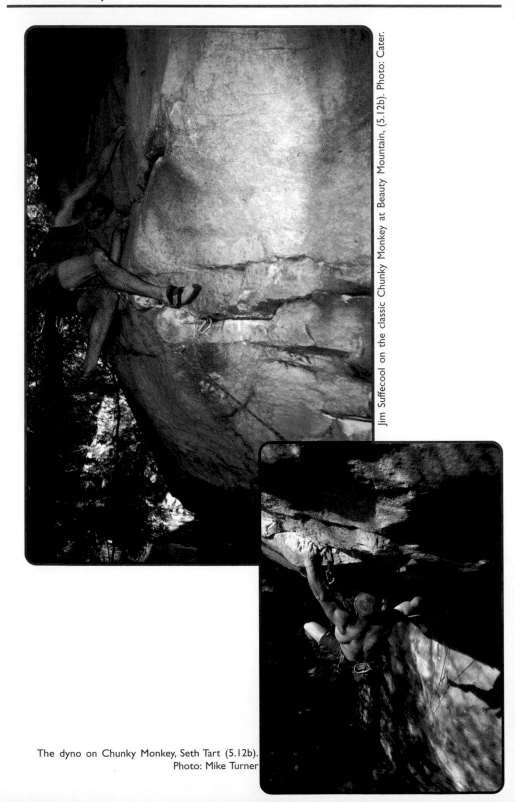

Jim Suffecool on the classic Chunky Monkey at Beauty Mountain, (5.12b). Photo: Cater.

The dyno on Chunky Monkey, Seth Tart (5.12b).
Photo: Mike Turner

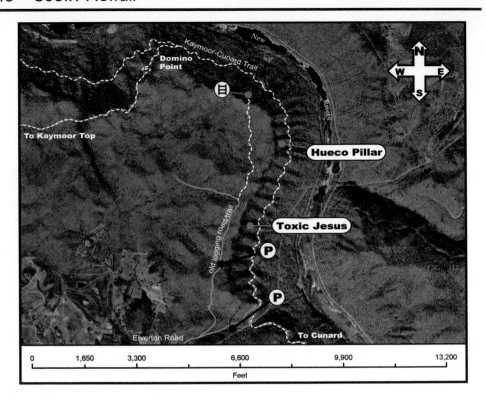

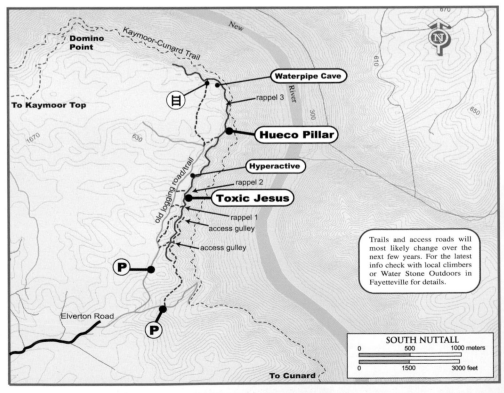

9

South Nuttall

87 routes • 27 sport • 60 trad/mixed

South Nuttall is one of the least visited climbing areas in the New River Gorge. The cliff is actually one of the longest unbroken sections of cliff in the gorge and in the past has been largely ignored by most climbers. There are several reasons for this. For one, the access has always been tricky with private property, logging and various other things hindering a pleasant climbing experience. Another factor is that the wall faces northeast and tends to be either to cold in the spring and fall or to damp in the summer. Access has improved in the past few years and a spurt of activity in the mid 1990's has resulted in a

assortment of quality routes. One of the problems with the area is that no one ever kept track of routes, especially the trad routes. This guide has attempted to put in as many known routes as possible but please keep in mind that not all routes will be in this guide. Hopefully with the inclusion of this area in a guidebook it will rekindle past memories of older routes that climbers established in the past. If you have not been to South Nuttall it is definitely worth visiting but be prepared for some adventure. Needless to say, there are some exceptional routes and a potential for many more.

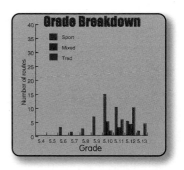

South Nuttall is located on Park Service land so please be mindful of all Park Service rules and regulations. For instance, power drills are not allowed.

Access
From the beer store in Fayetteville, turn left onto Gatewood Road, drive past the Kaymoor turnoff and continue until you see the Elverton Road sign. Turn left here and drive to the end of the paved road. Continue down the jeep road until you reach an obvious intersection. This area is constantly changing so the key is to park around here or further down the road near a pulloff. Hike in from the top of the cliff by walking north along the dirt road until you see a faint trail that cuts off to the right. Follow this down to an access gulley. This will put you at the south end of the cliff. It is also possible to rap in from several points at the cliff top but this can be tricky for first time visitors.

If you continue driving down the jeep road, you eventually reach a road block. It is also possible to park here and hike in from this parking area although this can be a bit of a bushwhack. The only hike out is the access gulley on the south end of the cliff and the scramble (not actual ladders) at the far north end just past the water pipe cave. Do not try and access the cliff from the Kaymoor- Elverton trail below the cliff. It is a heinous bushwhack. One reason for including South Nuttall in the book is the hope that this will facilitate a public access point for hiker and climber access. For the latest info on access go to Water Stone Outdoors or ask one of the local climbers. Hopefully in the next couple years the situation will be a little more user friendly.

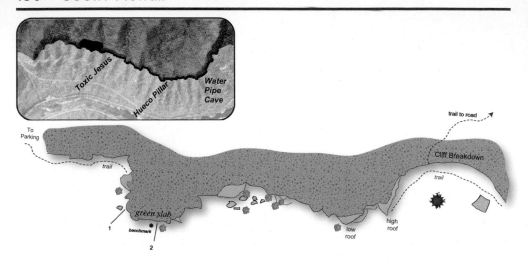

1. **Down Under** 5.11d *Sport,* 5 bolts. Short bulging wall. Possible Doug Reed route?

2. **Unknown** *Trad.* Handcrack that starts left of orange paint streak.

3. **Jungle** 5.10d *Trad.* Dihedral. Good climbing up to dirty crack.

4. **A & W Beer Route** 5.12d *Sport.*

5. **Unfinished** Abandoned project. *Mixed,* 4 bolts. Unfinished.

6. **Slice** (Uncompleted Project) *Mixed,* 1 bolt. Low bolt move up and left.

Toxic Jesus Wall

7. **Unknown** (Attempted but not completed) Left leaning dihedral up to wide V-slot.

8. **Unnamed** SN#1 5.10d *Trad.* Start on left flake, move up to corner crack. Huge death block on this one.

9. **Unknown** SN#2 *Trad.* Overhanging dihedral to roof, move right and continue to top. Hasn't been completed.

10. **Assholes and Elbows** 5.12c *Mixed.* Wide crack out roof. Three bolts out wide crack up to anchor. 2nd pitch- Up crack to top.

11. **Hyperactive** ✪✪ 5.10a *Trad.* Clean orange dihedral to top. Good landmark climb. Very obvious with great climbing.

12. **Kistler-Pesolja** ✪ 5.10a *Mixed,* 5 bolts Start on thin crack, move left at arete and follow bolts to anchor.

13. **Banal Tendencies** 5.12 *Mixed,* 1 pin. Shallow dihedral with pin, traverse right into larger crack.

14. **Unnamed** SN#3 5.6 *Trad.* Corner to top.

15. **Stoat's aren't Dangerous** ✪ 5.9 *Trad.* Wide crack up to dihedral and roofs.

16. **Absolon-Burgher** 5.9 *Trad.* Dihedral up to top of pillar.

17. **The Beckoning** ✪ 5.12a *Trad.* Thin crack to top.

18. **The Bitch** ✪ 5.11a *Trad.* Start on crack on left side of cave, up to roof, traverse right to overhanging crack and belay. Traverse out huge roof crack and continue following crack to top.

19. **Captain Crunch** 5.6 *Trad.* Crack.

20. **Stress Intolerance** 5.9 *Trad.* Nice arete.

21. **Unnamed** SN#4 5.11c *Sport,* 6 bolts. Starts at crack, move up and left around bulge to anchors.

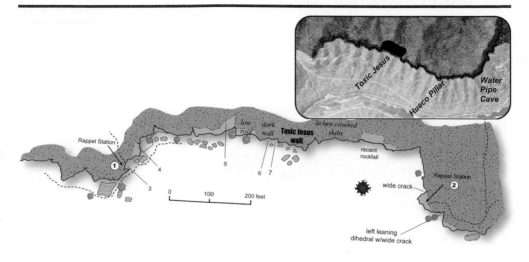

22. Unnamed SN#5 5.12b *Sport,* 10 bolts. Face route that starts right of crack.

23. Unnamed SN#6 5.11c *Sport,* 9 bolts.

24. Headless Mouse Memorial ✪ 5.10d *Trad.* Traverse in from the left to crack and continue following crack to top. Direct Start 5.11d- Pull straight over low roof at beginning.

25. Unnamed SN#7 5.9 *Trad.* Layback flake to ledge.

26. Wasted Daze 5.8 *Trad.* Layback

27. Izod 5.8+ *Trad.* Layback

28. Five Ten 5.8 *Trad.* Up ramp to face then right facing corner to roof at top.

29. The Reckoning 5.11b/c *Trad.* Corner crack to ledge, move left to crack up high.

30. Unnamed SN#8 5.10c *Trad.* Start on wide crack behind boulder, follow crack to roof, pull small roof, and continue to top. Same start as route below.

31. Unnamed SN#9 5.10+ *Sport.* Up crack then move out right onto face.

32. Project *Sport,* 12 bolts.

33. Heaven Cent ✪ 5.13a *Sport,* 12 bolts. Starts in shallow dihedral. 100'

34. Project ? *Sport,* 10 bolts.

35. Get Shorty ✪ 5.12a *Sport,* 11 bolts. Obvious line up arete then out right on face near top. 120'

36. Fat Daddy 5.10a *Trad.* Wide corner crack to chimney, then smaller crack to top.

37. Whimpering Puppies 5.11b/c *Trad.* Start in dihedral, up to thin crack, pull small roof then up to anchors. Doesn't go to top. Original route traverses out to arete and continues to top.

38. Offwidth Your Head 5.11 *Trad.* Wide crack to top. 10 to 15' of grunting then a little run to top. Bring two #5's. May have originally been called Inchworm.

39. Nut 5.10 *Mixed.* Finger crack, traverse left to bolt on face.

40. Corn 5.9 *Trad.* Wide crack to V-slot, continue up crack to finish.

41. Unnamed 5.11c *Mixed.* Old bolt 10' off the ground. May have been started by Howard Clark.

42. Desperately Seeking Susan ✪ 5.9 *Trad.* Chimney to nice zig zag crack and top. Standard rack.

43. Unnamed SN#10 5.11 *Trad.* Up thin dihedral, traverse right to start of zig zag crack (avoids chimney start).

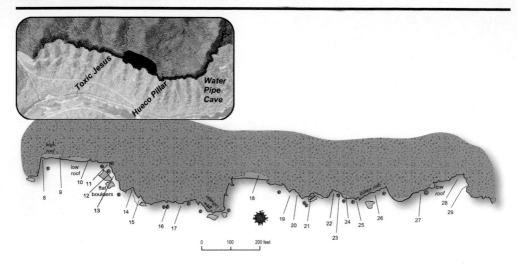

44. Guillotine 5.10+ *Trad*. Dihedral with very wide crack at the start. Big gear!

45. Unnamed SN#11 5.11a *Trad*. Corner crack to wide slot under roof. Finish up and left.

46. New Traditionalist ✪✪ 5.12b *Trad*. Hand and finger crack to top. Originally aided by Pete Absolon and Bob Burgher at 5.11d A1.

47. Tower of Power 5.6 *Trad*. Face to top of tower.

48. Kistler-Houghton Arete ✪ 5.10b *Trad*. Arete on large block.

49. Unnamed SN#12 ✪ 5.12b *Mixed*, 1 bolt. Crack up through overhang then clip bolt.

Hueco Pillar Area

50. Unnamed SN#13 5.10 *Trad*. Wide chimney/crack system to top. Double cracks, wide at top.

51. Sink or Swim 5.11a *Trad*. Wide crack. Two pitches.

52. Pushing Virgin Passage 5.10 *Mixed*. Starts in large roof. Three pitches out roof and up headwall.

53. Unnamed SN #15 A3 Aid pitch. Rack, hook and beaks.

54. Temporary Insanity ✪✪ 5.13a *Trad*. Start at broken crack in overhang, up 25', then traverse right 20' to beginning of thin crack.

55. Munson Burner ✪✪ 5.12c *Trad*. Start at ledge/crack system, up to thin crack and then traverse right into right-hand crack. First top roped by Tim Toula many years ago.

56. Unnamed SN#3 5.10+ *Trad*. Wide crack. Rap in from top.

57. M&M ✪✪ 5.12a *Mixed*, 2 bolts. Discontinuous thin crack up to face. Toproped by Munson and then retro-equipped by McCray and led free in 1997.

58. Unnamed Project *Sport*. Same start as *Women in Black*, move up and left after roof.

59. Women in Black 5.11d/12a *Mixed*, 8 bolts. Dihedral to roof move left then face to shuts staying right at the top.

60. Broken Vowels ✪✪ 5.10a *Trad*. Left side of large flake up to fixed anchors. (55+m rope required to lower).

61. Horst Play ✪✪ 5.12b *Sport*, 4 bolts. Right side of nice flake up to fixed anchors.

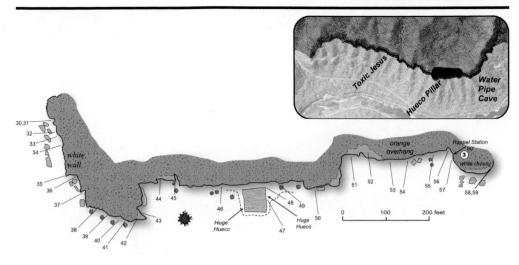

62. **Unnamed SN #16** 5.12c *Sport,* bolts/shuts. Left side of arete.

63. **The Sword and the Stone** ✪ 5.12a *Sport,* bolts/ shuts. Same start as above route but move right around corner.

64. **Unnamed SN#17** ✪ 5.12a *Mixed,* 2 bolts/ shuts. Low angle flake up to small roof, move right and follow crack to large roof and fixed anchors.

65. **Killing Fields** ✪ 5.13a *Sport,* bolts. Straight up nice orange wall. (55+m rope required to lower).

66. **Judgement Night** ✪ 5.12d *Sport,* bolts/shuts. Up and right.

67. **Reign in Blood** Project *Sport,* bolts/shuts. Red hangers up overhanging crack.

68. **Cool Corner** 5.10c *Trad,* Undercling out low roof, follow corner to top.

69. **Unnamed SN#18** 5.11c *Sport,* 7 bolts. Starts on blunt arete.

70. **Unnamed SN#19** ✪ 5.7 *Trad.* Broken crack up to dihedral. Shuts under roof.

71. **Timber** 5.10c *Trad.* Start as *Luv Nothing* but move left at Hueco and follow dihedral to top.

72. **Love Nothing** ✪ 5.12c *Trad.* Corner crack up to hueco, follow crack out hueco roof and continue to top.

73. **Unnamed SN#20** ✪ 5.11d *Trad.* Crack and flake system.

74. **Poop Ship Destroyer** 5.10a *Trad.* 1st: 5.9 Start on wide crack, up to face. 2nd: 5.10a, Finish out right under roof.

75. **Water Pipe Route** 5.11a *Trad.* Wide overhanging crack. Three pitches- 5.11a, 5.10a, 5.8

76. **The Abyss** 5.10a *Trad.* Overhanging chimney crack. 2 big pieces required.

77. **Unnamed SN#21** 5.9 *Trad.* Starts 5' left of tree. Broken crack system to top.

Climb Out. Scramble up ledge system to access the top of the cliff.

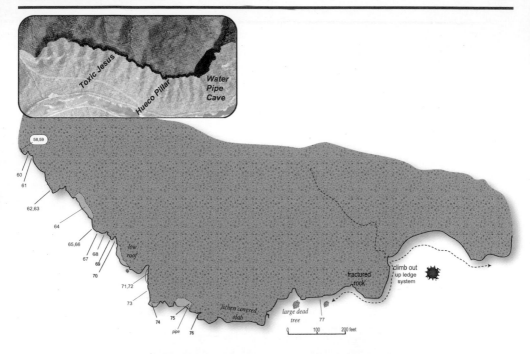

Toxic Jesus

Hueco Pillar

Water Pipe Cave

58,59

60
61

62,63

64

65,66
67
68
69
70
71,72
73

74 75
pipe 76

low roof

lichen covered slab

large dead tree
77

fractured rock

climb out up ledge system

0   100   200 feet

Andrew Barry on first ascent in 1986 of The Beast In Me (5.12), Beauty Mountain.
Photo: Burcham

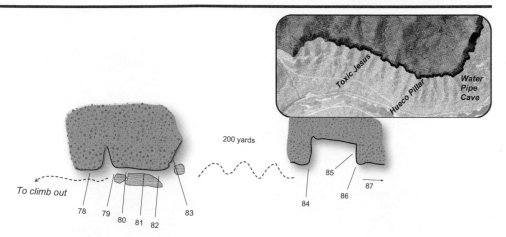

To climb out

200 yards

78   79   80   81   82   83   84   85   86   87

Toxic Jesus   Hueco Pillar   Water Pipe Cave

78. Unnamed SN#22 5.10c *Mixed*, 1 old bolt. Handcrack to arete.

79. Persistence of Memory ✪ 5.12a/b *Sport*, bolts/shuts. Arete.

80. The Scoop ✪ 5.12d *Sport*, bolts/shuts.

81. Unnamed SN#23 Project. *Sport*, bolts/shuts. Incomplete project.

82. Zend 5.13b *Sport*, bolts/shuts.

83. Evil Dick ✪ 5.11d/12a *Sport*, bolts/shuts.

Follow the cliff line for 100 yards and the next nice section of wall has several bolted lines on it.

84. Rox's Arete ✪ 5.11b *Sport*, 8 bolts.

85. Fun Hog ✪ 5.13a *Sport*, 9 bolts. Seam.

86. Land of the Lost ✪ 5.12c *Sport*, 10 bolts.

87. Dave Whitlock Needs an Enema 5.12a *Trad*. Steep squeeze chimney. Dave Whitlock took a grounder on this one and broke his back during the first attempt in 1996.

Brian McCray on Son of Thunder (5.11+), Beauty Mountain. Photo: Burcham

Steve Cater on Pocket Pool 5.12c, Endless Wall.
Photo: Cater Collection

10

Domino Point

18 routes • 5 sport • 13 trad/mixed

Domino Point is located on the southern rim of the gorge upstream of Kaymoor. This section of cliff is remote and receives very little climber traffic. From the Kaymoor parking area follow the gravel road that starts at the steel gate across from Roger's Campground. It takes about 30 minutes to walk to the cliff and about 10 minutes to ride out on a mountain bike. The road out to the cliff is a casual and the climbs are actually very good. To access the Domino Point Buttress, follow the road until it drops down through the cliffline and continue walking another 100 yards to where white graffiti is spray painted on a boulder. From here cut up right to the cliff.

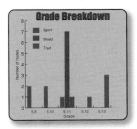

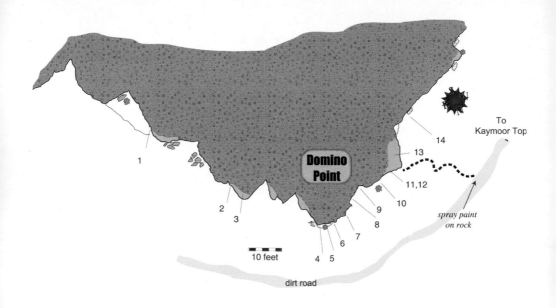

1. Unnamed ✪ 5.10 *Trad.* Splitter handcrack to top.

2. Unnamed 5.10 *Trad.* Wide crack to top.

3. Unnamed ✪ 5.11 *Trad.* Crack to roof, pull through roof and continue following crack to top.

4. Victims of Fury 5.11c *Mixed,* 3 bolts. Start from ledge and continue up arete.

5. Dr. Science 5.11c *Mixed,* 3 bolts. Start from ledge and follow middle route up face.

6. Jvie Stella ✪ 5.11c *Mixed,* 2 pins. Step off right edge of ledge, up face and right to blunt arete.

7. Harmony ✪ 5.11c *Sport,* 9 bolts. Face up and left to arete.

8 EEK! 5.11d *Mixed,* 1 bolt, 1 pin. Start on short flake, pull through roof, continue up face to shallow corner passing one bolt.

9. Dominaire ✪✪ 5.7 *Trad.* Flake system up to small ledge then right leaning dihedral to top. Excellent route. Makes it worth the hike!

10. Unnamed ✪✪ *Sport (5.13?)* Project, 10 bolts. Awesome looking line up overhaning wall. This may have been redpointed but by who?

11. Unnamed ✪✪ 5.12 *Sport* 10 bolts. Shares start with route below but moves left.

12. Mind Games ✪ 5.13a *Sport ,* 9 bolts.

13. Unnamed *Sport (5.13?)* 7 bolts. Project.

14. Limber Girl ✪ 5.11c *Trad.* White flakes to overhanging finger crack.

15. Fats 5.11d *Mixed,* 3 bolts. Face climb starting right of blunt arete. Missing hangers.

16. Lycra Victim 5.11c *Trad.* Thin finger crack to ledge, step right, chimney to top.

17. Sausage 5.12a *mixed,* 3 bolts. Face to shallow corner. Finish on ledge.

18. Checkers 5.12a *Mixed,* 3 bolts. Short arete.

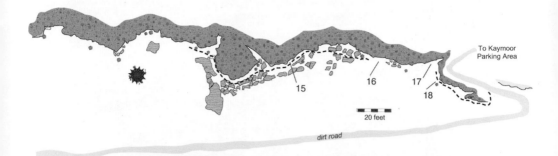

Tracy Martin on Four Sheets to the Wind (5.9), Junkyard Wall. Photo: Cater

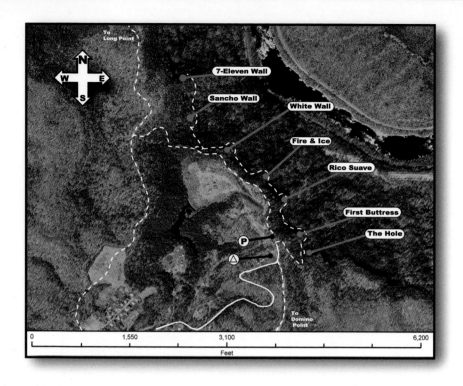

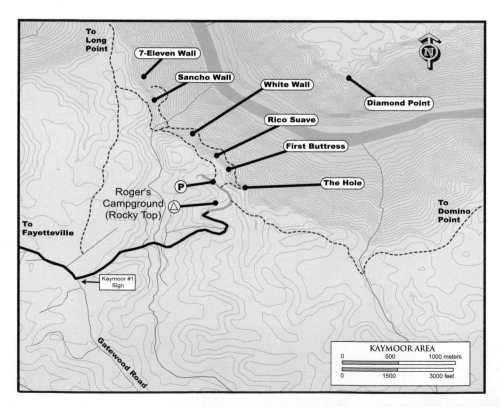

11

K a y m o o r

110 routes • 87 sport • 23 trad/mixed

At one time Kaymoor was the center of a large mining community. Hundreds of men and their families lived and worked at Kaymoor. Things have settled down and the only action now days is the rock climbers who hang out at Roger's Campground and lots of cragging on the cliff below. Kaymoor is one of the most popular climbing areas at the New. An abundance of bolted sport routes attract many of the modern day climbers. In the mid 1980's a handful of moderate crack routes were established by several climbers who discovered the area. It wasn't until the early 1990's, that the ever present, tall southern powerhouse of climbing, Doug Reed, began establishing new routes in what is now known as "The Hole". The Hole contains some of the classic test pieces of the New such as *Lactic Acid Bath* (5.12d) and *Yowsah* (5.12a).

Kaymoor is located on the southern rim of the gorge and faces north. The cliff remains cool on hot days and is popular during late spring, summer and early fall when the temperatures are still warm for climbing in the sun. The cliff varies from 50' to 90' in height and ranges from vertical to extremely overhanging. The majority of routes are sport routes but there are some excellent crack routes that are recommended. Many parts of the cliff remain damp after rainy days.

Access

From Sherries Beer Store in Fayetteville, turn left onto Gatewood Road and drive 2 miles. Turn left at the Kaymoor #1 sign and follow this road about one mile to its end. Park in the established parking area. There is also a pay camping area at the end of this road. The Hole and First Buttress are only a 5 minute walk from the parking area and Butcher's Branch is a 10 minute walk. Domino Point is a 30 minute walk from the parking area.

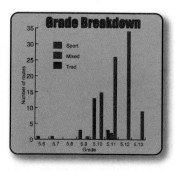

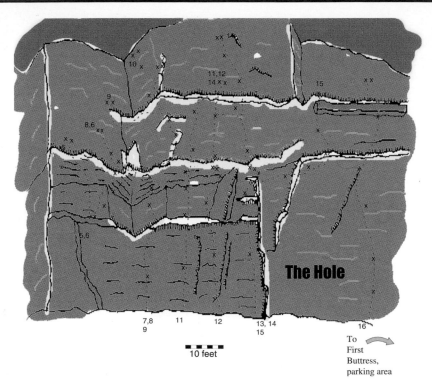

The Hole

7,8   11   12   13, 14   16
9   15

10 feet

To
First
Buttress,
parking area

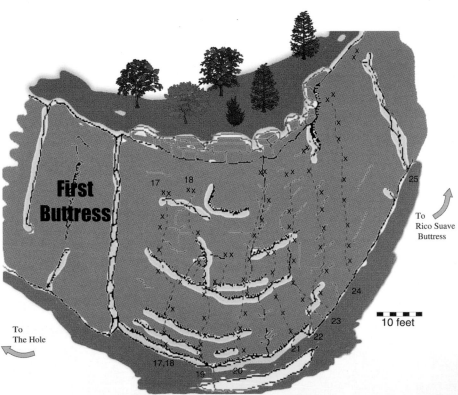

First Buttress

To
The Hole

To
Rico Suave
Buttress

10 feet

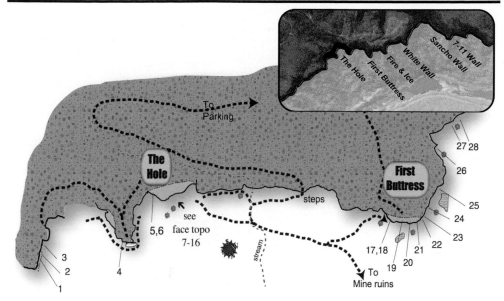

1. Clock's On ✪ 5.11b *Sport*, 7 bolts. May need one piece of gear between 3rd and 4th bolt.

2. Nutter Butter ✪ 5.10b *Sport*, 5 bolts.

3. Flat Motor'n 5.11b/c Sport, bolts.

4. Smell the Glove 5.11c *Sport*, 6 bolts.

The Hole

5. Against the Grain *Sport* 5.13b. Short route that moves up and left off ledge.

6. Mojo Hand 5.12d *Sport*, 6 bolts.

7. Lactic Acid Bath ✪✪ 5.12d *Sport*, 9 bolts. Up to roof flake, out large flake to underclings moving up and right. Pull two small roofs then finish in juggy corner. The classic pump fest!

8. Devil Doll ✪✪ 5.12d *Sport*, 8 bolts. Link-up between *L.A.B.* and *Mojo Hand*. Move left after 5th bolt on *L.A.B.*

9. In the Flat Field ✪✪ 5.13b/c *Sport*, 10 bolts. Moves left after 7th bolt on *L.A.B.*

10. Massacre 5.13a *Sport,* 10 bolts. Left from last bolt of *L.A.B.* Ends at anchors.

11. Blood Raid ✪✪ 5.13a *Sport*, 6 bolts. Velcroe clip on second roof.

12. Skull F--k ✪✪ 5.12b/c *Sport*, 6 bolts. Straight-up at 2nd roof it's 5.12c, avoiding crux and moving right makes it 5.12b.

13. Burning Cross ✪✪ 5.13a *Sport*, 9 bolts.

14. Yowsah ✪✪ 5.12a *Sport*, 7 bolts. *Burning Cross* to bolt six and link-up with *Skull F--k*.

15. Scar Lover ✪ 5.12c *Sport*, 7 bolts.

16. Final Exit ✪ 5.12a *Sport*, 7 bolts.

First Buttress

17. The Haulage ✪✪ 5.12c/d *Sport*, 7 bolts. Move left at bolt 3 of *World's Hardest*.

18. World's Hardest ✪✪ 5.12a *Sport*, 7 bolts. Steep face to overhang.

19. The Tantrum ✪ 5.12d *Sport*, 7 bolts.

20. Sanctified ✪✪ 5.12d *Sport*, 10 bolts.

21. Tarbaby ✪ 5.12a/b *Sport*, 5 bolts.

22. Oh, it's You Bob ✪ 5.11b *Sport*, 8 bolts.

23. Magnatude ✪✪ 5.11c *Sport*, 7 bolts.

24. The Leather Nun 5.13a A0 start *Sport*, 8 bolts.

25. Weinie from the Past 5.10c *Trad*. Crack system to anchors.

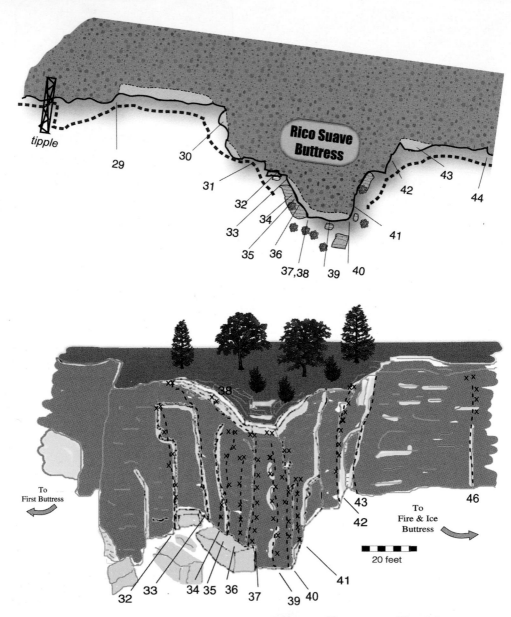

Rico Suave Buttress

26. **Unnamed** KM #2 5.12c *Sport*, 7 bolts. No anchors

27. **100% Real Cheese** 5.11a *Sport*, 4 bolts.

28. **Attack of the Moss Clods** 5.10a *Sport*, 4 bolts.

29. **Unnamed** KM #3 5.12c *Sport*, 4 bolts

30. **Trouble In Paradise** ✪ *Sport*, 5.13b 5 bolts.

31. **The Uninflatable Ewe** 5.12a *Sport*, 7 bolts.

32. **Totally Tammy** ✪✪ 5.10a *Sport*, 5 bolts.

33. **Second Thoughts** 5.10b *Trad*. Left leaning corner to roof, move left 15' to anchors.

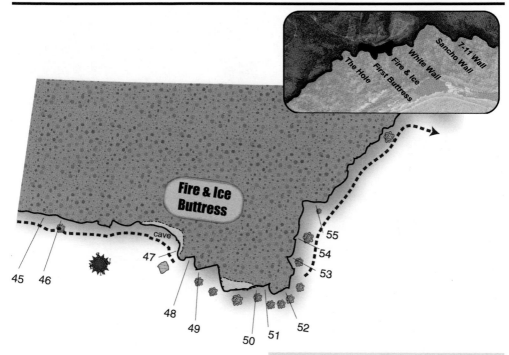

34. Grit & Bear it 5.11a *Sport*, 5 bolts.

35. Cuddle Monkey 5.7, *Trad*. Starts right of above route and moves diagonally left. Finishes to the right on anchor of above climb.

36. Not on the First Date 5.11c *Sport*, 4 bolts. A broken flake has made this more difficult.

37. Rico Suave ✪✪ 5.10a *Sport*, 7 bolts. Great climbing up blunt arete.

38. Coal Miner's Tale 5.12b *Sport*, 5 bolts. From anchors on *Rico Suave*, climb out roof and traverse left 40" to anchors.

39. Out of the Bag ✪✪ 5.11c/d *Sport*, 8 bolts.

40. Preparation H ✪ 5.11d *Sport*, 6 bolts. Arete.

41. Pockets of Resistance ✪✪ 5.12a *Sport*, 4 bolts. Slightly overhanging pocketed face.

42. Nude Brute ✪✪ 5.13a *Sport*, 7 bolts.

43. The Good Old Days 5.9 *Trad*. Corner.

44. Collateral Damage 5.11a *Sport*, 4 bolts.

45. Consumer Liability 5.9+ *Trad*. 2 shuts for anchor.

46. Buried Treasure ✪ 5.11c *Mixed*, 3 bolts. Starts on thin crack and finishes on face.

Fire and Ice Buttress

47. Albatross ✪ 5.13b *Sport*, 4 bolts. Overhanging thin crack right of cave.

48. Bovine Seduction ✪ 5.10c *Trad*. Start two cracks left of SLAP, thru flakes and overhang. 2 shut anchor.

49. SLAP 5.12a *Sport*, 4 bolts. Arete.

50. Carolina Crocker and the Tipple of Doom ✪✪ 5.12a *Sport*, 10 bolts. Start below small roof, up and right at first roof then back left.

51. Raiders of the Lost Crag ✪✪ 5.10b *Trad*. Follow nice crack system to top.

52. Malfunction Junction 5.10b *Trad*. Corner.

53. Ice ✪ 5.11c *Trad*. Obvious left hand crack.

54. Fire ✪ 5.10c *Trad*. Crack on the right.

55. The Sound and the Slurry 5.11c *Sport*, 5 bolts.

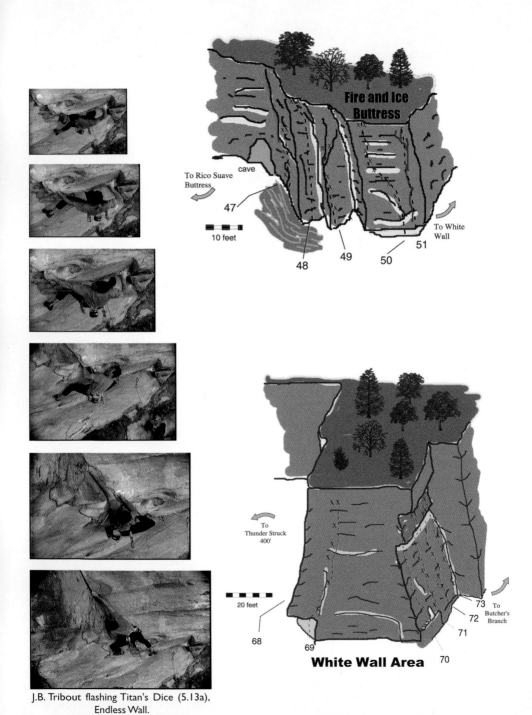

Fire and Ice Buttress

To Rico Suave Buttress

cave

47

10 feet

48

49

50

51

To White Wall

To Thunder Struck 400'

20 feet

68

69

White Wall Area

70

71

72

73 To Butcher's Branch

J.B. Tribout flashing Titan's Dice (5.13a), Endless Wall.
Video Capture: Steve Cater

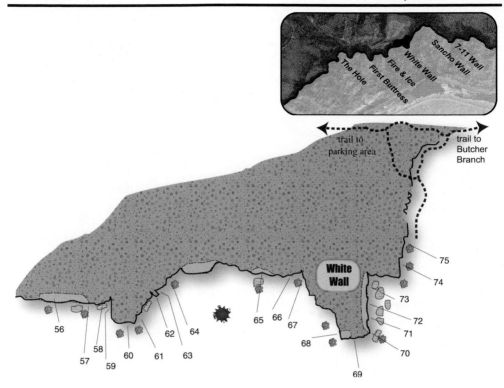

White Wall

56. The Shining 5.11b *Trad.* Start at overhanging crack and follow it to the fixed anchors (old pins).

57. White Lightning ✪ 5.13b *Sport*, 9 bolts. Obvious line up white streak.

58. Thunder Struck ✪✪ 5.12b *Sport*, 7 bolts. Start at large flake at base of cliff. Good climbing up beautiful orange rock.

59. Almost Heaven ✪ 5.10b *Sport*, 4 bolts. Short warm-up on left facing wall.

60. Unnamed KM #5 5.10b R *Trad.* Face.

61. Ride'em Cowboy 5.12a *Sport*, 8 bolts.

62. The Cow Girl 5.12b/c *Sport*, 4 bolts. Bolt line up fin of rock.

63. Damn the Layback, Full Stem Ahead! 5.10 *Trad.* Corner.

64. Swinging Udders 5.12a *Sport*, 6 bolts.

65. Boss Cocky ✪ 5.12b/c *Sport*, 8 bolts. Shallow corner up to roof.

66. Unnamed KM #6 5.10d *Trad.* Crack.

67. Jane Fonda's Total Body Workout 5.11c *Trad.* Crack.

68. Moon Child Posse ✪✪ 5.11c *Sport*, 8 bolts.

69. Half and Half 5.11b *Mixed*, 5 bolts.

70. Unnamed KM #7 5.11c *Sport*, 7 bolts.

71. Dining at the Altar ✪✪ 5.12a *Sport*, 7 bolts.

72. Shang ✪✪ 5.12d/13a *Sport*, 7 bolts.

73. Pettifogger ✪✪ 5.12b *Sport*, 7 bolts.

74. New Clear Potato Meltdown 5.11b *Sport*, 4 bolts. Crack to left leaning wide flake.

75. J-Crack 5.10 *Trad.* Crack and corner.

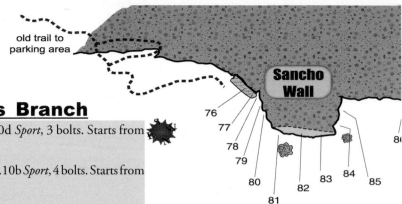

old trail to parking area

Sancho Wall

76
77
78
79
80
81
82
83
84
85
80

Butcher's Branch

76. Arpeggio 5.10d *Sport*, 3 bolts. Starts from ledge.

77. Play it by Ear 5.10b *Sport*, 4 bolts. Starts from ledge.

78. Just Another Glitch 5.6 *Trad*. Corner that is often wet.

79. The Green Piece ✪ 5.10b *Sport*, 6 bolts. Starts right of grungy corner. Nice face climbing and good warm up.

80. Low Voltage ✪ 5.10b *Sport*, 7 bolts.

81. Ministry 5.12b *Sport*, 4 bolts.

82. Sancho Belige ✪✪ 5.11b/c *Sport*, 7 bolts. Center route up bulging wall. Great route that will leave you pumped!

83. The Bicycle Club ✪✪ 5.11d/12a *Sport*, 5 bolts. Pull low roof then straight up to anchor. fun moves with tricky finish.

84. Boing 5.10d *Sport*, 6 bolts. Slab on left side of wall.

85. Springer ✪ 5.10b *Sport*, 6 bolts. Slab on right side of wall. Enjoyable climbing but seeps.

86. The Bag 5.10d *Trad*. Crack through bulging wall.

87. Lost Souls ✪✪ 5.11d/12a *Sport*, 6 bolts. Slightly overhanging wall. Pumpy climbing on excellent rock.

88. Jumpin' Ring Snakes ✪ 5.9 *Trad*. Large corner and crack system to top. Nice trad route hidden amoung the sport routes.

89. Flight of the Gumbie ✪✪ 5.9 *Sport*, 9 bolts. Starts on face move up and right then arete to top. Technical climbing up arete and face.

90. Bourbon Sauce ✪✪ 5.11d/12a *Sport*, 4 bolts. Move left at roof. Cranky moves out roof.

91. Control ✪✪ 5.12a *Sport*, 7 bolts. Move right at roof. Nice climbing out steep roof.

92. Kaos ✪ 5.12c *Sport*, 4 bolts. Hard bouldr moves.

93. Mo' Betta' Holds ✪✪ 5.11c/d *Sport*, 6 bolt. Fun climbing out steep roof then pumpy moves to finish.

94. All the Right Moves ✪ 5.11d *Sport*, 8 bolts. Long route with some hard moves after you think it is over.

95. Hard-Core Female Thrash ✪✪ 5.11c *Sport*, 6 bolts. Up short arete to ledge then up and left into dihedral. Pull roof and move right near top. Great route that keeps you on your toes.

Seven-Eleven Wall

96. Unnamed KM #8 5.10a *Sport*, 7 bolts.

97. Fearful Symmetry ✪ 5.11d *Sport*, 6 bolts.

98. The Sting ✪✪ 5.12a *Sport*, 7 bolts. Named after being stung by wasps on the route. Good face climbing.

99. Tit Speed ✪✪ 5.11c *Sport*, 7 bolts. Another great face climb!

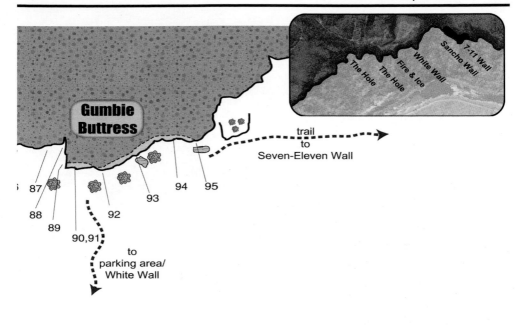

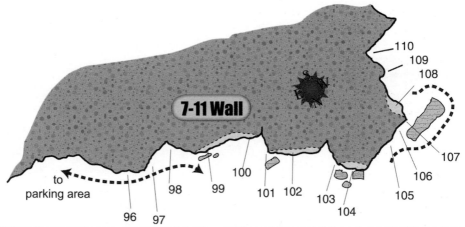

100. Tony the Tiger ✪ 5.11c *Sport*, 9 bolts. Fun face climbing.

101. Scenic Adult ✪✪ 5.11c *Sport*, 10 bolts. Obvious line up arete. 55m rope required. great climbing and nice exposure. One of the best!

102. Bimbo Shrine ✪ 5.11b *Sport*, 8 bolts. Nice climbing up face.

103. Mr. Hollywood ✪ 5.11d/12a *Sport*, 5 bolts. You'll look like a star on this one!

104. Slash and Burn ✪✪ 5.12d *Sport*, 9 bolts. excellent route up awesome overhanging face!

105. Buzz Kill ✪ 5.12c *Sport* 10 bolts. Wandering bolt line with difficult slab crux.

106. Fairtracer ✪✪ 5.10d *Trad*. Excellent hand crack that starts left of large boulder.

107. First Steps ✪✪ 5.10c *Sport*, 6 bolts. Scramble up to top of large boulder to start this climb.

108. Fuel Injector ✪ 5.13b *Sport*, 8 bolts. Classic New River reach problem crux.

109. The Butcher Man 5.11a *Sport*, 4 bolts. Short arete.

110. Ed and Bill's Excellent Adventure 5.10a *Trad*. Corner.

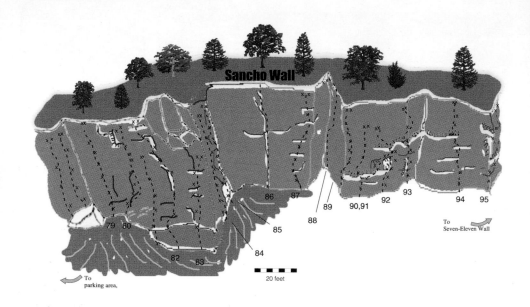

Sancho Wall

86 87
89
90,91 92 93
94 95
88
85
79 80
84
82 83
To
Seven-Eleven Wall
To
parking area,
20 feet

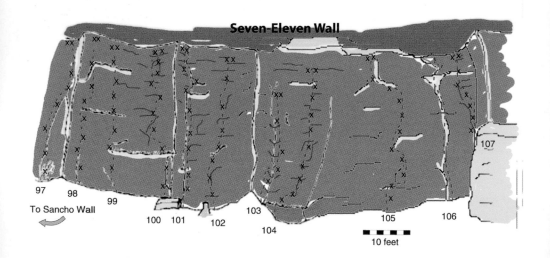

Seven-Eleven Wall

107
97 98
99
To Sancho Wall
100 101 102
103
104
105 106
10 feet

Video capture of Shannon Langley on Moon Child Posse (5.11c). Photo: Cater

One of the Butcher Branch classics, Flight of the Gumbie (5.9). Photo: Cater

Adam Wisthoff on Out of the Bag, (5.11). Photo: Dan Braysack

Kerry Allen in The Hole. Photo: Cater

Kenny Parker getting lit up on Magnatude (5.11d), Kaymoor. Photo: Cater

Bill Chouinard nailing the dyno on The Haulage (5.12c). Photo: Cater

Christina Austin, Pockets of Resistance (5.12a). Photo: Daniel Brayack

Kenny Parker on Greenpiece (5.10a). Photo: Cater

Mike Helt on crux of Bloodraid (5.13a), Kaymoor. Photo: Dan Hague

Kenny Powell on The World's Hardest at Kaymoor, (5.12a). Photo: Cater

12

Sunshine Buttress

24 routes • 15 sport • 14 trad/mixed

Sunshine Buttress is a small cliff located on the southern rim of the gorge just off Fayette Station Road. The main buttress, which is highly visible off to the right when driving south across the bridge, contains the majority of routes. The upstream section of cliff only has a couple established routes. The cliff faces southeast and receives sun most of the day making it an enjoyable place to climb during chilly days. This cliff also receives very little attention, has easy access and is usually not crowded during the weekends if you are looking to escape the crowds.

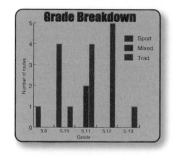

Access

Starting spring 1999 access on Fayette Station Road became one-way from north to south so to access the crag climbers will have to drive in from the Bridge Buttress, cross the lower bridge and then drive up to the parking area. Park at the pull-off at the obvious hairpin turn, cross the road and follow the short trail up to the cliff. This will put you at the base of Mother's Milk.

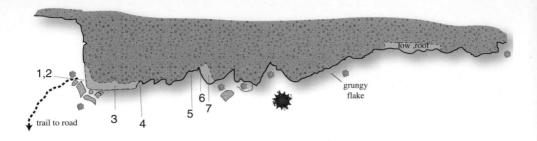

Climbs 1-7 are located about 15 minute walk along the base of the cliff upstream from the Orange Wall. These climbs can also be accessed by walking down the paved road from the sharp turn parking area and cutting up a steep trail to the base of the cliff. None of the routes are very good so it's not really worth the effort.

1. Unnamed SB #1 5.12a *Sport,* 4 bolts. Same start as below but move out left.

2. Unnamed SB #2 5.12b *Sport,* 5 bolts.

3. Unnamed SB #3 5.10 *Trad.* Wide flake to sling anchors.

4. Unnamed SB #4 5.10 *Trad.* Flake to crows nest.

5. Unnamed SB #5 5.9 *Sport,* 7 bolts.

6. Unnamed SB #6 5.9 Trad. Flake to roof, move left at roof and continue following corner to top.

7. Unnamed SB #7 5.12b *Sport,* 5 bolts. Starts under large roof.

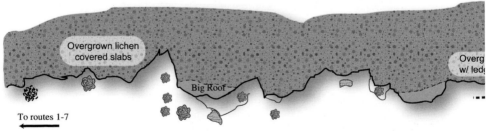

One-way from Fayette Station

This area has the best routes at Sunshine and sees the most climber traffic.

Mango Boingo Wall

8. Head Like A Hole ✪ 5.11c *Sport*, 5 bolts. This route starts from the upper ledge. Stem corner then move right onto face.

9. Disco Apocalypse ✪ 5.12c *Sport*, 8 bolts. Same start as *Mango Boingo* but move left at 4th bolt then 4 more bolts to anchor.

10. Mango Boingo 5.12b *Sport*, 6 bolts.

11. He Man Adhesive 5.11c/d *Mixed*, 3 bolts. Starts at thin left facing flake, up and right to ledge. Finish at anchors or finish on *Head like a Hole*.

12. Popeye Syndrome ✪ 5.11d *Sport*, 6 bolts. Starts from anchors of *Necromancer*.

13. Necromancer ✪ 5.10c *Sport*, 3 bolts.

14. Just Say Yo To Jugs 5.10c *Trad*. Wide corner and crack system to roof crack. Loose block near top.

15. Syndicate Fool ✪ 5.12b *Sport*, 8 bolts. Same start as *Original Crankster* moving up and left.

16. Original Crankster ✪ 5.13a *Sport*, 6 bolts. Right bolt line, steep face through bulge.

17. Unnamed SB #8 5.11c *Sport*, 6 bolts.

18. Unnamed SB #9 5.11d *Sport*, 4 bolts. Stops under roof.

19. Unnamed ✪ SB #10 5.12a *Sport*, 9 bolts. Move left at bolt six .

20. Unbroken Chain ✪✪ 5.12a *Sport*, 8 bolts. Up face then move right to arete.

21. Unnamed SB #11 Project.

22. Mother's Milk ✪ 5.12c/d *Sport*, 11 bolts.

23. Love Puppy ✪ 5.11c *Mixed*, 2 bolts. Crack system out roof and up face.

24. Afro-Sheener 5.9 *Trad*. Left side of arete.

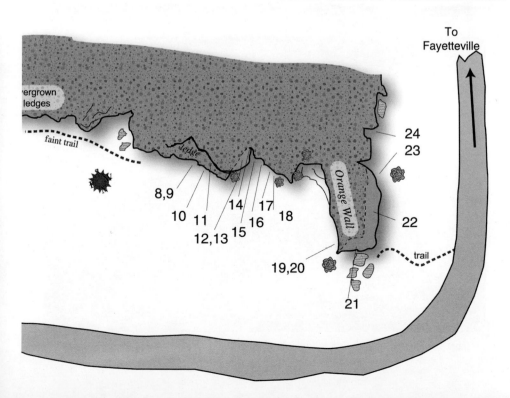

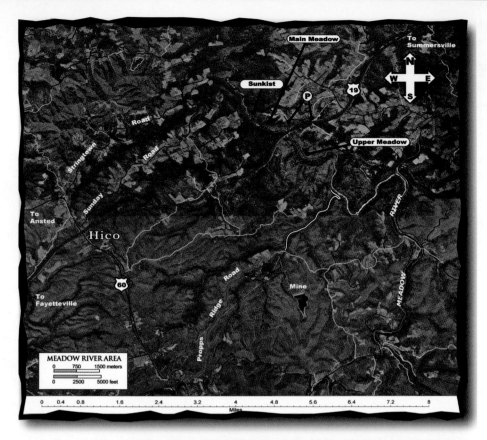

John Burcham on Wicked Gravity, later renamed Greatest Show on Earth after it was free climbed. Photo: John Burcham Collection

13
M e a d o w   R i v e r

183 routes • 83 sport • 100 trad/mixed

The Meadow River described in this book is actually comprised of several different developed climbing areas; The Main Meadow and Upper Meadow . Several other less developed areas, Orange Wall, Fragle Rock ,Hedricks Creek, Bik Pelahol and Area 51 are shown on the map but routes have not been described since the access is not as developed and route information has not been disseminated amongst the climbing community. All Meadow River climbing areas are included in one chapter since the climbing areas tend to have fewer routes. The climbing at the Meadow is some of the best in the area and several of the areas most famous climbs are located at the Meadow River. Routes such as *Mango Tango*, *Puppy Chow* and *World's Greatest Show* all exist only a couple hundred yards away from Route 19.

The Main Meadow was the first area at the Meadow to see route development. The close proximity to Route 19 made it an obvious target for climbers. Driving across the bridge headed north, the Puppy Chow Roof can be seen to the left towering above the trees.

The cliffs at the Meadow range from 45' to 110' in length. The rock is very similar to the stone in the New River Gorge, and is in fact the same formation. The cliffs tend to be steeper at the Meadow River with very little slab climbing. Although the Meadow River is a smaller gorge it contains excellent rock with tons of great climbing. In the past the area was not publicized due to access problems but in recent years access has improved well enough to not cause many problems by including the cliffs in a guidebook. Special thanks to Kenny Parker, Heather Musante, Gene Kistler and Craig Lewis for route info and double checking maps and route placements.

Access

Access to most of the Meadow climbing areas is surprisingly easy. The Main Meadow and Upper Meadow are within easy walking distance of the road and require no major uphill hiking with very casual approaches. To access the Main Meadow, Sunkist Wall and Upper Meadow (Three Buttress Area), park at the pull out on CR24/12 where the dirt road has been blocked. Do not block the paved road. If no parking is available park back at the intersection and walk up the road. Follow the dirt road down towards the river paralleling Rt. 19. Turn right to access the Main Meadow and Sunkist Wall. Turn left to access the Upper Meadow.

The other areas shown on the maps will have access descriptions revealed as they become available. Check in at Water Stone in Fayetteville or go to their website (www.waterstoneoutdoors.com) for updates. (See notes on maps)

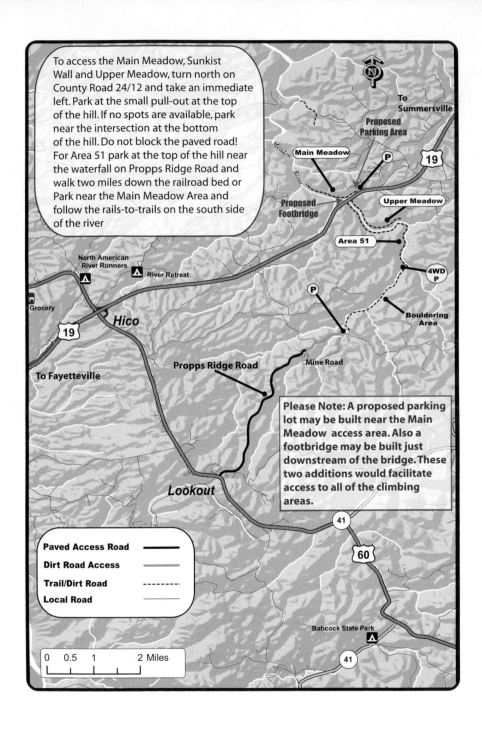

To access the Main Meadow, Sunkist Wall and Upper Meadow, turn north on County Road 24/12 and take an immediate left. Park at the small pull-out at the top of the hill. If no spots are available, park near the intersection at the bottom of the hill. Do not block the paved road! For Area 51 park at the top of the hill near the waterfall on Propps Ridge Road and walk two miles down the railroad bed or Park near the Main Meadow Area and follow the rails-to-trails on the south side of the river

To Summersville

Proposed Parking Area

Main Meadow

P

19

Proposed Footbridge

Upper Meadow

Area 51

4WD P

North American River Runners

River Retreat

Grocery

P

Bouldering Area

Hico

19

Mine Road

To Fayetteville

Propps Ridge Road

Lookout

Please Note: A proposed parking lot may be built near the Main Meadow access area. Also a footbridge may be built just downstream of the bridge. These two additions would facilitate access to all of the climbing areas.

41

60

Paved Access Road

Dirt Road Access

Trail/Dirt Road

Local Road

Babcock State Park

0   0.5   1   2 Miles

41

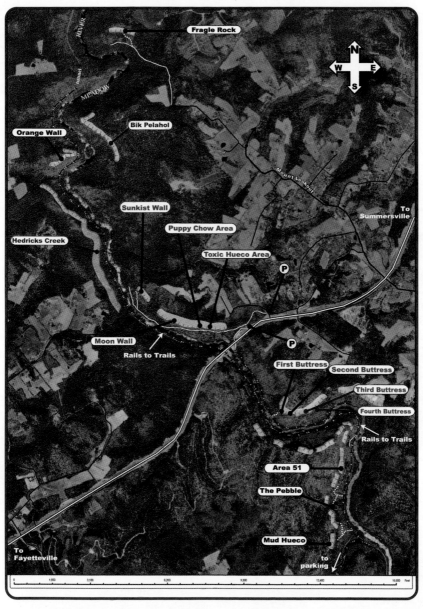

Names in purple are featured in this guidebook. Other areas will be added as access and route information become available.

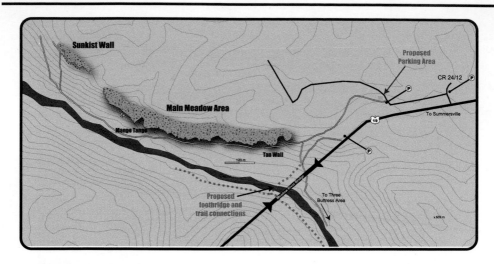

Sunkist Wall

Sunkist Wall is a 25 minute walk from the parking area near Rt. 19. It is a small cliff but contains some fun sport climbing on good stone. To find the cliff continue walking down the logging road past the Main Meadow Area . When the road forks, take the right branch that goes uphill. Continue walking until the road aproaches the cliff then look right. The first climbs are near the road. This wall was developed by Kenny Parker, Gene Kistler, Blaze Davis and friends in the mid 1990's.

1. Winter Fest 5.10c *Trad* Leaning corner with crack on the right wall.

2. Dead Varment 5.8 *Trad* Crack.

3. Turtle Power 5.9 *Trad* Crack.

4. Howard Corner 5.10a *Trad* Corner/crack syatem. Up roof and move right to crack.

5. Mr. Mogely ✪✪ 5.11c *Sport*, 5, bolts.Stick clip first bolt. Starts under low roof. A couple moves out steep roof lead to nice face climbing.

6. Fresh Boy✪ 5.12a *Sport*, 4 bolts. Stick clip first bolt. Starts under low roof. Same start as *Mr Mogely* then up middle of face

7. Soul Patch✪5.11a *Sport*, 5 bolts. Stick clip first bolt. Starts under low roof. Low roof to crack.

8. The Hand Out ✪ 5.11b *Sport*, 4 bolts. Stick clip first bolt. Starts under low roof.

8a. Begoon/Cote 5.11a *Trad.*

9. Arachniphobia ✪✪ 5.9 *Trad.* Dihedral.

10. Woodstock 5.11d *Sport*, 5 bolts. Move up face then right around corner.

11. Crusade 5.12a *Mixed*, 1 pin. Steep face just right of arete.

12. Victory Stroke 5.11c *Mixed*, 1 bolt. Up face right of *Crusade*.

13. Give Me Oxygen 5.11d *Trad*. Up middle face on right of wall.

14. Shteep! ✪ 5.11b *Trad*. Up steep start to right angling small corner to anchors on *Clip Trip*.

15. Clip Trip 5.12a *Mixed*, 5 bolts, 2 pins. Mixed route up face.

16. I Just Pinched! ✪✪ 5.11d *Mixed*, 1 bolt, Mixed route up orange face.

17. Mixer 5.12b *Mixed*, 1 bolt. Up middle of face past bolt to top

18. Pigs from the Pitt ✪ 5.11a *Mixed*, 2 bolts. Left of large corner. Goes up orange face.

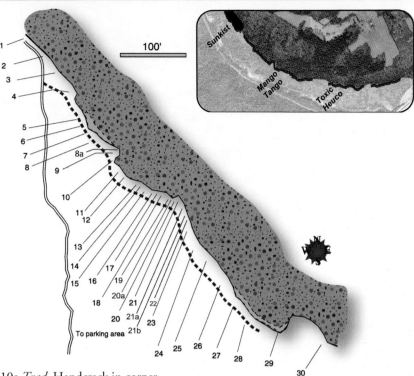

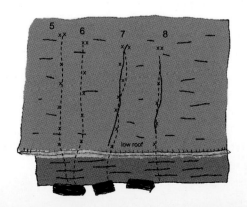

19. Moochie 5.10a *Trad.* Handcrack in corner, then right out roof.

20. Pay the Troll ★★ 5.11c *Mixed*, 2 bolts. Starts right of corner. Up to anchor.

20a. Pay the Mortgage ★★ 5.11d *Sport*, 7 bolts.

21. The Reed Parker ★★ 5.11d *Sport*, 6 bolts. Very nice climbing on colorful rock up right leaning corner.

21a. Unnamed 5.9 *Trad.* Fist crack corner.

21b. Ram/Davies 5.9 *Trad.*

22. Zippity Doo Dah 5.9 *Sport*, 4 bolts. Slabby route up green face. Was originally a trad route. Always seems kind of grungy.

23. Zippity Day 5.9 *Trad.* Up green slabby face.

24. Bulgarian ★ 5.9 *Trad.* Obvious crack on left end of wall.

25. Nominative 5.11d *Trad.* Face right of *Bulgarian*. Same start as *Artz vs. Parker*

26. Artz vs. Parker ★★ 5.12a *Trad.* Obvious finger crack up middle of wall with roof start.

27. Adapter ★ 5.11d *Mixed*, 1 pin. Face right of obvious finger crack.

28. The Instigator ★★ 5.11b *Trad.* Nice crack starts from low overhang.

29. Opulence 5.9 *Trad.* Obvious crack and corner system.

30. Doin' the Manly Jackson ★★ 5.11d *Mixed*, 3 bolts. Up obvious areteto anchors.

31. Babooshka O'Brien 5.10a *Mixed*, Short arete past pin w/ slings.

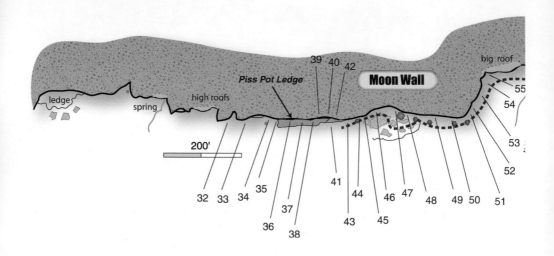

Moon Wall

32. Wooshka Man 5.10c *Mixed,* Face to bolt on headwall.

33. Unnamed 5.6 *Trad.* Start at bottom of *Wooshka* and finish on the top of *Truancy.*

34. Truancy 5.7 *Trad.* Crack to top.

35. Home Schooled 5.9 *Trad.* Right of *Truancy.*

36. Easy To Slip ? Unfinished Project. Flake and crack to face.

37. **Making Whoopie** 5.8 *Trad.* Face climb up steep wall to top.

38. Giggle Box 5.6 *Trad.* Up face following crack jug up to top.

39. Little Feat 5.5 *Trad.* Start left side of block, face thru slot to top.

40. Rocket In My Pocket 5.5 *Trad.* Start right of block face to top.

41. Short Arse 5.11b *Mixed,* Short face to ledge past two bolts.

42. Neon Parks 5.6 *Trad.* Corner to ledge, prominent crack to top.

43. Spanish Moon 5.8+ *Trad.* 10 ft. Left of deceptive crack, up face to top.

44. Deception ✪ 5.11b/c *Trad.* Obvious deceptive right leaning crack below and just right of *Piss Pot Ledge.* Deceptive moves, starts left of tree.

45. **Sky is Crying** ✪ 5.11b/c *Mixed,* Face past 3 bolts to ledge, then up to top.

46. Tripe Face Boogie 5.11c *Mixed.* Face past two bolts to overhanging hueco wall.

47. Welcome to the Meadow ✪✪ 5.11b *Mixed,* Up hueco face past 3 bolts.

48. Welcome To Hell 5.12d *Mixed* 1 bolt. Thin crack with bolt on right side 10 ft. off the ground. Up to horizontal then right to broken crack to top.

49. **Death by Chewing Insects** 5.9 *Trad.* Crack to ledge, rap from nearby tree.

50. Phase Four 5.11a *Trad.* Starts just right of *Death by Chewing.* Climb face to obvious crack and ledge, traverse right to arete or rap from neighboring tree.

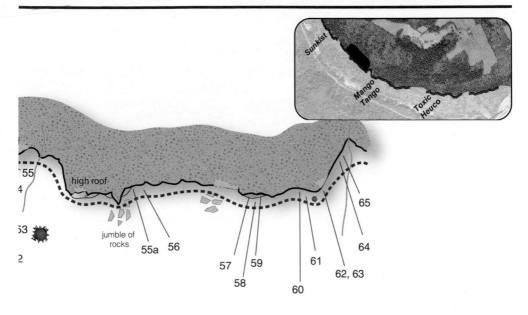

51. Mockingbird 5.10c *Trad.* Face climb left of the long blunt arete (*Tabasco Fur*).

52. Tabasco Fur 5.10a *Trad.* Long blunt arete.

53. Tabasco Fart 5.7 *Trad.* Same start as *Tabasco Fur*, follow crack (10' right of arete) to its end and angle up and left on face to the top.

54. Hand Job 5.9 *Trad.* Crack.

55. Lip Lock 5.10d *Trad.* Climb thru overhangs.

55a. Kistler/Clark 5.10 *Trad.* Goes thru roof and obvious crack

56. Hueco the Flood ? *Trad.* No info on this one.

57. Jugnasium 5.8 *Trad.*

58. Pickled Eggs 5.7 *Trad.* Obvious fault line to ledge.

59. Ledge Access 5.6 *Trad.*

60. Fritz Crack 5.8 *Trad.* Obvious crack with huecos. Left leaning crack to horizontals.

61. Nodes 5.12b *Mixed* 4 bolts. To ledge then up orange wall past 4 bolts.

62. Winter Harvest ✹✹ 5.10c *Sport,* 5 bolts. Do *Golden Age* to 1st bolt traverse to arete up to anchors. This route was accidently retrobolted and is now a sport route.

63. Golden Age ✹ *Mixed* 5.11d 3 bolts. White corner to roof.

64. Bust A Move ✹ 5.10d *Mixed,* Bolted face to same rap as *Off My Rocker.*

65. Off My Rocker ✹ 5.11a *Mixed,* 4 bolts. Up face to anchor under roof.

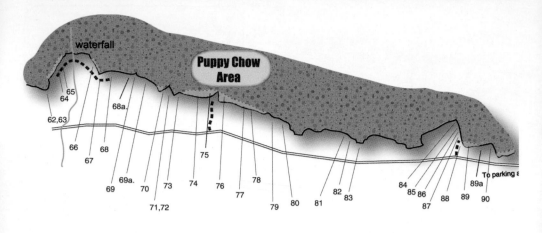

Puppy Chow Area

66. Sonnet ✪ *Trad.* 5.10d/11a. Flake to finger crack. Stops under roof at bolt rappel.

67. Mango Tango ✪✪ 5.13d *Sport* 5 bolts. Obvious beautiful orange arete. Thin moves to anchor the whole way. Has only seen a few ascents.

68. Fruity Pants ✪ 5.13a *Sport* 9 bolts. Up gently overhanging white face to anchors. Starts from ledge.

68a. Unnamed 5.10a *Trad.* Corner.

69. Ziggerknot ✪ 5.10c *Trad.* Wide zig zag crack up to bolt anchors at ledge.

69a. Jarrard/Kevin Parker 5.11c *Trad.* small corner through roof to big white scooped face, to anchor below top roof.

70. Just Another Pretty Face ✪✪ 5.11c *Sport* 6 bolts. Up and left to ledge. You might need a cam at the bottom. At ledge move up and left onto face. Ends at anchors right of arete.

71. Begoon/Artz Corner 5.9 *Trad.* Long corner

72. Begoon/Artz Variation 5.11b *Trad.* Hard variation start to 5.9 corner

73. Lavender Days ✪ 5.13a *Sport* 12 bolts. Up face until possible to traverse right to arete. Finish up arete. Use two ropes to reduce rope drag.

74. Puppy Chow ✪✪ 5.12c *Sport* Starts under giant roof. Up chossy rock to roof. Climb straight out huge roof to headwall. Most people use two ropes. After pulling roof there is a good stance to drop the first rope after clipping the second rope into two bolts. This dramatically reduces rope drag.

75. The Ringmaster 5.12d *Trad.* Face to awesome roof crack to radically overhanging juggy arete.

76. Greatest Show ✪✪ 5.13a *Mixed.* Starts under giant roof. Up chossy rock clipping several pins to base of roof crack. Hard climbing out roof puts you at the base of a beautiful dihedral. Thin climbing up dihedral.

77. Big Top 5.12a *Trad.* Obvious crack 40' right of *Greatest Show*, up white wall, pulls roof at top.

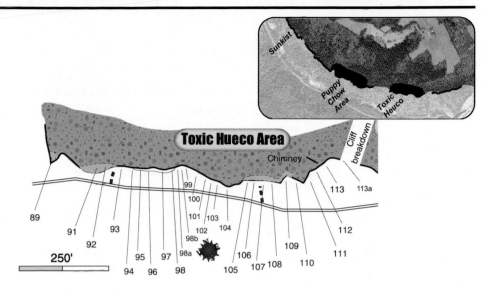

78. Peanuts 5.11 *Mixed,* Steep face past bolt to ledge.

79. Bearded Lady 5.12a *Mixed,* Up white face past 3 bolts to bulges, then on to slab and upper crack with a bolt then rap station.

80. Starvation Artist 5.11a *Mixed,* Face past bolt w/o hanger.

81. Unnamed 5.10 *Trad.* Crack.

82. Unnamed 5.10d *Mixed,* Short thin crack to pins w/ red sling.

83. Inadequate Length 5.6 *Trad.* Finger crack.

84. Begoon Solo 5.7 *Trad.* Obvious easy looking route.

85. Uncle Aremus 5.10b *Mixed,* 1 bolt. Arete on left end of wall

86. Tarbaby 5.11a *Trad.* Obvious thin crack on left side of face from *Ghandian Dilution.*

87. Wasted Wimper ✪ 5.10b *Trad.* Up middle of face left of *Ghandian Dilution.*

88. Ghandian Dilution ✪✪ 5.11c *Sport,* 6 bolts. Starts under left corner of roof. Up to roof, move right to broken crack then straight up to top.

89. Inertial Twists ✪✪ 5.12a *Sport,* 5 bolts. Up broken face to bottom of roof. Crank out a couple hard moves through roof then finish. Lower off last two bolts.

89a. Unnamed 5.12b

90. Jughead 5.8 *Trad.* Up dirty corner traverse right then up featured face.

91. Mind Bomb ✪✪ 5.12b *Mixed.* Face to roof. Jugs through roof to white wall. Continue up face to 2nd smaller roof then face to top.

92. Toxic Hueco ✪✪ 5.11d *Sport* Starts below obvious huge hueco. Cruxy climbing up through roof to stance above roof. Enjoyable and easier face climbing to top anchors. Great route!

93. Trojans ✪✪ 5.11d *Trad.* Obvious crack line. Good route with enjoyable climbing. One of the first routes on this wall. No top anchor.

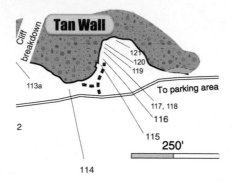

94. **By the Way, I Did Your Mom** ✷ 5.10b *Trad.* Up face through small overhang to dish. Left or right to finish at anchors.

95. **Canine** ✷ 5.12a *Sport,* 4 bolts. Good climbing.

96. **Crag Memorial** ✷✷ 5.12b *Sport,* 4 bolts. Crank through several hard boulder moves to anchors.

97. **White Trash** ✷✷ 5.12d *Sport,* 4 bolts. Nice line up bulging white face. It is good to place a medium size cam near the top to avoid a long runout (#1 Camalot). Starts from ledge.

98. **Chimpanzabubbas** ✷✷ 5.10d *Mixed.* Start at large flake, up to ledge then corner to juggy overhang. Fun climb on steep rock up high.

98a. **Machine Shop** 5.11a *Mixed,* 1 homemade hanger.

98b. **Year of the Gimp** 5.10d *Trad.*

99. **Revenge of the Gimp** 5.7 *Trad.* Left end of lichen covered wall straight up huecos to top.

100. **Gimpy** 5.8 *Trad.* Middle of hueco face to anchors.

101. **Boogie til ya Need Glasses** 5.8 *Trad.* Straight up hueco wall to anchors.

102. **Pine Trees and Hula Hoops** 5.9 *Trad.* Up cracks and huecos to same anchors.

103. **Night Time is the Right Time** 5.9 *Trad.* Up past pin then right to wide crack with huecos to top.

104. **Meadowlark** 5.12c *Mixed,* 1 bolt 1 pin Up to corner past bolt through overhangs and up and right to hanging white face to anchors.

105. **Cat Food** ✷✷ 5.11d *Sport,* 6 bolts. Starts on left side of overhanging wall. Up a series of underclings and flakes to roof. Most people lower from here (5.11b). Pull the roof and it is 5.11d.

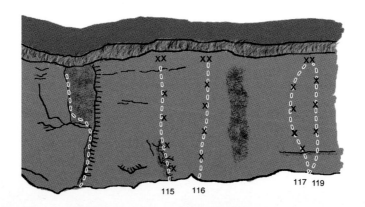

106. Go Cat Go! ✪✪ 5.12b *Sport,* 6 bolts. Good climbing on steep rock. Pulls small overhang at the top. Anchors just above roof.

107. Gato ✪✪ 5.12a *Sport,* 6 bolts. Another pumpy route on this wall. Pull small overhang at the top then up slab to anchors.

108. Rocket to My Brain 5.12c Trad. Face left of white corner past huecos to big lunge then left to finger crack to top.

109. I'll Buy That For a Dollar ✪✪ 5.12a *Trad.* Pull roof at bottom. Up and right to white corner. Thin gear in corner to upper roofs. Finish by moving right. Need small wires and TCU's.

110. Natural Selection 5.10c *Trad.* Traverse out of corner at first horizontal to arete.

111. Touchstone Productions ✪ 5.12c *Mixed,* 1 bolt. Up to bolt then face and crack to top.

112. Palm Trees and Hula Girls ✪ 5.11d *Mixed,* 1 bolt. Starts right of large overhang. Up shallow corner then right to face.

113. Mega Dosage 5.10d *Mixed,* Face past pin and bolt w/o hanger.

113a. Unnamed Project. 4 bolts. Starts in obvious corner up to roof.

Tan Wall

As you walk down the dirt road from the parking area, a cliff band appears on the right. Continue walking down the road another couple hundred feet until an obvious tan wall with several bolted routes appears on the right.

114. Unnamed 5.10 *Trad.* Wide crack.

115. Crack Puppy ✪✪ 5.12a *Sport,* 4 bolts. Up left leaning crack. Then some face climbing to anchors.

116. Czech Tech ✪ 5.11d *Mixed,* 4 bolts. Bolt line that moves up and right to anchors under high roof.

117. Campground Sluts ✪ 5.10a *Sport,* 4 bolts. Left bolt line to anchors.

118. Where the Hell is Ansted? 5.9 *Sport,* 3 bolts. At top of *Campground Sluts* move right and pull roof to arete to top.

119. DC Memorial Face 5.11c *Sport,* 4 bolts. Short thin face.

120. Game Face 5.12a *Sport,* 4 bolts. Short thin face.

121. Roy Davies 5.8 *Sport.* Starts at far right side of Tan Wall behind hemlocks.

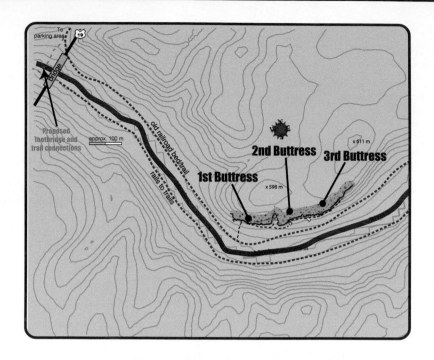

Climber on Chimpanzabubbas, 5.10d. Photo: Cater

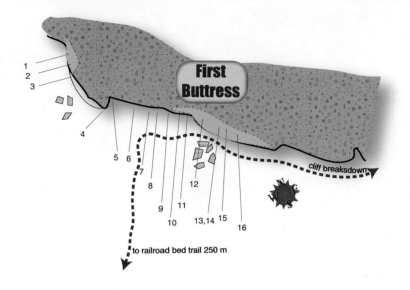

Upper Meadow Walls

From the main Meadow Area under the bridge, walk upstream one mile (15-20 minutes). There is a faint trail that leads up and left to the First Buttress. It is also possi ble to continue down the trail and cut up to the Second and Third Buttress but bushwhacking will be required. Most people walk the cliff from the First Buttress to access the other two areas. The First Buttress is a large overhanging wall 120' to 140' high. The right side of the wall has a sh ort overhanging section with three short routes on it.

First Buttress

1. Typical Situation 5.13b ✷ *Sport*, 7 bolts. Starts from ledge. Up white face to roof. Pull roof and move left, up through 2nd smaller roof to anchors.

2. Twostep 5.13a ✷ *Sport*, 6 bolts. Starts from ledge. Face climbing up to small roof. Pull roof then up to anchors.

3. Creature 5.12c ✷ *Sport*, 6 bolts. Starts from ledge left of orange rock. Up through small roofs to anchor.

4. Floaters ✷✷ 5.10d *Mixed*, 7 bolts. Start left of dead tree. Up to bolt, move left and continue up ledges to bottom of arete. You might want to place a cam before clipping the second bolt. Technical and tricky climbing up arete. At last bolt move straight up then right to anchor.

5. Ben Dunne ✷ 5.10a *Trad*. Large corner/crack system. Finish at the anchors for the sport climb to the left.

6. Cross-Eyed and Blind ✷✷ 5.10d *Sport* 6 bolts. Start at large hueco and go up and slightly left. Quintessential horizontal pulling. This route is 5.11a if you are shorter.

6a. Lamda ✷✷ 5.12a Sport, 8 bolts. Start at large hueco and go up and slightly right. Goes up past ledge and ends below headwall.

7. Push ✷✷ 5.12a Sport, 7 bolts. Start on small corner and climb up to pod between 3rd and 4th bolts. Then traverse left on ledge. Pull thru small roofs to anchor under headwall.

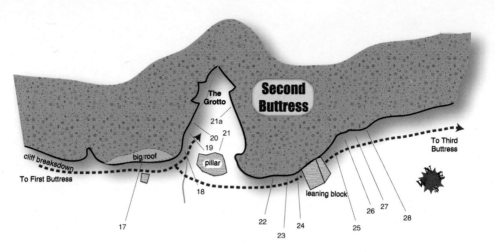

14. **Superman** ✪✪ 5.12b *Sport*, 4 bolts. Short overhanging route that starts from blocks behind two trees.

15. **Andoullie** ✪✪ 5.11c *Sport*, 5 bolts. Short route that cranks out steep wall to anchors below roof.

16. **Sausage** ✪✪ 5.11b *Sport*, 4 bolts. Slightly easier version of above route. Shares anchors with above route.

8. **Boomerang** 5.13a/b *Sport*, Same first 4 bolts of the above climb. Go straight up at ledge. Climb thru overhanging corner.

9. **Stolen Dreams** 5.12c *Mixed*. Climbs broken crack system thru overhanging roof at top. This route was another unfinished "Project" of Doug Reed but was quickly dispensed of by Peter Croft on one of his visits.

10. **Corner Pocket** ✪ 5.13a *Sport*, 10 bolts. Starts on above climb. Continue straight up thru roofs to top.

11. **Eye of Mordor** ✪ 5.13b *Sport*, 11 bolts. Starts on left side of overhang near iron stained oval. Climb up and right to white corner. You need a 60m rope for this one!

12. **Toy Maker** 5.13a *Sport*, 8 bolts. Start below orange corner. Up and right to roof. Straight thru roof and overhang to chain anchors.

13. **Pinochio** 5.12+ *Sport*, Starts behind tree under steep overhanging wall. Up 4 bolts to anchor then continue up and right eventually heading around corner near the top. Long route, 60m rope required.

Second Buttress

17. **Unnamed** *Trad*. Crack thru large roof. May not be completed.

18. **Unnamed** *Trad*. Right leaning dihedral out large overhang. May not be completed.

19. **Pete's Got A Beaver** ✪✪ 5.12b *Sport*, 5 bolts. Left hand bolt line under bulging roof.

20. **Little Shavers Club** ✪✪ 5.12b *Sport*, 6 bolts. Right hand bolt line that climbs through roof. There's just one SUPER HARD move on it that's difficult to stick and pull through.

21. **Shroomage** 5.10a *Trad*. Climb the mushroom pillar on the side facing away from the river.

21a. **Thief** 5.8 *Mixed*, 2 bolts. Short crack to face then up to anchors.

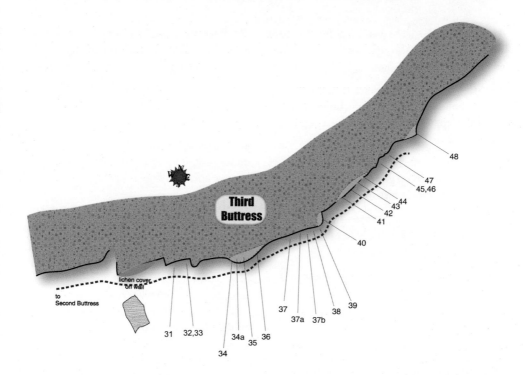

22. Load ✪ 5.10d *Sport,* 6 bolts. Starts right of low overhang. Up to overhang then right up slab to anchors.

23. Schneezal ✪ 5.12a *Sport,* 8 bolts. Starts left of giant round iron stained dish. Up thru crack in bulge. Then continue up face and cracks to anchor. Great climbing. One of the best routes out here. Long route, maxes out 60m rope!!

24. Red Bull ✪✪ 5.12d *Sport,* 8 bolts. Starts right of iron stained dish. Up bulging wall to anchors. Good route.

25. Bullocks ✪✪ 5.9+ *Sport,* 4 bolts. Starts just right of the leaning pillar after going thru the tunnel.

26. Minotaur ✪ 5.11c *Mixed,* 6 bolts. Starts at broken dihedral. Up crack system to ledge. Pull through roof at top. No top anchor.

27. Pistol Whip ✪✪ 5.11c *Sport,* 8 bolts. Start at purple streak near bottom. Up white face to roofy finish.

28. Madmen Rule the World ✪ 5.10d *Sport,* 7 bolts. Starts left of huge flake. Up slabby rock to slightly overhanging finish. Fun climbing with a pumpy finish.

Third Buttress

29. Unnamed Project.

30. Unnamed Project.

31. Unnamed *Mixed* 2 bolts. Project.

32. Ken's Routes 5.11d *Sport,* 8 bolts. Start right of corner. Up 4 bolts then follow left bolt line thru overhangs.

33. Gary's Route 5.11c *Sport,* 8 bolts. Same start as above, move right after 4th bolt.

34. Tsunami Bob ✪ 5.10d *Sport,* 6 bolts. Starts in left hueco, move up and right to anchor below large roof.

34a. Unnamed ✪✪ 5.10d *Sport,* 8 bolts. Starts in right hueco. Traverses right after first bolt, then back left. Shares same anchors as above route.

35. Meathead ✸ 5.11c *Sport*, 8 bolts. Bouldery start. Straight up through roof finishing out crack in high roof.

36. Starry ✸ 5.12b *Sport*. Starts under broken corner. Follow corner up then climbs horizontal out steeper section pulling over high roof near the top.

37. Unnamed ✸✸ 5.11c *Sport*, 9 bolts. Starts between rock slabs on ground. Up broken crack to left side of roof. Over roof then straight up to anchors.

37a. Half Mast ✸ 5.12b *Sport*. Starts right of tree and left of below route.

37b. Unnamed 5.11c *Sport*. Starts right of tree and left of below route.

38. The Prow ✸ 5.12b *Sport*. Starts on clean white wall. Up 35' to ledge and slab. Then large orange overhang.

39. Skull in Hole ✸✸ 5.12a *Sport*, 6 bolts. Starts above pocket. Stay right of arete.

40. Strip Tease ✸✸ 5.12a *Sport*. Obvious crack that splits roof. Retro bolted so now it has 4 or 5 bolts on it and stops at the roof.

41. Dragon's Tooth ✸ 5.12d *Sport*. Starts 20' right of giant corner. Up and right passing thru 2 small roofs then anchor.

42. Unnamed 5.12b *Sport*, 9 bolts. Starts at large overhang. Up 4 bolts to slab. Trend right to anchors under roof.

43. Bittersweet ✸✸ 5.13a *Sport*, 10 bolts. Pull out horizontal overhang at the bottom. Up bulging wall to anchors near top.

44. Shake and Not Stir ✸✸ 5.12d *Sport*. Out bulging overhang. Fixed draw on 3rd bolt.

45. Deans' Route 5.12a *Sport*, 9 bolts. Starts right of big undercling. Up 7 bolts and then move right to finish. Need a 60m rope!

46. Beer Pressure ✸✸ 5.11d *Sport*, 9 bolts. Same start as above but straight up at bolt 7. Need a 60m rope!

47. First, Last and Always 5.12a *Sport*, 9 bolts. Starts below crack in black rock. Straight up passing thru roofs.

48. Unnamed 5.10b *Sport*, 5 bolts. Up to shuts under roof. This is a truly awful climb. Missing one anchor.

Fourth Buttress

The Fourth Buttress is difficult to find when coming from the Third Buttress. The cliffline breaks down and you have to wander across a large expanse of rocky terrain. It can more easily be found by heading back down to the old railroad bed and heading upstream. When you come to a stream, head towards the cliffs. There is a waterfall in view of the bolted Fourth Buttress climbs. This was a last minute addition and bolt counts were not available

49. Sandbox ✸ 5.12c *Sport*. Bouldery start. Goes through steep roof up high.

50. S.N.A.F.U. ✸✸ 5.12a *Sport*. Starts on top of boulder. Fall across to thin face climbing for a couple of bolts. Then head up thru steep tiered climbing.

51. Ich Bin Ein Auslander ✸✸ 5.12d *Sport*. Starts on top of boulder. Very steep climbing to chain anchor under roof.

52. Project *Sport*. Goes out huge roof.

53. The Excuse ✸ 5.12c *Sport*. Starts on left side of ledge. Steep climbing to cliff top.

54. Anchors Away 5.11c *Sport*. Starts on middle of ledge.

55. Skintimate ✸ 5.11c *Sport*. Starts on right side of ledge.

Doug Reed on the first ascent of My Stinking Brain (5.13a), Fern Buttress. Photo: Cater

Gene Kistler on another awesome New River Gorge corner. Photo: Cater

Eddie Begoon works his way up another awesome New River Gorge arete! Photo: Cater

Climber on Floaters at First Buttress, 5.10d. Photo: Mike Turner

Climber on Ghandian Dilution, 5.11b.   Photo: Cater

Jim Suffecool on the classic Toxic Hueco at the Main Meadow, 5.11+. Photo: Cater

Robert Thomas looking smooth on Push at First Buttress, 5.12a. Photo: Mike Turner

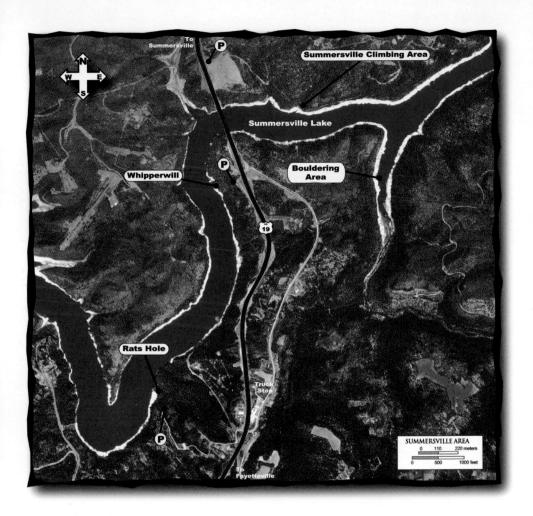

14

Summersville Lake

148 routes • 129 sport • 19 trad/mixed

Summersville Lake is not actually located in the New River Gorge. It lies approximately 20 miles north of Fayetteville on Rt. 19. The rock at Summersville is the same Nuttall Sandstone formation that forms the cliffs of the New River Gorge. The rock is very similar in texture and quality as to the rock at the New and Meadow. Cliff height varies from 30' to 80' in height and the walls range from slightly overhanging to extremely overhanging. The majority of routes are slightly overhanging face climbs with horizontal edges, pockets and jugs. The area contains predominately sport routes but there are some excellent trad routes that should not be overlooked. The cliff location beside the lake also gives it a unique feel. During the summer, it's great fun to rent a boat and float around the lake bouldering out of the water. The lake also keeps the area a bit cooler on warm days. During the fall, winter and spring the water level is low creating an interesting desert-like landscape. There is also a good collection of boulder problems that appear during low water levels.

There is a free camping area (no facilities) at the Summersville Lake Dam and a pay area, Mountain Lake Camping, just a few minutes from the crag. Just a few miles further north on Rt. 19 there are some fast food joints, grocery stores, motels and the town of Summersville.

Access

From Fayetteville drive about twenty miles north on Rt. 19. After crossing the second bridge (Gauley River Bridge), look for a pull-off on the right. Park at the pull-off on the right just north of the bridge. Make sure your car is at least 4' off the road and that it is not blocking other cars or vehicles. From the pull-off on Rt. 19 follow the trail up through the clear-cut and continue down to the bottom of the hill to a small bridge. If the water level is low turn right and follow the road down to the lakebed. This will access the Pirates' Cove area. If the water is high, turn left and walk back to a small wooden bridge, cross the bridge and pickup the trail across the clearing. Stay right and at the second branch turn right, descend about 100 meters and cross the stream. From there follow the stream down to a waterfall and descend the ladder. This will put you behind the D.C. Memorial Boulder.

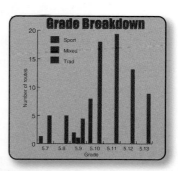

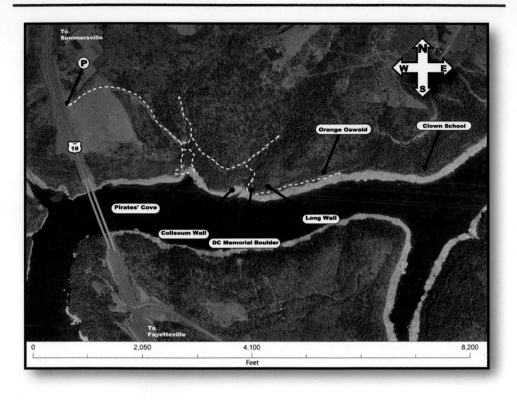

Harrison Dekker on Mutiny (5.11d), Summersville Lake Photo: Cater.

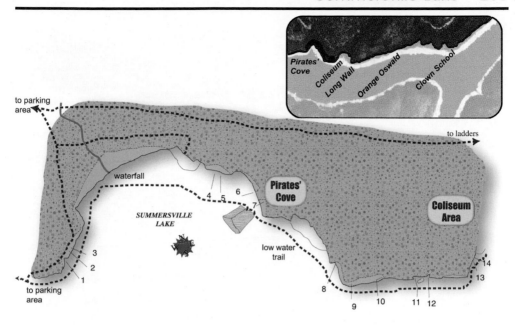

The Pirates' Cove Area is only accessible from mid-September to mid-April. During this time, it is possible to walk from Armada to the Coliseum Wall by following the lake bed. This area is southwest facing and is excellent for those cool fall days. During the summer months, the water level rises partway up the cliffline making it impossible to climb in this area.

Pirates' Cove

1. Unnamed SL #1 5.7 *Trad.* Overhanging crack.

2. Armada ✪✪ 5.12c/d *Sport*, 7 bolts.

3. The Skull In the Stone ✪✪ 5.12c *Sport*, 7 bolts.

4. Walk the Plank ✪ 5.11b *Sport*, 4 bolts.

5. Man Overboard ✪ 5.11d *Sport*, 4 bolts.

6. Mutiny ✪✪ 5.11c/d *Sport*, 6 bolts. Obvious left leaning arete.

7. Unnamed SL #2 5.10 *Trad.* White dihedral to roof, move left and continue up crack to top.

8. Unnamed SL #3 5.9 *Trad.* Start right of short chimney crack, follow crack system to top.

9. Unnamed SL #4 5.10b *Trad.* Follow flake and crack system to roof, pull large roof out flakes and continue to top or lower off fixed gear. (Boat start)

10. Unnamed SL #5 5.10c *Trad.* Splitter crack to ledge.

11. Unnamed SL #6 5.10a *Trad.* Dihedral to top.

12. Unnamed SL #7 5.10 *Trad.* Left facing dihedral to ledges or continue to top.

13. The Good, the Bad and the Boltless ✪ 5.10 *Trad.* Start left of pillar follow crack system and small roofs to cold shut anchors.

14. Vertical Plains Drifter ✪ 5.10 *Trad.* Start right of pillar, up to shuts.

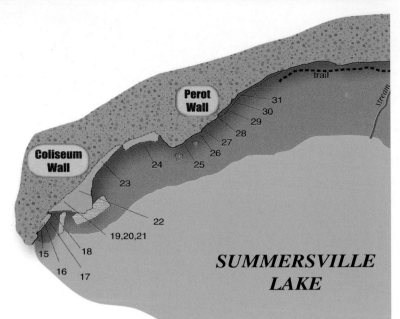

The Coliseum Wall

15. Reckless Abandon ✪ 5.12b/c *Sport*, 8 bolts.

16. Surfer Rosa ✪ 5.12d *Sport*, 8 bolts.

17. Obitchuary 5.12b *Sport,* 8 bolts. Starts on Surfer Rosa. Move right at 2nd bolt.

18. Tobacco Road 5.12b *Sport*, 8 bolts. Starts on the left of the wall and traverses right up and thru tiered roofs.

Climbs 19, 20, 20a,20b, and 21 share the same start.

19. Mercy Seat ✪✪ 5.13a/b *Sport*, 9 bolts. Moves left after the third bolt.

20. Apollo Reed ✪✪ 5.13a *Sport*, 11 bolts. Moves right after third bolt. Straight up thru steep roof, One of the classics of the area and fun.

20a. Metz Hill Parking 5.13c *Sport*, 11 bolts. Start on Apollo, climb to 5th bolt (do not clip). Traverse right to bolt on the Project on the right, climb up one more bolt and thru the crux to a rail, traverse 10' to the right and finish on the last 3 bolts of B.C.

20b. Kill Whitey Traverse 5.13a *Sport*, 11 bolts. Start on Apollo, climb to the 5th bolt (do not clip). Traverse right all the way to B.C., climb 3 bolts to the rail below the crux of B.C. Traverse 15' right to finish on The Pod.

21. Unnamed SL #8 Project. Start on Apollo, traverse right then straight up thru dihedral.

22. B.C. ✪✪ 5.13b *Sport,* 11 bolts.

23. Pod ✪✪ 5.13a/b *Sport*, 9 bolts. Starts on the right side of the wall.

24. Still Life ✪✪ 5.13d *Sport*, 7 bolts. Impressive steep overhanging face on far right. Broken hold and has not had repeat.

Perot Wall

These routes are verticle to slightly overhanging. Fun and pumpy climbing on moderates. Good warm-ups for the Coliseum Wall.

25. Do It (a.k.a Snub Nose) 5.11a *Sport,* 2 bolts.

26. Trigger Happy ✪ 5.10a *Sport*, 3 bolts.

27. Talk About It (a.k.a. Stick Em Up) ✪ 5.10b *Sport*, 4 bolts.

28. Gun Lust ✪ 5.10c *Sport*, 4 bolts.

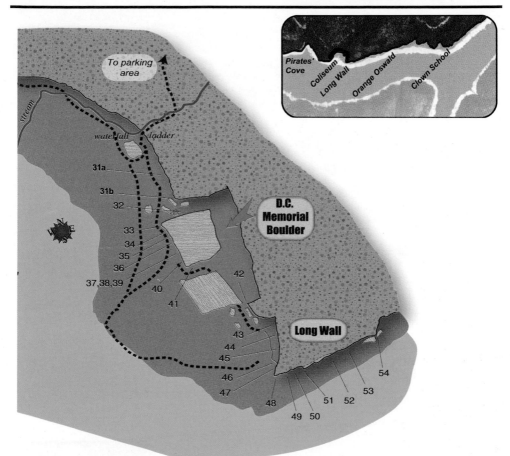

29. All Ears (a.k.a. Armed and Dangerous) ✪ 5.10b *Sport*, 4 bolts.

30. How'Bout'em Apples (a.k.a.Gun but not Forgotten) 5.10d *Sport*, 4 bolts.

31. The Deficit (a.k.a. Line of Fire) 5.10d *Sport*, 4 bolts.

D.C. Memorial Boulder Area (Mega Boulder)

This is a large boulder tilted sideways that has some great climbing on it. Routes are short.

31a. Power Outage 5.12c *Sport*, 5 bolts. Short face up thru two small roofs.

31b. Unnamed 5.11b *Sport*, 5 bolts. Outside corner in corridor.

32. Spider Needs A Thesaurus 5.11d/12a *Sport*, 5 bolts.

These routes are located on the lakeside of the boulder. Short, steep and pumpy climbing!

33. Angle of Attack ✪✪ 5.12c *Sport*, 4 bolts. Overhanging arete.

34. All the Way Baby ✪✪5.12b *Sport*, 3 bolts. Short overhanging route stops short of top.

35. Skinny Legs ✪5.13b *Sport*, 4 bolts.

36. Pro-Vision 5.13a *Sport*, 4 bolts.

37. Unnamed SL #10 Project.

38. Vaseline Vision (a.k.a. Straight Up and Narrow) ✪ 5.12a/b *Sport*, 3 bolts.

39. Delayed Stress Syndrome (a.k.a. Process of Elimination) ✪ 5.11a *Sport*, 3 bolts. Starts at big flake, traverses to the right then straight up flake to anchors.

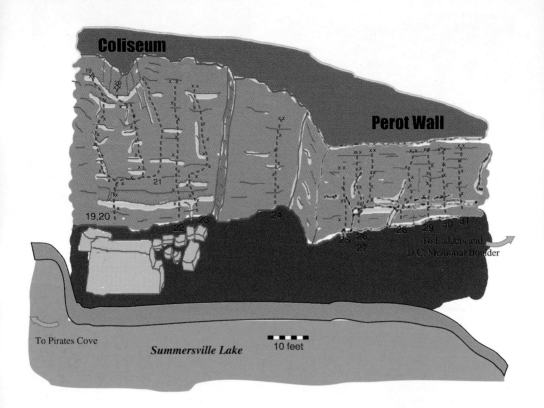

Coliseum

Perot Wall

19
20
21
19,20
22 23
24
25 26, 27
28 29 30 31
To Ladders and
D.C. Memorial Boulder

To Pirates Cove

Summersville Lake

10 feet

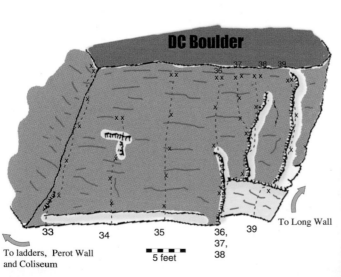

DC Boulder

37 38 39
36

33 34 35 36, 37, 38
39

To Long Wall

To ladders, Perot Wall
and Coliseum

5 feet

Climber on Under the
Milky Way (5.11b).
Photo: Cater Collection

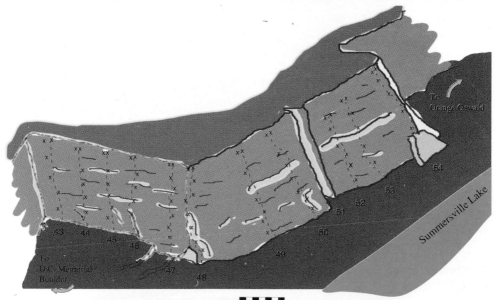

10 feet

Steve Cater on first ascent of Sunny Daze (5.8), Whipperwill.
Photo: Cater Collection

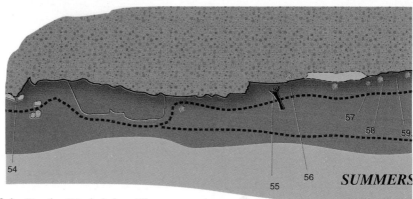

40. The Year of the Psycho Bitch (a.k.a. The Route of All Evil) ✪ 5.11b *Sport*, 3 bolts. Starts under slopping ledge. Straight up staying left of arete to anchors.

41. Psycho Babble 5.12a *Sport*, 6 bolts. Start 5' right of arete. Technical climbing up face right of arete.

The Long Wall

Great selection of moderates on The Long Wall. Perfect stone and some of the most enjoyable face climbing in the area.

42. Ingrate (a.k.a. Meat Wave) ✪✪ 5.9 *Sport*, 3 bolts. Short arete.

43. Chewy ✪✪ 5.10b *Sport*, 4 bolts.

44. Personal Pronoun (a.k.a. Menace Alert) ✪✪ 5.9 *Sport*, 4 bolts.

45. Jesus Is My License Plate (a.k.a. Flight Time) ✪✪ 5.10d *Sport*, 5 bolts.

46. For What? (a.k.a. Hot 'n' Bothered) ✪✪ 5.10b *Sport*, 4 bolts.

47. Six Dollars ✪✪ 5.11d *Sport*, 6 bolts.

48. Under the Milky Way ✪✪ 5.11d *Sport*, 7 bolts. Very nice climbing up arete.

49. World At War (a.k.a. Flirting with Empty) ✪✪ 5.11d *Sport*, 6 bolts.

50. Maximum Over Drive ✪✪ 5.11c *Sport*, 6 bolts. Nice face climbing!

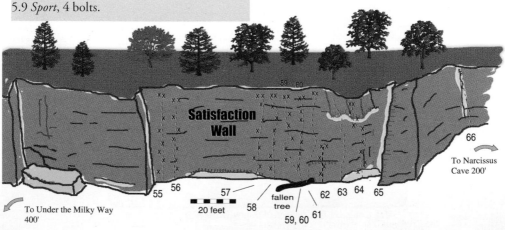

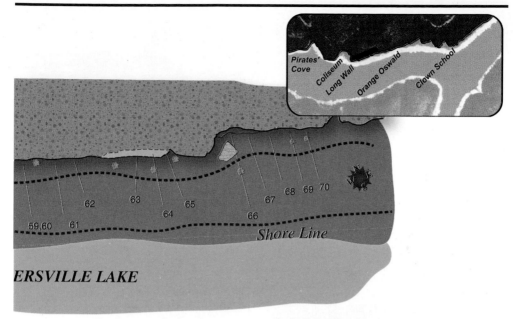

ERSVILLE LAKE

51. **Unnamed** SL #11 5.10d *Trad.* Dihedral to top.

52. **Spice** 5.11b/c *Sport,* 5 bolts.

53. **Gimme Some Tongue** 5.11c *Sport,* 5 bolts.

54. **No Way, Jose'** ✪ 5.11b *Sport,* 4 bolts. Start from top of boulders. Arete to face.

Satisfaction Wall

55. **BSIAGE** 5.11a *Sport,* 6 bolts.

56. **Bored Spitless** ✪ 5.10b/c *Sport,* 6 bolts.

57. **Tequila Maria** 5.10 *Sport,* 6 bolts.

58. **Lichen8er** 5.10 *Sport,* 6 bolts.

59. **Two Finger Limit** 5.8 *Sport,* 6 bolts. Same start as *Make Way for Dykling* but move left.

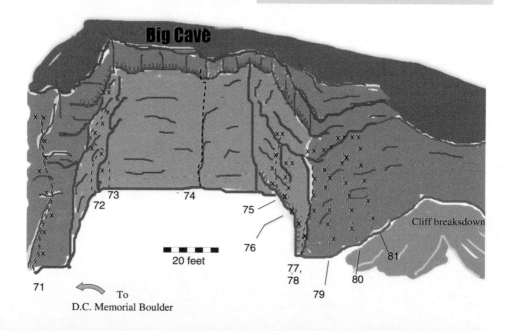

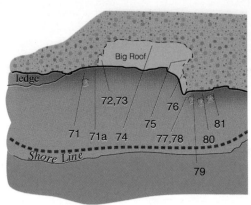

60. **Make Way for Dyklings** 5.10a *Sport,* 6 bolts.

61. **Lickty Split** ✪ 5.9 *Sport, 7 bolts.* Thin crack up to ledge then crack to top finishing at shuts on left.

62. **Short Pirouette** 5.10d *Sport,* 3 bolts.

63. **Hunda Scrunda** 5.10b *Mixed,* 1 bolt. Face to roof move left out roof and continue up corner to top.

64. **Satisfaction Guaranteed** ✪✪ 5.11a *Sport,* 8 bolts. Pull low roof, continue up slab moving left into high roof. Pull this roof and continue up bulging face to anchors.

65. **No Refund** 5.10 *Sport,* 7 bolts. Starts at overhanging block. Up left of wide crack then short face to top.

66. **Unnamed** SL #12 5.9 *Trad.* Crack to featured face and anchor.

67. **Bad Hair Day** 5.9 *Trad.* Face and crack to anchor.

68. **Useless Beauty** 5.10 *Sport,* 7 bolts.

69. **Unnamed** 5.8 *Trad.* Broken crack.

70. **Unnamed** SL #13 5.10 *Mixed,* 3 bolts.

Narcissus Cave

71. **Smilin' Jack** ✪ 5.11c *Sport,* 7 bolts. Right leaning crack. Occasionally wet at top.

71a. **Unnamed** 5.12d *Sport,* 7 bolts. Starts on arete. Up arete then small roof to face and anchors

72. **Narcissus Direct Start** ✪5.12d *Sport,* 6 bolts. Start left of normal start and climb pocketed face up to where it joins with regular route. Boulder problem start makes Narcissus a little bit harder!

73. **Narcissus** ✪✪5.12a *Sport,* 6 bolts. Steep route up left side of big roof. great route with lots of pumpy climbing.

74. **Unnamed** SL #14 Project. 10 bolts. Crack out big roof.

75. **Long Dong** ✪ 5.12d *Sport,* 8 bolts. Start at back of cave. It is recommended that two ropes be used to avoid heinous rope drag. Drop one rope after 4th bolt.

76. **Deep Throat** ✪5.13c *Sport,* 7 bolts. Starts on boulder and moves straight out horizontal roof.

77. **Suicide Blond** ✪✪5.13b *Sport,* 6 bolts. Start on arete and move left after first bolt up steep wall.

78. **Simple Minds** ✪5.11d *Sport,* 4 bolts. Start on arete, move up staying on right side of arete

79. **Jeff's Bunny Hop** ✪✪5.8 *Sport.* 6 bolts. Fun and easy. Very popular.

80. **Sniff the Drill** ✪✪5.8 Sport. 6 bolts. Fun and easy. Very popular.

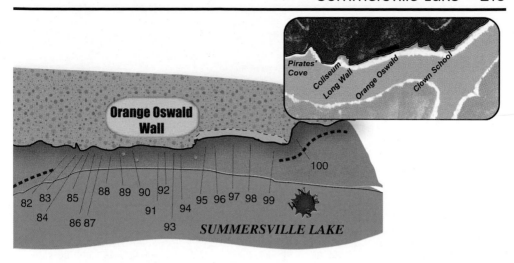

81. **That Eight** ✪✪ 5.7 *Sport.* 5 bolts. Fun and easy. Very popular.

Orange Oswald Wall

This is one of the most popular walls at Summersville. Lots of easy to moderate climbing on incredible stone! Faces south and is in the sun. Cliff diagram on next page.

82. **Fabulous Groupies** ✪✪ 5.9 *Sport,* 5 bolts.

83. **Unnamed** SL#15 5.6 *Trad.* Corner up to ledge, then up and left to anchors of *Fabulous Groupies.*

84. **Hippie Dreams** ✪✪ 5.7 *Sport,* 7 bolts. Starts on left side of arete then move around right to face.

85. **Souled Out** ✪✪ 5.9 *Sport,* 7 bolts. Starts from small vegetated ledge.

86. **Chunko Goes Bowling** ✪✪ 5.9 *Sport,* 8 bolts. Starts at small layback flake. Up through bulge to ledge then up through orange face to second bulge and anchors

87. **Voodoo Surfing** ✪✪ 5.10b *Sport,* 8 bolts.

88. **Orange Oswald** ✪✪ 5.10a *Sport,* 7 bolts. Starts at obvious ground level left facing dihedral.

89. **Just Say No** 5.9 *Trad.* Starts 15' left of *Strong Arming.* Finish at *Strong Arming* anchor.

90. **Strong Arming the Little Guy** ✪✪ 5.10b *Sport,* 6 bolts. Starts right of curving flake. Immediately right of Orange Oswald.

91. **No Bolts About It** 5.10 *Trad.* This line is just left of *Baby Has A Bolt Gun.* Follows flake and crack system up and right.

92. **Baby Has A Bolt Gun** ✪✪ 5.10c *Sport,* 8 bolts. This route is a combination of the two trad lines. First holds are high off the ground. Wanders up the face following bolts.

93. **Bolts, Just Say No** 5.10 Trad.

94. **She Got the Bosch, I Got Drilled** ✪✪ 5.10a *Sport,* 7 bolts. Starts left of large right facing corner/arete.

95. **Moon Pie Deluxe** ✪ 5.10c *Sport,* 7 bolts. Ramp, white face to roof.

96. **Barfing Butterflies** ✪ 5.11a/b *Sport,* 7 bolts. Up ramp to first bolt line. Face and roof.

97. **Unnamed** SL#16 5.9 *Trad.* Crack to open dihedral.

98. **Scoot Your Muffin** ✪ 5.10b *Sport,* 7 bolts. Starts directly behind thin tree.

99. **Thou Shall Not Chum** 5.11a *Sport,* 5 bolts.

100. **Snub Nose** ✪ 5.11b *Sport,* 3 bolts. Short overhanging face climb around the corner.

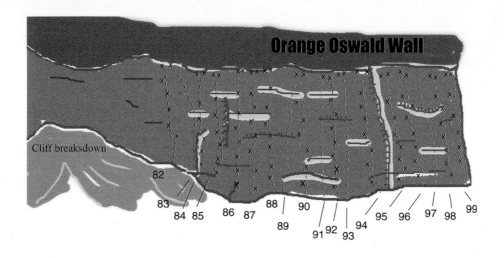

Dan Hague on the Reckless Abandon (5.12b/c), Summersville Lake.
Photo: Dan Hague

Mike Helt on crux of Mercy Seat (5.13a/b), Summersville Lake.
Photo: Dan Hague

Gary Land on the starting moves of Apollo (5.13a), Summersville Lake.
Photo: Dan Hague

The next routes are a bit spread out along the cliff the cliff breaks down twice before reaching the Clown School Wall.

101. Unnamed SL# 5.11 *Sport*, 6 bolts. Starts at orange flake, up to large ledge move right then up and right to blocky roof.

102. Unnamed SL# 5.11 *Sport*, 6 bolts. Starts from high ledge. Up orange featured rock thru small roof to anchors.

103. Unnamed SL# 5.11 *Sport*, 6 bolts. Starts from ledge just left of small roofy corner. Straight up to anchor.

104. Unnamed SL# 5.11 *Sport*, 8 bolts. Starts on right side of overhang. Up to slabs to roof. Face then second roof up to anchors.

These routes are located on an overhanging section of wall just after passing over a small stream and cluster of small boulders.

105. Board Out of My Mind 5.12a *Sport*, 6 bolts. Starts right of flake. Up thru roof move right traversing over roof up to anchors.

106. Overboard 5.11b *Sport*, 6 bolts. Starts 6' right of detached flake leaning against wall. Up to roof, pull roof then straight up to anchors.

107. Unnamed SL# 5.11 *Sport*, 5 bolts. Follows arete to anchor in middle of orange face.

A couple hundred yards beyond the last several routes the cliff breaks down. Continue walking on the faint trail until the wall picks back up. The next four routes are located near a huge boulder that is leaning against the cliff.

108. Unnamed SL# Project *Sport*, 5 bolts. Starts in middle of white face at bright green lichen. Straight up thru roof then crack to anchor.

109. Slim Pickens 5.12b *Sport*, 7 bolts. Up arete to roof. Move right at corner flake then up steep face to anchors.

110. Unnamed SL# 5.11b *Sport*, 4 bolts. Up inside of arete to anchors.

111. Unnamed 5.11a *Sport*, 4 bolts. Starts on outside of cave. Stays on left side of arete up to anchors.

Continue walking along the cliff until the cliff breaks down again. Near where the cliff picks up again is a high section of wall with some very nice routes. The next 6 routes are located here.

112. Unnamed SL# Project *Sport*, 10 bolts.

Eerie landscape of Summersville Lake.

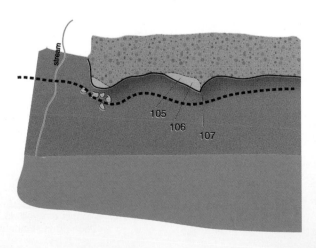

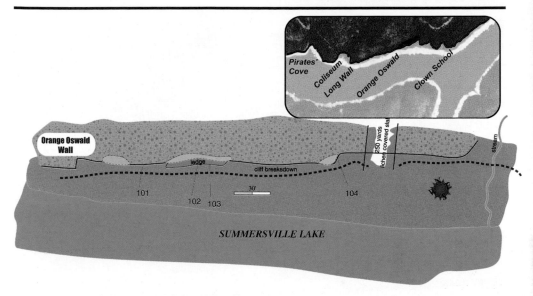

113. Ly'n' and Stealin ★★ 5.12b *Sport*, 8 bolts. Starts under the roof. Follow blunt arete to face. The climber should stick clip the second bolt and then clip the lead end of the rope through the first bolt. Unclip the first bolt as you climbs by it.

114. Trapezius ★★ 5.12b *Sport*, 8 bolts. Starts at pocketed wall. Up to small prow then follow left bolt line to anchors.

115. High Wire Act ★★ 5.12b/c *Sport*, 8 bolts. Same start as above. Move right after first bolt.

116. The Contortionist ★ 5.12a *Sport*, 6 bolts. Up to overhanging arete. Continues to anchors.

117. Clown School 5.10a *Sport*, 5 bolts. Directly around the corner from Contortionist. Hard start then climb the face.

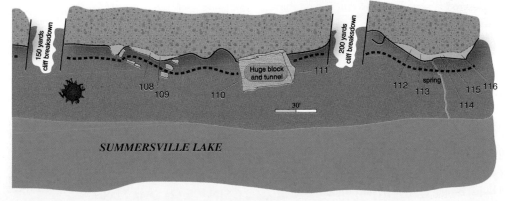

Rats Hole

1. Lavender Line 5.10c *Trad.* Wide flake that has a purple streak on left edge.

2. Dirty Stinkn' Rat 5.11c *Sport,* 7 bolts. Start at wide crack then face to anchors.

3. Rat Race ✪✪5.12b *Sport,* 7 bolts. Steep face.

4. Rat Hole 5.10a *Trad.* Start at Spray painted "RAT HOLE" and follow bubbly face to top.

5. Rat Fink 5.9 *Trad.* Crack and corner to top.

6. Unnamed RH #4 5.12a *Sport,* 5 bolts.

7. Unnamed RH #3 5.11c *Sport,* 4 bolts.

8. Unnamed ✪RH #2 5.10b *Trad.* Long corner to top.

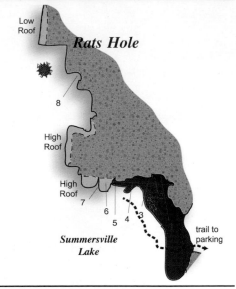

Whipperwill

1. Whinerlamer 5.8 *Sport,* 5 bolts.

2. Unnamed 5.9 *Mixed,* 1 bolt. Crack to face.

3. Wafer 5.12a *Sport,* 4 bolts.

4. Waverley 5.12b *Sport* , 4 bolts. Steep face left of arete.

5. Mojo JoJo Crack 5.12a *Trad.* Obvious finger crack right of corner under roof to shuts.

6. Davies/Hill 5.10d *Sport.*

7. Blaze Got A New Job 5.11b *Sport.*

8. Gimme A Clown ✪✪ 5.8 *Sport,* 6 bolts.

9. Cowboy in the Dirt ✪✪ 5.8 *Sport,* 7 bolts.

10. Bongo 5.7 *Trad.* Face up to anchors on above route.

11. Nonameyet 5.11a *Sport,* 5 bolts .

12. Bender 5.11d *Sport,* 7 bolts.

13. Masuko ✪✪ 5.11a *Sport,* 6 bolts. Great climbing on this one!

14. Jason and the Arguenuts ✪✪ 5.11d *Sport,* 6 bolts. Starts under horizontal roof.

15. Stop the Presses, Mr. Cater ✪✪ 5.12d *Sport,* 4 bolts. Boulder problem start under roof.

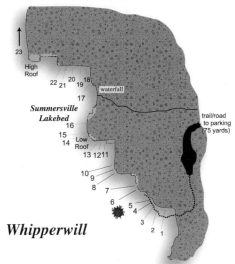

16. Java ✪ 5.9 *Trad.* Corner crack system then up and left at roofs following clean streak.

17. Sunny Daze 5.8 *Trad.* Up obvious corner, crack system to small roof. Move out left then to top. Dirty finish at tree. No fixed anchors.

18. Blimey ✪✪ 5.10b *Sport,* 6 bolts.

19. Playa ✪✪ 5.11a *Sport,* 5 bolts.

20. Rehab ✪✪ 5.12b *Sport, 6 bolts.* Hang draws on this one. Several of the bolts are very difficult to clip if you are of normal height. Excellent route.

21. SIN ✪ 5.12a *Sport,* 7 bolts.

Rats Hole

The Rat's Hole is a small crag located at Summersville Lake. This cliff was discovered in 1993 by climbers but it has always been a well-known and popular hangout for partiers during the summer. Spray paint, broken bottles and beer cans are common sites at the cliff. Although it is unsightful, there are some excellent routes, especially the super steep *Rat Race*. It is best to visit this cliff during the fall and winter when the water level is low. Only four of the routes are accessible during high water. The cliff also faces southwest making very toasty on cool days. Access may change due to land issues.

Access

The Rats Hole is located a couple miles from the main Summersville Lake climbing area. Driving north on Rt. 19 from Fayetteville, turn left just before reaching the Go-Mart Truckstop. Immediately after turning left, take another left and then an immediate right onto a dirt road. Turn left at the next intersection and follow the dirt road down into the hollow. Park at the end of the road and walk down the path 100 yards to the shore. The climbing area is on the right.

Whipperwill

This area has a small selection of nice sport routes. The climbs are only accessible during low water (mid Oct.- mid April). Bolt hangers occasionally disappear in this area and may become damaged by water, so be cautious. The cliff faces southwest and is perfect for cool days. The cliff name comes from the road name and also a huge 30' fall that Will Laird took from the anchors of Blimey.

Access

Driving north from Fayetteville, turn left onto the small access road called Whipperwill about 1/2 mile or so past the truck stop and about 1/2 mile before the Summersville Lake bridge. Park at the bottom of the paved road and follow the rough dirt road back to the lake. Drop down to the lakebed. All the routes are to the right after dropping down to the lakebed.

22. Unnamed ❂ 5.12 *Sport*. Toprope line up and left out roofs. May be bolted in the near future.

23. Max Paine 5.12b Steep sport route behind large boulder on right side of wall. (This route is off this map upstream a hundred yards or so.)

Early photo of Porter Jarrard on Libertine (5.12d), Endless Wall.
Photo: Jarrard Collection

Alphabetical Index
and First Ascent Information

R

Graded Index
Sport, Trad and Mixed* Climbing Routes

AB - Ambassador Buttress
BM - Beauty Mountain
BA - Bridge Area
BC - Bubba City
DP- Domino Point

EW- Endless Wall
FB - Fern Buttress
JW - Junkyard Wall
K - Kaymoor
MR - Meadow River
RH - Rat Hole

SL - Summersville Lake
SB - Sunshine Buttress
SN - South Nuttall
WW - Whipperwill

*Route may have some fixed bolts or pins and
requires stoppers and/or camming units.

5.3

Pony Ride .... Trad ...... BC

5.4

Dairy Area* .... Trad ...... BA
Doo-Wah-Woof* ,,,,,,,,,, Trad ...... BC
Easy Street .... Trad ...... EW
Impulse Power .... Trad ...... FB
Just Plain Dirty .... Trad ...... BC
Newd Scientist .... Trad ...... EW
Quantum Meruit .... Trad ...... BA
Slip Sliding Away .... Trad ...... BC
The Glitch* .... Trad ...... AB
Tosha Goes to the Gorge Trad ..... BC

5.5

Afternoon Delight* .... Trad ...... BA
Bush Battle .... Trad ...... BC
Good-bye Mr. Lizard ..... Trad ...... BC
Gospel Trek, The .... Trad ...... BA
Guides Route Left* .... Trad ...... BM
Guides Route Right .... Trad ...... BM
Little Feat .... Trad ...... MR
Micro Brew* .... Sport ..... BC
Monkey See Monkey Do Trad ..... BA
Rocket In My Pocket ..... Trad ...... MR
Save the Human Race .... Trad ...... EW
The

5.6

A Wild Hair .... Trad ...... FB
Beam Me Up, Scotty* ... Trad ...... FB
Beech, Beeech, Beeeech! .... Trad
FB
Beginner's Climb .... Trad ...... BC
Bobby D's Bunny** ...... Sport ..... BC
Captain Crunch .... Trad ...... SN
Cowabunga .... Trad ...... FB
Crack of the Klingons* . Trad ...... FB
Distortionist, The* .... Trad ...... JW
Five-Five My Ass* .... Sport ..... BC
Giggle Box .... Trad ...... MR
Gunky Heaven* .... Trad ...... BA
Inadequate Length .... Trad ...... MR
Jaded Vision .... Trad ...... BC
Just Another Glitch .... Trad ...... K
Keep It Tight, But etc. ... Trad ...... JW
McStumpy's Sandwich Crack .... Trad
FB
Mossy Groove .... Trad ...... BA
Nasty Poodle Chew* ..... Trad ...... JW
Near Beer .... Sport ..... BC
Neon Parks .... Trad ...... MR
Orange Blossom Special* .... Trad
BA
Plumber's Crack .... Sport ..... BC
Potato Chip .... Trad ...... BM
Prickly Bubba .... Trad ...... BC

5.7

Short'n Sweet .... Trad ..... BM
Silly Little Corner .... Trad ..... BC
Solitary Hang .... Trad ..... BA
Spams Across America .. Trad ..... BA
Themetime* ....,,,,, Trad ..... JW
Tower of Power .... Trad ..... SN
Transporter Crack* .... Trad ..... FB
Unnamed .... Trad ..... MR
Unnamed JW #3 .... Trad ..... JW
Unnamed SL#15 .... Trad ..... SL
Unnamed SN#3 .... Trad ..... SN
Wang Way, The .... Trad ..... BC
Wunderkind .... Sport ..... BC

An Affair with the Heart Trad ..... BC
Beginner's Luck .... Trad ..... BM
Beginners Only* .... Trad ..... BA
Begoon Solo .... Trad ..... MR
Bongo .... Trad ..... WW
Brain Wave* .... Trad ..... BM
Butterfly Flake* .... Sport ..... BC
Chasing Spiders to the Right * ..... Trad
JW
Cheap Thrill .... Trad ..... BA
Comic Relief .... Trad ..... BC
Crack'n Clutch .... Trad ..... BA
Crescent Moon** .... Trad ..... EW
Daisy Cutter** .... Sport ..... BC
Dominaire** .... Trad ..... DP
Ducks Unlimited .... Trad ..... BA
Eating Bimbo Pie .... Trad ..... BC
Fiesta Verde .... Sport ..... BC
Garden Weasel .... Trad ..... EW
Gilded Otter* .... Sport ..... BC
Gone with the Bubba ..... Trad ..... BC
Gut Feeling .... Trad ..... EW
Helmeted Warrior Of Love .... Trad
BC
Hippie Dreams** .... Sport ..... SL
Horton's Tree .... Trad ..... BA
In Tribute to Skid .... Trad ..... BA
It Comes in Spurts .... Trad ..... BC
Journey to the Center of the Brain**
Trad .... BM
Jumpin' Jack Flash .... Trad ...... JW
Lollipop* .... Trad ...... BA
Midnight Moonlight* ... Trad ...... BA
Moonraker* .... Trad ...... EW
Nasty Body O'Dour .... Trad ...... BC
New River Gunks** ...... Trad ...... JW
No Sign of Intelligent Life .... Trad
FB
Pickled Eggs .... Trad ...... MR
Purity Made .... Trad ...... EW
Rat's Alley * .... Trad ...... EW
Ratz Holm .... Trad ...... BC

Revenge of the Gimp ..... Trad ...... MR
Seventh Sign* .... Trad ..... EW
Shady Lady* .... Sport ..... BC
Stalking The Wild Toad . Trad ...... BC
Steppin' Out .... Trad ..... EW
Stoat Goes to Joshua Tree and Tears A
Flapper on Baby Apes ... Trad ...... FB
Spamling, The .... Trad ..... BA
Supersymmetry .... Trad ...... EW
Tabasco Fart .... Trad ...... MR
That Eight** .... Sport ..... SL
The Hopfenperle Special* .... Trad
BA
Thought Crime* .... Trad ...... EW
Throw in the Rack .... Trad ...... BA
Toxic Waste .... Trad ...... FB
Truancy .... Trad ...... MR
Unnamed JW #4 .... Trad ..... JW
Unnamed SL #1 .... Trad ...... SL
Unnamed SN#19 .... Trad ...... SN
Up to Disneyland .... Trad ...... BA
Verde Suave .... Sport ..... BC
Wasted Woute .... Trad ...... BC
Who Knows? .... Trad ...... JW
Wong Woute, The .... Trad ...... BC

5.8

Air Wailing .... Trad ...... BC
Ambiance .... Trad ...... EW
Ann's Revenge .... Trad ...... JW
Assman .... Sport ..... BC
Barefoot Alley .... Trad ...... BA
Bat Cave .... Trad ...... EW
Bearpaw Crack .... Trad ...... BM
Beat Me Daddy, Eight to the Bar .. Trad
FB
Beer Wench .... Sport ..... BC
Betty's Boop .... Trad ...... BC
Black Dog .... Trad ...... JW
Boogie til ya Need Glasses .... Trad
MR
Brain Storm .... Trad ...... BM
Bubba Safari .... Trad ...... BC
Bubbalicious .... Trad ...... BC
C. T. Crack .... Trad ...... BC
Carcus Tunnel Syndrome* .... Trad
EW
Cerveza Verde* .... Sport ..... BC
Chew Electric Death You Snarling Cur
Trad .... FB
Chuckles .... Sport ..... BC
Cow in A China Shop ... Trad ...... FB
Cowboy in the Dirt** .... Sport ..... WW
Creamy .... Trad ...... BC
Czech Vacation* .... Sport ..... BC
Dark Hollow .... Trad ...... BA
Dead Varment .... Trad ...... MR
Dr. Ruth's Variation .... Trad ...... EW

5.10a/b

Hardcore Female Rash .. Sport ..... BC

5.10b

All Ears* .... Sport ..... SL
Almost Heaven* .... Sport ..... K
Angel's Arete** .... Mixed ... BA
Aye Aye Captain .... Trad ...... BM
Badass Tattoo** .... Sport ..... BC
Bat Crack Direct Finish . Trad ...... BM
Beach, The .... Trad ...... EW
Bisect* .... Trad ..... FB
Blimey** .... Sport ..... WW
Blind Sight .... Trad ...... EW
Blunder and Frightening* .... Trad
BA
Brain Tweezers** .... Sport ..... BM
Bubbarete .... Trad ..... BC
Burning Calves** .... Trad ...... BM
By the Way I Did Your Mom* ..... Trad
MR
Catatonic Conflicts .... Mixed ... BA
Cell Block* .... Sport ..... EW
Chameleon, The* .... Sport ..... FB
Chewy** .... Sport ..... SL
Clumsy Club Crack** ... Mixed ... AB
Consenting Clips .... Trad
AB
Constant Velocity .... Trad ..... FB
Crazy Ambulance Drive Mixed ... BC
Dab Hand .... Trad ...... EW
Daily Waste .... Trad ...... BC
Danger in Paradise .... Mixed ... JW
Daughter of Dracula ...... Mixed ... FB
Decameron, The* .... Sport ..... BC
Dementing Situations .... Mixed ... BC
Dog Fight .... Trad ...... BA
Dr. Rosenbud's Nose* .... Mixed ... BA
Dumbolt County .... Mixed ... BC
Durometer 64 .... Trad ...... EW
Eat at the Wye .... Trad ...... BC
Emergency Room Exit .. Mixed ... BC
Exoduster** .... Sport ..... EW
Exquisite Lace .... Trad ...... EW
Eye of Zen .... Mixed ... FB
F. U. B. .... Trad ...... BC
Fat Factor, The .... Trad ...... BA
Fire and Waste .... Mixed ... FB
For What?** .... Sport ..... SL
Frigidator .... Trad ...... JW
Gift from the Mayor ..... Trad ...... BC
Glass Onion** .... Sport ..... EW
Green Piece, The* .... Sport ..... K
High and Lively .... Trad ...... EW
Hot Flash .... Trad ...... BM
Hunda Scrunda .... Mixed ... SL
Hunger Artist, The .... Trad ...... BC
Impaled .... Trad ...... BA
Imperial Strut .... Trad ...... EW
Insertum Outcome .... Trad ...... EW
Insistent Irony .... Sport ..... BC
Jams Across America ..... Trad ...... BA
Jimmy's Swagger .... Mixed ... BA
Joey's Face .... Trad ...... BA
Junk Food .... Trad ...... BA
Kistler-Houghton Arete . Trad ...... SN
Let Them Eat Pancakes . Sport ..... BC
Lewd Operator .... Trad ...... FB

Liddlebiddanuthin' .... Trad ...... AB
Lippo* .... Trad ...... MR
Little Wing .... Sport ..... BC
Lotus Land .... Trad ...... BA
Low Voltage* .... Sport ..... K
Malfunction Junction .... Trad ...... K
Men Who Love Sheep ... Mixed ... BC
Mud and Guts .... Trad ...... FB
My Wife Is A Dog* .... Mixed ... BA
Naked Potatoes .... Trad ...... FB
Nestle Crunch Roof * .... Trad ...... EW
Nutter Butter* .... Sport ..... K
Ode To Stoat .... Mixed ... BA
One-Eyed Viper .... Trad ...... JW
Party All the Time** ..... Mixed ... EW
Party in My Mind* .... Mixed ... EW
Party Till Yer Blind* ..... Mixed ... EW
Pit Bull Terror* .... Mixed ... JW
Plastic Sturgeons .... Mixed ... BC
Play it by Ear .... Sport ..... K
Promised** .... Trad ...... BA
Raiders of the Lost Crag* .... Trad
K
Remission** .... Trad ...... EW
Rod Serling Crack** ..... Trad ...... BM
S.T.A.N.C.* .... Trad ...... EW
Scoot Your Muffin * ..... Sport ..... SL
Scott's Turf Builder .... Trad ...... JW
Second Thoughts .... Trad ...... K
Skiggle Van Wiggle .... Trad ...... EW
Sojourners .... Trad ...... BM
Solitude Standing .... Sport ..... BC
Spider Wand** .... Trad ...... BM
Springer* .... Sport ..... K
Strike a Scowl** .... Sport ..... EW
Strong Arming the Little Guy** ... Sport
SL
Sundowner .... Trad ...... BA
Talk About It* .... Sport ..... SL
Team Jesus** .... Trad ...... JW
Technarete** .... Trad ...... EW
Thing Foot .... Trad ...... BC
'Til The Cows Come Home .... Trad
BA
Timberline* .... Trad ...... EW
Two-Tone Arete** .... Sport ..... FB
Unamed .... Trad ...... MR
Uncle Aremus .... Sport ..... MR
Underfling** .... Trad ...... BA
Undeserved, The** .... Trad ...... EW
Unnamed .... Sport ..... MR
Unnamed .... Sport ..... MR
Unnamed KM #5 .... Trad ...... K
Unnamed SL #4 .... Trad ...... SL
Voodoo Surfing** .... Sport ..... SL
Wasted Weeblewobble, The .... Trad
EW
Wasted Wimper* .... Trad ...... MR
We're Having Some Fun Now ...... Trad
BC
Wham Bam Thanks for the Jam** Trad
BM
Wishbone Left .... Trad ...... FB
Women Who Won't Wear Wool ..... Trad
BC

5.10b/c

Bored Spitless* .... Sport ..... SL
Lying Egyptian .... Mixed ... EW

5.10c

A Dog Always Returns to It's Vomit
Trad .... JW
Airwaves .... Sport ..... BC
Americans, Baby, The ... Trad ...... EW
Arthur Murray Crack .... Mixed ... BC
Baby Has A Bolt Gun** Sport ..... SL
Back in the Saddle .... Trad ...... EW
Between Coming and Going .... Trad
EW
BM #1 .... Sport ..... BM
Boltus Prohibitus .... Trad ...... BA
Born Under A Bad Smell Trad ...... JW
Bovine Seduction* .... Trad ...... K
Brain Death .... Trad ...... EW
Breach Birth .... Trad ...... FB
Brown Dirt Cowboy* .... Trad ...... JW
Can I Do It Till I Need Glasses?** Trad
EW
Celibate Mallard** .... Trad ...... EW
Common Ground .... Mixed ... FB
Cool Corner .... Trad ...... SN
Cross-Eyed and Blind** Sport ..... MR
Double Twouble .... Trad ...... BC
Eclectic Mix .... Sport ..... BC
Enemy Line .... Trad ...... JW
Erogenous Zone, The .... Trad ...... EW
Esse Crack* .... Trad ...... BA
Eurobubba .... Trad ...... BC
F. A. B. .... Trad ...... BC
Faith Crack .... Trad ...... JW
Fire* .... Trad ...... K
First Person* .... Sport ..... FB
First Steps** .... Sport ..... K
Furry Nerd .... Trad ...... FB
Gemini Crack - Left** .. Trad ...... BA
Good Life, The .... Trad ...... JW
Gun Lust * .... Sport ..... SL
High Octane .... Mixed ... EW
High Times* .... Trad ...... BA
Hummingbird* .... Trad ...... FB
Ichabod Crane* .... Sport ..... BC
Icon of Control, The ...... Mixed ... BC
Intimidation .... Trad ...... FB
Just Say Yo To Jugs .... Trad ...... SB
Kansas Shitty .... Mixed ... JW
Kinesthetica** .... Sport ..... BC
Labor Day* .... Trad ...... BA
Lavender Line .... Trad ...... WW
Le Brief .... Trad ...... BA
Lone Rhinoceros .... Trad ...... BM
Maranatha** .... Trad ...... BA
Meto Power .... Trad ...... BA
Mockingbird .... Trad ...... MR
Moon Pie Deluxe * .... Sport ..... SL
Natural Selection .... Trad ...... MR
Necromancer* .... Sport ..... SB
New Speedway Boogie . Trad ...... EW
New Tricks for the Old Dog* .... Sport
FB
Nutcrafter Suite, The .... Trad ...... EW
Parsimony .... Trad ...... FB
Perpendiculus .... Mixed ... BC
Petrified Pink Puke .... Trad ...... EW
Pipe Dreams .... Trad ...... BA
Poison Ivy .... Trad ...... JW

5.12a/b

5.12b

Notes